The Sovereignty Cartel

Sovereignty is the subject of many debates in international relations. Is it the source of state authority or a description of it? What is its history? Is it strengthening or weakening? Is it changing, and how? This book addresses these questions, but focuses on one less frequently addressed: what makes state sovereignty possible? *The Sovereignty Cartel* argues that sovereignty is built on state collusion – states work together to privilege sovereignty in global politics, because they benefit from sovereignty's exclusivity. This book explores this collusive behavior in international law, international political economy, international security, and migration and citizenship. In all these areas, states accord rights to other states, regardless of relative power, relative wealth, or relative position. Sovereignty, as a (changing) set of property rights for which states collude, accounts for this behavior not as anomaly (as other theories would) but instead as fundamental to the sovereign states system.

J. SAMUEL BARKIN is author of ten books and some fifty articles and chapters on international relations theory and international organization, and is a leading authority on theories of sovereignty. His previous book with Cambridge University Press, *Realist Constructivism: Rethinking International Relations Theory* (2010) was named a Choice Outstanding Title.

The Sovereignty Cartel

J. SAMUEL BARKIN
University of Massachusetts Boston

CAMBRIDGE
UNIVERSITY PRESS

University Printing House, Cambridge CB2 8BS, United Kingdom

One Liberty Plaza, 20th Floor, New York, NY 10006, USA

477 Williamstown Road, Port Melbourne, VIC 3207, Australia

314–321, 3rd Floor, Plot 3, Splendor Forum, Jasola District Centre, New Delhi – 110025, India

103 Penang Road, #05–06/07, Visioncrest Commercial, Singapore 238467

Cambridge University Press is part of the University of Cambridge.

It furthers the University's mission by disseminating knowledge in the pursuit of education, learning, and research at the highest international levels of excellence.

www.cambridge.org
Information on this title: www.cambridge.org/9781316518809
DOI: 10.1017/9781009003490

© J. Samuel Barkin 2021

This publication is in copyright. Subject to statutory exception and to the provisions of relevant collective licensing agreements, no reproduction of any part may take place without the written permission of Cambridge University Press.

First published 2021

A catalogue record for this publication is available from the British Library.

Library of Congress Cataloging-in-Publication Data
Names: Barkin, Samuel, J. 1965– author.
Title: The sovereignty cartel / J. Samuel Barkin, University of Massachusetts, Boston.
Description: New York, NY : Cambridge University Press, 2021. | Includes bibliographical references and index.
Identifiers: LCCN 2021000166 (print) | LCCN 2021000167 (ebook) | ISBN 9781316518809 (hardback) | ISBN 9781009010009 (paperback) | ISBN 9781009003490 (epub)
Subjects: LCSH: Sovereignty. | International relations. | BISAC: POLITICAL SCIENCE / International Relations / General | POLITICAL SCIENCE / International Relations / General
Classification: LCC JC327 .B242 2021 (print) | LCC JC327 (ebook) | DDC 320.1/5–dc23
LC record available at https://lccn.loc.gov/2021000166
LC ebook record available at https://lccn.loc.gov/2021000167

ISBN 978-1-316-51880-9 Hardback
ISBN 978-1-009-01000-9 Paperback

Cambridge University Press has no responsibility for the persistence or accuracy of URLs for external or third-party internet websites referred to in this publication and does not guarantee that any content on such websites is, or will remain, accurate or appropriate.

Contents

Acknowledgments		*page* vi
1	Introduction	1
2	Sovereignty?	17
3	Sovereign Rights	36
4	The Sovereignty Cartel	55
5	The Sovereign	79
6	Sovereign Property	102
7	The Interstices of Sovereignty	124
8	Normative Dissonance	144
9	Conclusions	163
References		183
Index		199

Acknowledgments

This book collects several ideas about sovereignty in the contemporary states system that have been bouncing around in my head for quite some time. These ideas have appeared in a sufficient variety of different papers and talks and have been commented on by so many people that it would be unrealistic to list them all here even if I had done an adequate job of keeping track, which I have not. My thanks to all of those people, along with apologies for not keeping track.

I do have some acknowledgments for assistance specifically with the book project. Beth DeSombre and Laura Sjoberg both read and provided invaluable commentary on several versions. Patrick Thaddeus Jackson and Swati Srivastava, as well as an anonymous referee, read and commented on the penultimate draft. The final version would, of course, have been better if I'd done a more effective job of taking all their advice.

My colleagues in the Conflict Resolution, Human Security, and Global Governance Department at the University of Massachusetts Boston provided a supportive environment for the writing of the book. Thanks also to UMass Boston for the sabbatical leave during which much of the book was written, and the Watson Institute for International and Public Affairs at Brown University for an institutional affiliation during that sabbatical.

Finally, thanks to those who helped with the editorial side of getting this book published. John Haslam at Cambridge University Press waited patiently for a decade between the first time I pitched the idea of this book to him and the time I actually started writing it. William Krol copyedited the final manuscript; Kathryn Butterworth compiled the index.

1 | Introduction

Sovereignty is often talked about as central to, even definitional of, contemporary international relations. We assume it as the source of state authority or use it to describe state capabilities. We talk about whether it is getting weaker, and occasionally about whether it is changing in some fundamental way. But rarely do we get into details about what it is, how it works, how it maintains itself, and what the effects are of sovereignty specifically, as opposed to some other organizing principle, on contemporary international relations. In this context, some of the patterns of state behavior that are easy to take for granted as part of the sovereign states system are in fact striking. States do not just compete with each other to maximize their national interest or cooperate with each other to provide global public goods. They also collude with each other to reinforce the centrality of the sovereign state as a category of actor in international relations. This pattern of collusion is what I call the "sovereignty cartel."

Examples of this collusive behavior can be found in a wide range of international issue areas; the most obvious is legal standing. International law – the law of states – recognizes only sovereign states as having international legal personhood. In other words, states recognize each other as the people of international relations and no one else. Many examples can also be found in the international political economy. Corporations need to be legally domiciled in a state, even if they are neither physically domiciled nor do a significant amount of business there. Businesses need a state to legitimate them, even if the state plays little meaningful role in regulating or taxing the business. Ships at sea need to fly a national flag, lest they be treated as pirates. A flag from a state that is dysfunctional, or from a country that has no coast, legitimates the ship, but the flag of a large shipping company with a history of responsible operation of its ships does not.

States also recognize a right to the use of violence in other states that they do not recognize with respect to any other actors. Soldiers in the uniform of a sovereign state have, under some circumstances, the right to kill people in other countries. This right may be loosely circumscribed by principles such as proportionality and civilian immunity, but soldiers can still kill noncombatants in large numbers and remain within international law. Anyone else behaving in this way is subject to local laws for murder. The same sort of mutual recognition of the right to violence can be found in criminal justice. States will, as a general rule, allow their nationals to be incarcerated by other sovereigns, subject to due process. However, states do not accord the right to detain their citizens to any other category of international actor.

These examples seem at first to be unexceptional because they are simply the way international relations currently works and the way it has worked throughout recent memory. When examined in more detail, however, they are actually inconsistent with the assumptions of many international relations scholars both about how the world works and about how the world should work. The examples all involve states according rights to other states whether big or small, rich or poor, liberal or illiberal, status quo or revisionist – rights that allow other states to regulate and use force that might undermine their own ability to govern. These rights give small and poor states, for example, leverage in global governance and in the international political economy that they might not otherwise have. They can make it more difficult for bigger and richer states to govern illicit activities by creating alternative sources of legitimation for those activities. Why do the bigger and richer countries put up with this? What do they get in exchange for this dilution of their own practical ability to govern?

Political realists, for instance, begin with the assumptions that power is the key currency of politics, that states are the social actors with power in international relations, and that states will act in their national interest. This set of assumptions leads to a view of international relations in which states compete with each other to maximize their gain. But in the examples given above, states with more power are conceding rights to states with less power, without any clear quid pro quo and sometimes at significant cost to their ability to promote their own national interest. Realists tend to either assume sovereign states as a starting point of their analysis or argue that it is states that matter in international relations because they are the organizations that have the power to matter. From neither of these perspectives does it make sense for the most powerful states to concede reciprocal rights to the least powerful. This is particularly true of neorealists, who tend to look at great powers specifically rather than states generally, highlighting the focus on power rather than sovereignty.

Nor does it make sense from liberal perspectives. These might include an institutionalist liberalism that sees states as cooperating to provide public goods, and a democratic liberalism that takes popular sovereignty to be representative of the general will. In the former case it means the concession of rights to states that may not have a meaningful ability to participate in the provision of public goods and may not, in fact, agree on what constitutes international public goods. Such concessions serve to create more potential veto players that can stymie cooperation and create interstices between multiple points of legitimate regulation, leading to situations in which various kinds of illicit activity can thrive. In the latter case, the assigning of these rights to sovereigns as determined by the community of sovereigns can undermine, rather than express, popular sovereignty by reinforcing the position of despots of various kinds.

Bigger and richer states support the rights of smaller and poorer ones because in doing so they support the principle of sovereign right, thereby reinforcing their own claim to the exclusive right to regulate their own place in the international system. States, in other words, act not only individually to protect their own sovereignty but also collectively, as a cartel, to protect the rights of sovereignty in general and of sovereign actors as a group. They do this because they recognize (whether explicitly or implicitly) that the social construct that is the sovereign state system needs to be constantly reconstituted through practice. The sovereignty cartel is part of the process of this reconstitution. This book argues that states, while they do compete with each other for power and cooperate with each other to deal with collective problems or provide collective goods, also collude with each other to protect the rights of sovereignty against all other actors. In other words, states act as a cartel to retain for themselves the exclusive right to govern. This cartel acts to reproduce sovereignty in the face of pressures both from other actors and from changes in the international system.

Sovereignty in International Relations

The concept of sovereignty holds an awkward position in the study of international relations. It is both ubiquitous and contested. It is understood variously as a legal principle, a set of powers, a set of rights, or a set of norms, among other things. Sovereignty is understood either as a principle or as a practice, as absolute or as changeable, as binary or as flexible, as legal or as political. It is often associated with the Peace of Westphalia of 1648, despite the likelihood that the modern state would be completely unrecognizable and in ways unintelligible to the princes who negotiated that Peace. In the thirty years since the end of the Cold War, the future of sovereignty has been questioned and regarded as threatened by putative forces such as economic globalization and political neomedievalism. These discourses suggest a sovereignty that does not change in meaning over time but gets stronger or weaker in response to the international political conditions of the time.

The various arguments about the decline of sovereignty provide a useful foil for the argument of this book. These arguments have used various languages, from "sovereignty at bay" in the 1970s[1] to globalization in the 1990s,[2] and neomedievalism[3] and empire[4] in the 2000s. The globalization argument is that as economies globalize, global forms of both public and private authority are replacing the sovereign state as the primary locus of governance in contemporary international relations. The neomedievalist argument is in a way the opposite, that governance is fracturing, and the sovereign state is being displaced by various overlapping layers of governance, for better or worse. The empire argument, conversely, is that the discourse of sovereignty is just a cover for new modes of rule by the powerful. Either way, the claim is that international forces are undermining the power, and in some versions the legitimacy as well, of the sovereign state to maintain its central role in governance.

These arguments may seem less compelling with the rise of populist nationalisms and of Chinese assertiveness on the international stage in the early years of the twenty-first century. But the extent to which what were seen as secular trends in one decade succumb so easily to reassertions of sovereign authority in the next is itself telling. It suggests that what some scholars saw as a weakening of sovereignty was in fact an example both of the flexibility and complexity of sovereignty as an

---

[1] Vernon 1981.
[2] See, *inter alia*, Barber 1995; Ohmae 1995; and Strange 1996.
[3] E.g., Cerny 1998; Kobrin 1998; and Khanna 2009.
[4] For an overview, see Nexon and Wright 2007.

institution. Flexibility suggests that what we think of as sovereignty is not fixed; it can change over time. Complexity, in turn, suggests that what we think of as sovereignty is not reducible to one definition. It is a set of interrelated characteristics that need not covary, such that, for example, sovereign capabilities can change in different ways from sovereign authority, which, in turn, can change in a different way from sovereign right.

The starting point of the analysis of sovereignty in this book is the opposite of that in arguments about globalization and neomedievalism. Rather than being seen as a definitionally fixed ideal type, sovereignty is seen here as a messy social construction. Instead of sovereignty being defined by a single characteristic – be it control within a demarcated border, recognition by other sovereigns, or some other characteristic – it is seen here as a complex set of attributes, relations, rights, etc. Rather than understanding sovereignty as a set of capabilities that can get stronger or weaker but the content of which is constant over time, it is seen as changeable and changing. Understanding sovereignty as a social construction entails looking at how it is understood and practiced at a particular point in time and looking at changes in those understandings and practices over time, rather than seeing it as a fixed and unchanging thing.

Some recent scholarship looks at sovereignty as a social construct, as a set of historically contingent practices in international politics that vary across time and space.[5] This book takes this body of scholarship as a starting point, and argues that sovereignty is in fact malleable – the practices and shared understandings that we think of as sovereignty can and do change over time. Seen through this lens, sovereignty was not getting weaker in the two decades following the end of the Cold War but was adapting to changes in the international political economy. Sovereignty has, in fact, changed radically over the years, and only since World War II has it come to be understood as a globally consistent construction into which all international relations should fit.

State sovereignty as a social construct is a set of related practices that can be understood in a variety of ways. One can look at where sovereignty resides, at what the constitutional rules of sovereignty are, at what powers are associated with sovereignty, and at what

---

[5] E.g., Biersteker and Weber 1996; Barkin and Cronin 1994; and Srivastava (forthcoming).

sovereign authority is. This book focuses on what sovereignty permits the sovereign to do. In other words, it focuses on sovereignty as a set of rights. These might be understood as property rights in the broadest sense, not just describing who owns what, but who has the right to do what and who does not. Sovereign states have many rights in the contemporary states system that no other entity or actor has. These include rights that are generally associated with sovereignty, such as the right to govern domestically and the right to international legal personhood. They also include a set of exclusive rights to regulate a variety of international transactions and to use violence internationally.

Property rights are claims to the use or control of goods in law or in theory ("good" meant here in a broad sense, as anything the claimant wants the right to use, control, or do). In practice, rights claims are only as good as their audience; a claim of property rights that is not recognized either by other potential claimants or by a mechanism for arbitrating such claims yields little benefit to the claimant. Rights therefore do not automatically maintain themselves over time. Claims need to be both documented and reinforced through practice. For a functional system of property rights to exist in the absence of a higher authority that is able to legislate and enforce rights (as is characteristic of international relations), tensions in rights claims need to be negotiated and mechanisms for arbitrating those tensions need to be created. Property rights, in other words, are not natural laws there for the taking, but claims that need to be made real through practice.

There are two aspects to sovereign property rights that provide the focus for this book. The first is that they are established through practice and need to be continuously reestablished to be maintained. This means that states as institutions have a collective interest in behaving in ways that protect their rights against other potential actors in international politics. This is what I call the "sovereignty cartel" – states acting together to exclude other actors from the right to govern. The second aspect is that there is no clear rational or coherent plan of what sovereign right consists of. The set of rights that constitutes sovereignty, in other words, is not necessarily internally consistent.

The Sovereignty Cartel

Property rights tend to be exclusionary: if one actor claims a right to a good, it generally means excluding other actors from that good. In any case, goods are generally more valuable when they are limited in supply. If anyone can regulate authoritatively or use force legitimately, we do not really need states to do it. The value of states is that only they can do these things. The value to sovereigns of rights to things like the natural resources within their borders is even more straightforward. To the extent that sovereigns as a group claim a set of exclusive rights to authority over violence and commerce internationally and to authority and resources domestically, it follows that they deny those rights to other actors, whether individuals or other social institutions. In order for sovereign states as a group to successfully claim exclusive rights to a set of goods and privileges, they need to effectively exclude other actors from enjoying those rights. They need, in other words, to collude both to enforce their claims to and to maximize the value of their sovereign rights.

But why focus on collective rights through a cartel? Why not simply claim rights as individual sovereigns? Because recognition by other potential claimants increases the value of property rights. A general recognition of the right to use force internationally, for example, protects soldiers and statespeople against prosecution abroad and makes it easier to organize collective suppression of the use of force by other actors. A general recognition of the sovereign right to regulate globally enables authoritative multilateral cooperation with respect to the international political economy. A general recognition of the sovereign right to resource royalties makes it easier to extract such royalties from third parties. Sovereign rights, in other words, are in many instances more valuable to individual sovereigns when those rights are generally recognized as systemic.

Sovereign rights, then, are not an abstract concept that give states capabilities and authority. They are a set of specific claims made through practice, tempered by the willingness of counterparties to recognize those claims. A cartel increases the likelihood that those claims will be recognized, in part by empowering other sovereign states as the key counterparties to the claims, and in part by regularizing claims of what counts as sovereign right. A cartel only makes sense to the extent that sovereign actors see themselves as competing with other categories of actor as rights claimants rather than competing with other sovereigns as rights holders. While much of the literature on international relations focuses on the latter form of competition, this book argues that the former form is a regular feature of contemporary international relations as well. A cartel in general can be thought of as cooperation among a set of actors to maximize the value of a good they collectively traffic in. They can do so using various mechanisms, ranging from restricting supply (e.g., the OPEC cartel) to shooting competitors from outside the cartel (e.g., drug cartels). The sovereignty cartel is in ways more like a drug cartel than a petroleum cartel, in that its members are willing to use force to maintain their collective monopoly on what they see as their sovereign prerogatives.

The term "cartel" may conjure images of sovereigns in smoke-filled rooms conspiring to keep their powers and keep others out. However, "the sovereignty cartel" works more through structural power rather than relational power; it can work through well-meaning people simply doing their jobs, with a cumulative cartel effect (and, of course, the rooms are no longer smoke-filled). Diplomats, for example, work through diplomatic channels and protocol; international lawyers, whether working for states or other actors, work through the mechanisms of international law. In both cases the social structures in which they work are the structures of sovereign right, which recognize states as having a role and privileges distinct from other actors. They reconstitute these structures not because doing so is their primary goal but as a corollary of working within them to achieve whatever proximate goal they are working toward. As such, the sovereignty cartel is more a side effect of the quotidian activities of international politics professionals than it is the intentional effect of state leaders.

This quotidian character in turn makes the cartel relatively invisible; it is part of the taken-for-granted internal mechanics in the background of the conduct of international politics rather than the more visible machinations of high politics. But invisibility does not mean irrelevance. Seeing sovereignty as a cartel explains the efforts that states put into maintaining the rights of states in general even when this undermines more proximate political and policy goals. It sheds new light on rules about the use of force internationally. It explains why states are willing to see regulation of international activity by foreign sovereigns as legitimate in principle, even when it is substandard, incompetent, or corrupt in practice. It helps to explain why states recognize governments as sovereign when they are neither popularly legitimate nor functionally in control of their countries. And it points to the absurdity of claims that foreign powers should keep out of domestic disputes over who should be sovereign, since nonintervention in effect means that the cartel concedes valuable rights to the actor identified by the cartel as sovereign.

Seeing sovereignty as a cartel also provides a new way of looking at debates about globalization and sovereignty, and, by extension, at concepts such as neomedievalism. Proponents of the argument that sovereignty is being weakened by either private actors (globalization) or non-state public actors (neomedievalism) generally understand sovereignty as a set of outcomes: it is weaker if we see regulation or governance coming from elsewhere. The implicit assumption underlying these arguments is that this weakness is imposed on states by forces beyond their control. Why, after all, would states allow this to happen if they could prevent it?

Seeing sovereignty as a set of rights rather than a set of outcomes, however, paints a different picture. States may be interested in, or ambivalent to, the existence of specific processes of global governance without necessarily wanting to be responsible (individually or collectively) for providing that governance. Allowing other actors to provide governance in these specific instances therefore makes sense. But states can relinquish control over specific processes of global governance without relinquishing the ultimate right to such governance. Sovereignty-as-outcomes misses this distinction. Sovereignty-as-rights can allow states to give up control as a practical matter in specific instances without weakening the institution of sovereignty more broadly.

Sovereignty-as-rights also provides the mechanism for states to reclaim control when it is in their collective interest to do so. It may, in fact, be difficult for individual states to reclaim control, depending on the state and the circumstances in question. It may even be difficult for an individual state to reassert the right to govern in a particular situation that it had previously ceded in practice, because the right to govern (as opposed to asserting a material capability to govern) requires recognition by others. But for sovereigns acting as a cartel it is much less difficult, because the members of the cartel (the community of sovereigns) provide the recognition. It may well be the case that non-state actors – for example, those that had been providing the governance – are less interested in recognizing a reassertion of state right. But they have much less purchase in resisting a claim by sovereigns collectively than they would claims by individual states.

Seeing sovereignty as a set of rights claims supported by the community of sovereigns, as a recognition cartel, also allows for the possibility of viewing sovereignty as something more flexible than an absolute condition and something that can vary along more than a single dimension of stronger or weaker. Much as the specific content of property rights can change over time, the content of sovereign right can change over time. Sovereign rights, in this analysis, are whatever the community of sovereigns at a particular time collectively claim them to be. Change in the content of this claim can represent the interests of states as states, which vary over time in response to changing global economic and political conditions.

Change can also be driven by evolution in the normative substructure of sovereignty, the sets of beliefs shared by governors and governed alike about who should be sovereign and what good governance entails. Examples of such change can be found in decolonization and multilateralism – the ideas that all peoples should have their own sovereignty and that formal sovereign cooperation should be the default form of governance for a broad range of global issues. Neither idea existed as a norm a century and a half ago, but both were broadly accepted and firmly institutionalized in international relations by half a century ago. Both are fundamental to the contemporary practice of sovereignty and are reinforced by the cartel.

Inconsistent Sovereignties

The second aspect of sovereignty understood as a set of property rights that provides the focus of this book is the observation that there is no clear rational or coherent plan of what sovereign right consists of. The concept of property rights itself is a social construct and thus subject to different understandings across time and place. The set of rights that constitutes sovereignty, in other words, is not necessarily internally consistent. Furthermore, the set changes over time, and new rights can conflict with the old.

One way of distinguishing among different rights constructs in general is to distinguish between negative and positive rights – the right against interference versus the right to participate with others. An illustration of this distinction can be found in property rights. Take, for example, the way in which property is understood by an archetypical rancher in the American west. For the rancher, property is exclusion, the right to keep others out. There is a fence around the property, and anyone who crosses it without permission is liable to get shot. This is analogous to one way that sovereignty was understood for much of the history of the European states system. Sovereignty understood through this lens means autonomy – sovereignty as the right of the sovereign to be free from constraint in dealing with its own territory and population as it sees fit.

Contrast this view with the way property is understood by investors in public companies. For the shareholder, property rights are the claim both on a financial stake in and to a specified vote in the management of an asset, rather than physical control over that asset. Property rights understood in this way are not about exclusion or sole physical control. They are about participation in governance and fractional benefit from operations. A (loosely) analogous understanding of property in the sovereign states system is multilateralism – sovereignty as the right to participate in the making of international rules, regulations, and norms that bind all sovereigns.

Both of these understandings of rights inform the discourses and practices of contemporary international politics. But the two understandings are in principle mutually incompatible. Sovereignty-as-autonomy suggests an inalienable right to control what goes on within an internationally recognized set of borders. Sovereignty-as-participation, however, is premised on the idea that states need to give up that very autonomy to participate in global governance. The former understanding of sovereignty is generally understood to have the longer history in the Westphalian international system, with the idea of multilateralism developing more recently (over the past century or so). And yet, while norms of multilateralism have clearly embedded themselves deeply in the practice of international relations, particularly since the end of World War II, they do not seem to be displacing the discourse of sovereignty as autonomy. The two forms of sovereignty, although in principle incompatible, nonetheless seem in practice to be thriving in parallel to each other.

This parallel structure of different definitions of the rights underlying sovereignty leads to a set of discourses in international relations that cannot be fully reconciled with each other. In one of the best known recent books on the institution of sovereignty, Stephen Krasner points to this inability of political actors to reconcile the various discourses and practices of sovereignty, and concludes that sovereignty is a form of organized hypocrisy, a set of norms that is long-lasting but that statespeople do not take particularly seriously in practice.[6] My argument is the opposite of Krasner's. The specific norms of sovereignty do change over time, and statespeople take them very seriously – seriously enough that they put considerable effort into reconstituting those norms through practice. However, the process of change leads to practices that can be mutually inconsistent.

This inconsistency reinforces the need for a sovereignty cartel. If the set of property rights associated with sovereignty was consistent both internally and over time, then much of the work of maintaining sovereign right could be done by simple inertia; sovereigns might generally be able to retain their property rights by default unless other categories of actors made active counterclaims. But a set of rights that is both changeable and internally inconsistent takes more effort to maintain because the specific default rights claims in any given case are unclear. When the content of the rights underlying specific claims are unclear, the claims themselves are less likely to succeed through deference and are more likely to require enforcement. This is precisely what the sovereignty cartel is for: to enforce claims of sovereign right in those circumstances when the community of sovereigns can collectively agree on what those rights are.

Concurrently, however, inconsistent sovereign rights claims may well undermine the credibility of those claims over time. Participants in inconsistent discourses of sovereign property therefore need some mechanism to reconcile specific dissonant claims without undermining the broader claim of sovereign right. Krasner's suggested mechanism is organized hypocrisy (which is, it should be noted, its own kind of sovereignty cartel). But this mechanism implies that invocations of sovereignty and sovereign right are self-consciously hypocritical, an implication that is inconsistent with even a cursory understanding of the practices and discourses of contemporary international relations. I suggest a different mechanism, which I call "normative dissonance." The term is a play on the theory of cognitive dissonance in psychology,[7] and posits that participants in the practices and discourses of contemporary international relations deal with an inconsistent normative structure to contemporary sovereignty through a set of cognitive mechanisms that allows them to deny or ignore the inconsistencies. These are, as a result, never really resolved but rather negotiated anew

[6] Krasner 1999.   [7] Festinger 1957; Jervis 1976.

as normative tensions between various understandings of sovereign property reappear in new political contexts.

Plan of the Book

This book first builds the groundwork for this view of sovereignty, and then develops and complicates the case for thinking of sovereignty as a cartel, over several chapters. Chapter 2 makes the case for looking at sovereignty as a social construction rather than as a definitional absolute. It reviews various ways in which sovereignty is understood in international relations, and the analytical utility and limitations of using the concept in this way. It discusses the Peace of Westphalia in this context, since "Westphalian sovereignty" is a sufficiently common trope in international relations theory that it cannot be ignored (this discussion reappears in various places throughout the book). It also briefly discusses methodology and how the analytic approach taken here can address questions of both power in and change of sovereignty in ways that conceptualizing sovereignty as a definitional absolute cannot.

Chapter 3 develops some of the basic arguments of the book. It develops the idea of using property rights as a lens through which to study sovereignty and contextualizes that lens in a broader ontology of sovereignty. It builds on the property rights lens to develop the core idea of the book, that sovereignty can usefully be seen as a recognition cartel in which a small group of actors arrogate to themselves, and work communally to protect, a set of exclusive rights to global governance. It also addresses the question of why the sovereignty cartel should be read as a social construction, as the political expression of a set of norms of sovereignty, rather than as a simple interest-based argument. Yes, interests matter and power matters, but both matter in the context of, and can only be understood as expressions of, an ontologically prior set of norms associated with sovereignty.

The sovereignty cartel is unpacked and illustrated in Chapter 4, which looks at some of the individual-level practices through which the sovereignty cartel is reconstituted in the daily conduct of international politics. The chapter makes the connection between sovereignty as an abstract concept and the actual people who act on the international stage in the name of that concept. It complicates the idea of property rights by discussing the responsibilities that are often part and parcel of rights. These property rights include responsibilities to other sovereigns, but also include responsibilities to the citizenries in whose name states rule. In addition, the chapter provides examples of the sovereignty cartel in action, drawn from a variety of issues, including multilateral participation, human rights, and the governance of the commons. These all show ways in which sovereign right involves specific and historically contingent claims by states, and requires of those states specific behaviors, rather than being a generic claim that can be understood and studied out of context.

The discussion of sovereignty to this point has mentioned the idea of sovereigns, as well as the state and individuals who speak for the state. But it has not delved into the relationship between sovereignty and the sovereign, and between the sovereign and the state. Who decides who is sovereign, which is to say who controls the property rights associated with state sovereignty? Chapter 5 addresses this question, arguing that the rules about who gets to be sovereign are, at least in part, both imposed and enforced by the cartel – which is to say that the sovereign is a member of the cartel because she is recognized as sovereign by the other members of the cartel. The norms underlying this recognition change over time, and the chapter notes five different major changes in these norms since the Westphalian settlement. But these norms are sticky, and new ones often do not fully displace earlier ones. Sovereignty disputes are therefore often messy: not only are the norms that govern what constitutes sovereign property mutually contradictory, but the norms governing whose property it is are mutually contradictory as well.

Having made a general case for property rights as a lens through which to study sovereignty and having addressed the question of who is the sovereign who holds those rights, Chapter 6 circles back to the question of what we understand property rights to mean. It looks at the roots of different aspects of contemporary sovereign rights in both Roman law and English contract law. It looks at what these different traditions of property have to say about sovereignty with respect to both domestic politics and international relations, and how they interact with other ideas that legitimate the modern state such as popular sovereignty and nationalism. It connects the Roman tradition with a national interest in autonomy and the English tradition with a national interest in multilateralism. And it highlights the conceptual tensions between these traditions as practiced in contemporary international relations.

Plan of the Book

But what of the practical effects of these tensions? One of the key practical effects is a governance gap between autonomy and multilateralism into which a variety of illicit activities falls. Chapter 7 looks into these interstices of the contemporary sovereign states system. It argues that the tensions not only create spaces in the system in which illicit activity can find a home but actually force some activity there by definition. This often involves non-sovereign actors engaged in economic pursuits, either finding the interstices of sovereignty to arbitrage regulatory gaps or forced into the interstices by those gaps. It also often involves sovereign actors taking advantage of the market value of their sovereign property rights to enrich either their states or themselves. These gaps in governance in the sovereign states system introduce places where sovereign right can be challenged; to this extent the globalization and neomedievalism arguments have a point. This is (in part) why a sovereignty cartel is necessary to maintain these rights. The cartel is the mechanism by which the sovereign states system polices its interstices and keeps them from undermining the prerogatives of its members.

Chapter 8 fills in the last piece of the theoretical story of this book. It looks at the various normative tensions and governance gaps in contemporary state sovereignty and asks how sovereignty can be maintained as a set of broadly recognized norms, rather than simply as rights claims, in the face of those tensions. It introduces the idea of normative dissonance and connects it to arguments from political psychology about the cognitive mechanisms people use to navigate dissonant information and beliefs. It runs this idea past normative tensions in questions both of what sovereign property rights are and of who should hold those rights. This introduction of political psychology into the story of the sovereignty cartel provides a mechanism for thinking about state sovereignty as a system that cannot be reduced to a rational set of rules or to a simple discussion of interests, but that reconstitutes itself nonetheless. It is in this sense like any other social system: it does not make coherent sense, but it functions, so we make what sense of it that we can.

The concluding chapter addresses the "So what?" question: what do we learn from studying sovereignty through a property rights lens? One key upshot of the argument is that changes in international patterns of economic regulation and use of force are not necessarily indicative of either the strength of or the content of claims of sovereign right. Sovereignty maintains its centrality in the international system not only (arguably not even primarily) through the practice of governance, but also through collusion to reinforce a normative structure of sovereign right. Another is that it is to a significant degree the members of the cartel who decide who benefits from sovereign property rights. This means that sovereignty is inseparable from the international system. To argue that sovereign actors should keep out of each other's domestic politics is therefore disingenuous.

Finally, the chapter concludes with some thoughts about the "So what?" question for international relations theorists. For theorists of foreign policy, the sovereignty cartel helps to explain deference by bigger states to the sovereign rights claims of smaller states when national interest would argue against such deference. For globalization theorists, the cartel shows that globalization and sovereignty do not vary inversely on a unidimensional spectrum. For theorists of the social structure of the international system, it highlights the often-overlooked agentive processes needed to maintain existing social structures rather than just agentive mechanisms for changing structures. And for theorists of sovereignty, the cartel is an example of the complexity of sovereignty and of the value in studying this complexity from a variety of perspectives rather than arguing over what sovereignty means in some abstract sense.

2 | *Sovereignty?*

The idea of a sovereignty cartel is based on a view of sovereignty as a specific set of property rights claimed by sovereigns in contemporary international politics. This chapter lays some of the groundwork for viewing sovereignty through this lens. It does so first by contrasting the property approach with how sovereignty is usually understood in the international relations literature: as a single unvarying attribute rather than as a changeable set of social practices. Viewing sovereignty as a changeable set of social practices, some of which can usefully be understood as property rights, allows for a much richer and more nuanced reading of international relations while avoiding sterile debates about whose definition of sovereignty is the "correct" one. These debates often center on the Peace of Westphalia as an origin story of the contemporary sovereign states system. The second section of this chapter makes the case that these debates miss the point. The rest of the chapter discusses some of the methodological and theoretical ramifications of looking at sovereignty as a changeable set of social practices, prior to the introduction of the property rights lens specifically in Chapter 3.

Whither Sovereignty

What does sovereignty mean? The word can be used in a number of contexts, ranging from the political to the religious.[1] The particular context that I am interested in here is as an attribute of states in the modern sovereign states system. In other words, sovereignty as a constitutive aspect of the state in contemporary international relations. This statement will be unpacked and elaborated upon both in this chapter and the next. But it needs to be stressed that I am not claiming

---

[1] On the latter see, e.g., Munn 2006.

to discuss sovereignty as a generic concept; rather, this book is about one specific aspect of contemporary international relations.

Having said this, a core element of the argument of this book is that state sovereignty is not a single identifiable thing. It is a set of norms, practices, and discourses that legitimate the role of the state in both domestic governance and international politics and law. The content of this set is neither static over time nor necessarily internally consistent, which is to say that some of the practices (for instance) of sovereignty may be similar to those of a century ago (such as the issuance of passports) while others are quite different (such as the absence of formal colonialism). In contemporary international politics, noninterference and respect for human rights are both norms of sovereignty, without any clear mechanisms for adjudicating between them when they (inevitably) clash.[2]

As such, the content of sovereignty is arguably impossible to define definitively. It is the way we think about, talk about, and behave with respect to the state as the legitimate ultimate source of governance. We can study it as a set of discourses,[3] as a set of authority relationships,[4] as a set of legal structures,[5] etc. All of these modes of study will yield different understandings of contemporary state sovereignty, built on epistemologically different bases, but none will be inherently more accurate or definitive than the others. The route taken in this book is to study sovereignty as a set of property rights, not based on a claim that doing so is *the* correct way to study sovereignty but on a claim that it is *a* useful way, and that it illuminates the cartel aspect of sovereignty that we otherwise do not see.

What I am arguing against in this book, then, is the essentialization of sovereignty, the idea that sovereignty is a specific thing or essence, whatever that thing is defined as. The essentialization of sovereignty is widespread in the international relations literature. Realists, for example, tend to assume a radical disjuncture between domestic and international politics that is premised on a "Westphalian" sovereignty of domestic autonomy and hierarchy and an international anarchy.[6] Globalization theorists often assert that an increase in globalization, however understood or measured, necessarily equals a decrease in

---

[2] E.g., Barkin 1998.　[3] E.g., Aalberts 2004.　[4] E.g., Lake 2003.
[5] E.g., Gross 1948.　[6] See, e.g., the example in Lake 2003: 305–307.

sovereignty.⁷ Sovereignty in this understanding is a specific measurable thing that correlates inversely with globalization. Liberal institutionalists in international relations theory, meanwhile, often understand sovereignty in purely legal terms, as the exclusive right to engage in legally binding multilateral treaty making and cooperation.⁸ This understanding of the essential meaning of sovereignty is, of course, incompatible with that of globalization theorists who argue that such binding cooperation is part of what is undermining sovereignty (not to mention populists who see globalization or the EU as undermining sovereignty).⁹

A very different view of sovereignty from that found within the mainstream Anglophone international relations literature can be found in the realm of critical theory. Carl Schmitt, for example, defined the sovereign as the individual who has the power to define the state of exception to the law.¹⁰ Building on this conceptualization, Giorgio Agamben speaks of sovereign power as the power to create zones of exclusion from the law or from politics.¹¹ Sovereignty is being used here as an analytical concept in service of a critique of the state. It is being defined as a different essentialized type from the Westphalian metaphor so often used in international relations theory (Agamben is drawing on classical Roman religious law rather than seventeenth-century treaty law for his metaphor), but it is being essentialized nonetheless.

All of these approaches to the examination of sovereignty have in common that they attempt to essentialize sovereignty.¹² In other words, they approach it as an abstract concept and then examine the extent to which practice accords with the concept that has been variously defined. The approach used in this book begins with practice, rather than with concept, and thus sees sovereignty as contextual to time and place. This approach requires a recognition that there is no essential core to something like state sovereignty. Such a recognition is not in itself new to the international relations literature, although existing arguments about the contextuality of sovereignty do not

---

⁷ E.g., Korten 2001. ⁸ E.g., Goldstein et al. 2001.
⁹ On the broader debate about whether sovereignty should be understood as a legal or political phenomenon, see Prokhovnik 2007.
¹⁰ Schmitt 2005. ¹¹ Agamben 1998.
¹² For a more detailed version of this argument, see Kalmo and Skinner 2010.

develop this observation into an argument about contemporary sovereignty as a cartel.[13]

Some analyses, in recognizing the contextuality of sovereignty, approach the complexity of actual practices of sovereignty by breaking the general concept up into various aspects. David Lake, for example, speaks of two kinds of sovereignty: the internal and the external.[14] Janice Thomson divides the concept using (among other things) two dichotomies, that between internal and external, and that between de jure, or legal, sovereignty, and de facto sovereignty, or practical autonomy.[15] Loosely following these distinctions, Stephen Krasner identifies four kinds of sovereignty:[16] (1) domestic sovereignty (located in the domestic/de jure box of a 2×2 of Thomson's two distinctions); (2) interdependence sovereignty (domestic/de facto); (3) international legal sovereignty (international/de jure); and (4) Westphalian sovereignty (international/de facto, somewhat ironically given that Krasner argues elsewhere against the interpretation of the Peace of Westphalia that this metaphor is built on).[17]

Attempts such as these to allow for the complexity of state sovereignty do go part of the way in addressing the variety of norms, practices, and discourses associated with sovereignty. But they nonetheless remain exercises in essentializing in that they attempt to create a comprehensive categorization of sovereignty. Each category has its own rules, but those rules are mutually compatible, and thus a particular political behavior either fits in the rules or fails to – it is either pro-sovereignty or anti-sovereignty. And although the categories allow for different aspects of sovereignty, they remain fixed categories. Sovereignty can, for this approach, mean different things but those things remain constant over time.

Oddly enough, the approach to conceptualizing sovereignty as a set of categories leads to quite different conclusions about the state of state sovereignty than does the approach that focuses on a single overriding feature in the definition of sovereignty. Definitions that focus on a single feature (such as exclusive control within a specified territory) often look back at an idealized "Westphalian" state and then note that this ideal is far from contemporary practice (the idealizing of Westphalia will be discussed at more length in the following sections).

---

[13] E.g., Biersteker and Weber 1996.   [14] Lake 2003.   [15] Thomson 1995.
[16] Krasner 1999.   [17] Krasner 1993.

The conclusion that is often drawn is that since we are far from the defined ideal, sovereignty must be getting weaker. When conceptualizing sovereignty as more multifaceted, however, it becomes more difficult to maintain that there was a point in time when international politics conformed to all aspects of the definition, when states were fully "sovereign" in all of the various categories. Thus Krasner ends up concluding that states were never sovereign, that state sovereignty is a myth hypocritically propounded by powerful states as a cover for the pursuit of their national interests.[18]

The approach taken in this book is to understand state sovereignty as a social construct, which is, in turn, to say that there is no single definition – be that definition essentialist or categorical – that applies across time and place. To understand sovereignty as a social construct we need to look at how it is practiced at a particular point in time and within a particular community.[19] The community that I am looking at here is the sovereign states system, the group of states that among them currently claim most of the territory on the planet and count the vast majority of its people as citizens, and that recognize each other as sovereign. The question I ask in this book is not "How well does this system currently conform to an abstract definition of sovereignty?" but rather "What are the norms, practices, and discourses associated with the term 'sovereignty' within this system at present?" These practices and discourses are multifaceted, and one book cannot do them all justice. The focus here, therefore, is on one lens through which to study contemporary sovereignty – what I call the property rights aspect of state sovereignty, because it is this lens that most clearly brings the self-reinforcing cartel practices of contemporary sovereignty into clearest focus.

Westphalia

The property rights aspect of state sovereignty, unlike many of the traits often associated with sovereignty in international relations

---

[18] Krasner 1999.
[19] While this is done in this book in the language of norms, practices, and discourses, it could be similarly done in the language of a series of specific rules associated with sovereignty that collectively describe sovereignty as a rule. This language would be compatible with the property rights lens used here. On rules and rule in international politics, see Onuf 1989.

literature, is one that can clearly be seen in the treaties that make up the Peace of Westphalia, a set of treaties signed in 1648 that marked the end of the Thirty Years War.[20] It might at first seem ironic that, after arguing that sovereignty should be studied as a contemporary practice, I am now claiming the same mantle of Westphalia as those I am criticizing. Nonetheless, a brief excursion through Westphalia to look at what is written in the treaties signed there in 1648 is worthwhile both to question the way in which reference to the Peace is used to legitimize various definitions of sovereignty[21] and to note that the property rights aspect of sovereignty that is the focus of this book has a long history within the European states system. It is, in this sense, one of the least novel of the practices associated with the contemporary sovereign states system.[22] The particular property rights of sovereignty have changed markedly since then, but the broader idea of sovereignty as property provides a useful lens through which to study the evolution of the modern international system. As such, I am discussing Westphalia not to legitimate my own definition of sovereignty, but to question the way in which it is used to legitimate other definitions, and to establish a point of reference for looking at ways in which the property rights aspect of state sovereignty has changed over time.

This is by no means the first effort to debunk the notion that the Peace of Westphalia created a principle of state autonomy within its borders or of noninterference in the affairs of other states.[23] The Peace spoke of rulers rather than states, but it did not give princes absolute control over their domains. The best known of these debunking efforts

---

[20] The Peace of Westphalia is generally thought to refer to the Treaties of Münster, between the Holy Roman Emperor and the King of France, and Osnabrück, between the Holy Roman Emperor and the Queen of Sweden. It is sometimes taken to refer as well to the Peace of Münster, also of 1648, between the King of Spain and the Dutch Republic. The Treaties of Münster and Osnabrück are similar in terms of content; the discussion in this chapter will draw mostly on the text of the former.

[21] For a seminal example of such use, see Gross 1948.

[22] Throughout this book, when I speak of the sovereign states system I am referring to relations among states specifically. When I speak of the international system, I am referring to the broader system of international politics within which the sovereign states system is embedded and which includes both those states and the various other actors (corporate and individual) with which those states interact and with which the sovereignty cartel competes.

[23] For a broader history of the Peace, see Croxton 2015. Croxton highlights the extent to which Westphalia is as much a medieval peace as a modern one.

within the mainstream international relations literature is probably Stephen Krasner's in "Westphalia and All That," and the most thorough may well be Andreas Osiander's in "Sovereignty, International Relations, and the Westphalian Myth."[24] Both authors point out that far from guaranteeing rulers absolute autonomy in determining religious affairs within their domains, the Peace actually withdrew from them the right to do so. The principle that the ruler has the right to determine the religion of the state (often noted in the Latin, *cuius regio eius religio*) was (arguably) a feature of the Treaty of Augsburg of 1555 and was explicitly limited in the Treaties of Münster and Osnabrück that constitute the Peace of Westphalia. In this sense, Westphalia can be seen as supporting the concept of constitutional limits on the domestic autonomy of sovereigns as much as creating the concept of the absolute autonomy of sovereigns.

Similarly, the Peace did not mark a clear watershed between a hierarchy of feudal patterns of rule before the Thirty Years War and an anarchy of a sovereign states system afterward.[25] The winners of the Peace – France and Sweden – were recognizable as independent states before the Thirty Years War, and the treaties did nothing to affect that status, although they did expand the territory of both monarchies. And the principalities within the Holy Roman Empire were not made fully independent by the Peace. In fact, Osiander argues that while the Peace did make the constitutional machinery of the Empire work more smoothly and transparently, it did not particularly undermine either the legal status or the legitimacy of the Empire. He notes that princes within the Empire remained subject to the rulings of its courts until well into the eighteenth century. Hugo Grotius, arguably the leading scholar of international law during the first half of the seventeenth century, and writing during the Thirty Years War, defined sovereignty as the right to appoint judges. The Peace did not give princes within the Empire this right (although it did give some of them the right to participate in the choosing of judges). This suggests that the framers of the Peace did not think that they were granting absolute sovereignty to said princes. Nor did the Peace set new constraints on either the legal rights or the diplomatic standing of the Emperor. Westphalia, in other words, does not seem to have been an attempt to construct the legal framework of a sovereign states system,

[24] Krasner 1993; Osiander 2001.   [25] Croxton 2015.

according to a then-prevailing understanding of the meaning of sovereignty.

What was the Peace about, then? A majority of both treaties (much of the text in both is identical) consists of the minutiae of the postwar settlement – who got what piece of territory, who owed how much reparations to whom, and which disputes were to be sent to arbitration. This is the stuff of property rights in a direct sense. Much of the rest of the text was devoted to detailing the constitutional structure of the Holy Roman Empire, its parliaments, councils, and courts. Article 64 of the Treaty of Münster guarantees to "Princes and States of the Roman Empire ... free exercise of territorial right," but far from being a radical novelty, the same article describes this as one of their "establish'd and confirm'd ... antient [sic] rights."[26] The next article, 65, after noting that major decisions relating to the military and foreign affairs of the Empire were to be taken with the advice and consent of the Assembly of States, also notes that "it shall be free perpetually to each of the states of the Empire, to make Alliances with Strangers for their Preservation and Safety," subject to the constraint that such alliances "be not against the Emperor, and the Empire, nor against the Publick [sic] Peace."

It has been noted that this right to make alliances, like the rights declared in Article 64, was not a new one – it represented continuity as much as change in the structure of seventeenth-century international politics.[27] Whether or not it was a new right, the right to make formal alliances and, more broadly, to make treaties is associated in contemporary international politics with sovereign states. It is a property right, in the sense that will be discussed in Chapter 3. But it is not, according to the terms of the Peace, an absolute right. It was not exclusive to princes (the guarantee of the right to princes in the treaties is not a derogation of the right of the Emperor to ally). And it is subject to limitation – states could not make formal alliances that threaten the Emperor, and the Emperor could make formal alliances without the collective consent of the states. The right to make alliances, in other words, was subject to ground rules which formed the constitutional structure that framed the rights of princes within the Empire.

Yet when international relations scholars invoke the Westphalian metaphor, they often use it to refer to internal sovereignty, even though

---

[26] Treaty of Münster 1648.   [27] Osiander 2001: 273.

the terms of the Peace itself played only a minor role in affecting patterns of domestic authority in seventeenth-century Europe.[28] One manner in which the Peace did have an impact upon the relationship between external and internal sovereignty, however, was by reinforcing the notion of rulership as a property right. Much of the text of the constituent treaties of the Peace focuses upon the monetary obligations of various combatants to each other, in recompense for physical damages, for territories lost, and the like.[29] In other words, the assumption was made that in some real way the territories involved were the properties of their princes, and those princes deserved compensation for damage or loss. The idea of compensation for property loss was in itself, of course, in no way novel. What the Peace did was clearly identify the German princes, rather than the Holy Roman Emperor, members of lesser nobilities, or the actual inhabitants of the lands (the peasantry) as the appropriate recipient of this compensation. In other words, the territory of a principality was officially accepted for the purposes of international relations as the property specifically of the prince, and not of anyone else. This is significant among other reasons because it represented a denial of such claims by the Emperor, even though he remained first in rank among European sovereigns, as suggested by the fact that his name preceded all others in the Westphalian treaties.[30]

Where does all this leave us in the discussion of what state sovereignty means? It suggests a number of things. It suggests that references to Westphalia as a source of legitimation for essentialist definitions of sovereignty are historically inaccurate and misleading. An easily defined Westphalian sovereignty never existed, and it is not even clear what such a concept might mean. It suggests that many of the rights and capabilities that we associate with the sovereign state system in fact predate that system. In other words, not only are the practices of sovereignty socially constructed, but discourses of sovereignty can coopt practices that had previously been outside the discourse. It suggests that the rights of states at the moment of the putative birth of the sovereign states system were contingent, rather than absolute. This in

---

[28] Krasner 1993.
[29] These were often very specific in terms of amounts owed, payment terms, interest rates, etc. See for example Articles XIII, XVI, and XXIV of the Treaty of Münster 1648.
[30] Treaty of Münster 1648, preamble; and Osiander 1994.

turn suggests that sovereignty need not be thought of in an absolute, all-or-nothing way. Sovereignty can be contingent, constrained, or embedded in a constitutional structure that delimits the rights of states. This is, in part, what it means to be a practice rather than an essence. Finally, it suggests that there is a long history to understanding, and practicing, sovereignty as the right to property associated with the state or its territory.

The Social Construction of Sovereignty

Associating the sovereign states system with Westphalia, a set of documents three-and-a-half-centuries old, has the effect of implying that the system has a certain timelessness to it. After all, if the core features of the system can last more than a dozen generations, it must be highly resistant to change. Some analyses of this system simply assume that it is changeless – Waltzian analysis, for example, assumes that sovereignty is a fixed feature of the system and does not allow any mechanism for it to change.[31] But more broadly, any analysis that begins with the assumption that the features of the international system can be defined *ex ante* is essentializing sovereignty. Beginning with an abstract and absolute definition, actual practice can presumably never fully conform to the essentialized Westphalian sovereign state. Two approaches to this methodological artifact were noted previously – arguing that past practice was in fact closer to the definition and that, therefore, sovereignty is getting weaker, and arguing that the definition is not particularly historically relevant. Either way, the course of the discussion is determined by the essentialized definition, and only those aspects of contemporary practice that speak directly to that definition are relevant to that discussion.

And in this case the essentialized Westphalia is misleading, in no small part because scholars do not agree on what it means. Is it about domestic control or international legal personhood? Does it refer to the capabilities, prerogatives, or legitimacy of the sovereign? Is it about control over people, territory, or law? Can it be all these things at once? And if it is all these different things at once, is it an analytically useful construct, given that these things do not necessarily covary, and that what they mean (both collectively and individually) changes over

[31] Waltz 1979.

time? If it means so many different things at once, we cannot meaningfully discuss change over time, because the essentialized definition is both fixed and nonspecific, leaving us no metric or clear anchor for analysis.

A core premise of this book is that, rather than an essentialized and ahistorical Westphalian metaphor (whatever the content of that metaphor is), state sovereignty can usefully be studied through the lens of property rights, which are in turn a type of social construct. A skeptic of sociological approaches to social science might ask, "So what?" What is gained by using the language of social construction to study sovereignty, rather than, say, the language of rational calculation? One can argue that we can study pretty much any phenomenon in politics as socially constructed; as is the case with a definition of sovereignty that includes everything, this makes the concept not particularly analytically useful. More specifically, since a political phenomenon such as sovereignty is self-evidently social in nature, what is gained from belaboring its social constructedness? Why belabor the obvious?[32]

To this challenge I offer three responses. The first is that, as already noted, most discussions of contemporary state sovereignty do not in fact look at it as a social construct. They look at it most often through the lens of an ahistoricized Westphalian metaphor, and less often as a category of things or as a highly contested concept,[33] but only infrequently do they examine sovereignty as a social practice.[34] As such, a discussion of the differences between looking at state sovereignty as essentialized and as a social construction, along with a discussion of what it means to look at it as a social construction, is in itself a useful contribution to the study of the topic. It is, as already noted, not a new contribution, but helps to balance the conversation by adding a voice to the less heard side.

The second is that the general observation of the social constructedness of sovereignty is not the point here. Rather, the point is identifying an analytically useful aspect of the content of that construct.[35] That sovereignty is a social construct is not in fact in itself inconsequential – it

---

[32] For a discussion of this question that is broader than the context of state sovereignty, see Hacking 1999.
[33] E.g., Kalmo and Skinner 2010.
[34] For exceptions to this generalization, see, *inter alia*, Biersteker and Weber 1996; Spruyt 1996; and Srivastava (forthcoming).
[35] On models and analytic utility, see Barkin 2015a.

suggests that international politics need not be organized the way it is, that there may be a meaningful difference between practices in the contemporary sovereign states system and other international systems, both past and future (and, for that matter, between the contemporary system and hypothetical, deductive analyses that assume that states are rational unitary actors). But the analysis of phenomena such as sovereignty as social constructions in general, and as sets of property rights more specifically, goes beyond the claim that they are socially constructed, and looks at the actual practices, norms, and discourses that constitute the phenomena. In other words, while the premise of this book is that sovereignty is socially constructed, the purpose of the book is more specific: to examine inductively how the particular forms of this construction affect and are reproduced by the practice of contemporary international relations.

The third response is that understanding a phenomenon such as sovereignty as a social construct allows for a more dynamic understanding of international relations than the more common essentialized approach. Analyzing a concept like sovereignty through essentialized metaphors such as that suggested by "Westphalian sovereignty" implies giving it a fixed definition, and doing so in turn limits the scope of the analysis to the terms of the definition. As the norms, practices, and discourses associated with the phenomenon change over time, these terms become increasingly less relevant as tools for understanding contemporaneous international politics. Analyzing the concept inductively, as a set of social constructions rather than as an exogenous definition, allows one to get at the ways in which norms, practices, and discourses change, rather than just the ways in which practices diverge from the definition. And the constructions associated with state sovereignty in the contemporary sovereign states system are changing in ways that makes sovereignty neither stronger nor weaker (whatever those measures might mean in this context), but rather different. It also allows clearer insight into what is necessary to maintain the system of sovereign states, a question that is more difficult to get at if one begins by assuming a deductive, exogenous definition of sovereignty rather than a contextual understanding of it.

Co-Constitution and Power

The rest of this chapter elaborates on the latter two of these responses; a focus on the social construction of state sovereignty allows us to look both at content and at change. With respect to content, the task is to ask what particular social norms, practices, and discourses are associated with contemporary state sovereignty. There is likely to be some overlap between the general sorts of things included in various essentialized definitions of "Westphalian" sovereignty and the contemporary understandings and practices of sovereignty because the definitions draw at least to some extent on observations of how international politics works. However, beginning epistemologically with contemporary practice rather than with the essentialized Westphalian definition allows us to avoid the limitations imposed by the need to reference a fixed definition. A focus on contemporary norms, practices, and discourses also highlights ways in which states and other actors actively work to reinforce norms of sovereignty, as well as ways in which they may fail to respect the norms.

I have so far used the phrase "norms, practices, and discourses" a number of times; this is a good point at which to unpack it. I use "norms" in the sense that John Ruggie does, to mean an element of a normative framework, a set of intersubjective understandings about "fact, causation, and rectitude, as well as political rights and obligations that are regarded as legitimate."[36] "Practices" are day-to-day patterned behaviors that respond to context and practical circumstance.[37] For example, Iver Neumann argues that Norwegian foreign affairs ministry speeches are uniformly boring not because of a principled belief in boring speeches, but because such speech-writing practices have been generated by the circumstances of working in the ministry.[38] "Discourses" are the languages that are used in any given undertaking, which both generate social structure and delimit the scope of how it is possible to talk about international politics.[39] Norms, practices, and discourses are all implicated in processes of reconstituting and changing sovereignty; norms are instantiated through practice and communicated through discourse.

Norms, practices, and discourses are understood here epistemologically as manifestations of the co-constitution of agents and structures. "Agents" in this context refers to actors who make decisions, think thoughts, and engage in discourses in ways that are not perfectly

---

[36] Ruggie 1982: 380. [37] E.g., Leander 2011; McCourt 2016.
[38] Neumann 2007. [39] See, respectively, Onuf 1989 and Goddard 2009.

predictable.[40] "Structures" in this context are social structures, existing intersubjective understandings, norms, discourses, practices, and the like that constitute the social setting within which individuals find themselves. The idea behind co-constitution is that neither agents nor structures precede the other, either temporally or ontologically.[41] Rather, they exist in a dialectical relationship with each other. Agents are both constrained by the social structures within which they find themselves and constituted by the social structures within which they developed.[42] To speak of what a person will do, say, or think without discussion of their social context is therefore meaningless. At the same time, however, structures are constituted by the agents within them. Norms and discourses have no independent material reality[43] – they are social structures only inasmuch as agents internalize and act upon them. Practices are actions that concretize expectations and norms embedded in social structures. This book focuses both on the effects of contemporary norms, practices, discourses, etc., of sovereignty on agents, on actors in international relations, and on the role of those actors both in reinforcing and in changing those norms, practices, discourses, etc.

A common critique of approaches to the study of international relations that focus on social construction is that they are naïve in believing that political actors privilege norms over political power. This critique draws on the premise that to assume that norms matter is to assume that people act in deference to norms, in an appropriate way, rather than in a strategic or calculating way designed to maximize interest.[44] But this premise is not inherent to arguments about social construction. These arguments are, for the most part, not that actors will generally hew to ideals at the expense of clear political interest, but

---

[40] For a more detailed discussion of this view of agents and agency, see Barkin 2010, chapter 7.
[41] See, for example, Onuf 1989.
[42] There is some debate in international relations theory about whether corporate bodies such as states can be understood as actors, or whether only people should be thought of as actors. I lean toward the former position (on which, see Wendt 2004), but this debate is not critical one way or the other to the arguments in this book.
[43] On social construction and materiality in international relations theory, see Onuf 1989 and Wendt 1999.
[44] For sympathetic statements of this premise, see March and Olsen 1998 and Ruggie 1998.

rather that ideas or norms, or practices, or patterns of discourse define actors' political interests and constitute the terrain of options available to actors.[45] Power, in this view, is, like everything else, socially constructed rather than a reflection of exogenous material conditions.[46] To the extent that power is the ability to affect the behavior of others, it depends as much (if not more) on what others will find persuasive as it does on the capabilities of the original actor.[47] One might object that an exception to this latter observation is when the actor can accomplish his or her ends through pure destruction; however, a set of interests compatible with pure destruction is actually exceedingly rare in politics and even in war.[48] And the destruction of a sovereign state has not happened in the post-World War II era.[49]

In the context of the argument in this book, then, a discussion of the norms of sovereignty does not suggest that states follow these norms out of altruism. Norms are, it is true, certainly followed at times because they define appropriate behavior for an actor. At other times, norms define interests for actors. Fighting for one's nation is a clear example of a social construct (the nation) playing a sufficiently strong role in individuals' definition of their own interests that in many instances they volunteer to put themselves in harm's way for it. But norms also serve some interests: political actors can and do act strategically to promote norms that serve their interests and use norms to justify actions in their own self-interest. This does not mean that those actors do not believe in the norms (although it does not mean that they do, either). More importantly in this context, it does not

---

[45] E.g., Wendt 1999.
[46] And claims on power are themselves acts of social construction. See, e.g., Guzzini 2005.
[47] "Power" is being used here in a relational sense, as used in realist international relations theory, whence this particular critique of the social construction of international politics comes. For a critique of the realist use of power, see Guzzini 1998. For a broader discussion of power in international relations theory, see Barnett and Duvall 2005.
[48] E.g., Morgenthau 1948: 13–14.
[49] Note that this refers to a sovereignty rather than a government. Sovereignties have been divided (e.g., the USSR, Czechoslovakia, Malaya); there have been secessions (e.g., South Sudan); expulsions (e.g., Singapore); changes of state (e.g., Rhodesia to Zimbabwe); and amalgamations of sovereignties that proved reversible (the United Arab Republic), but none of these involved the destruction of a sovereign state. Perhaps the closest to such an example is South Vietnam, but South Vietnam was never recognized by the international community as being fully sovereign in the first place.

make those norms any less relevant as central features of international relations. In other words, it is not a choice between a focus on power or a focus on ideas. Understanding uses of power in international relations requires understanding the ideas that underlie and motivate behaviors and discourses.

Co-Constitution and Change

The third and final of the responses offered above to the "So what?" challenge to a focus on the social construction of state sovereignty is that it is dynamic, that it allows for change in a way that a definition-driven approach to the study of sovereignty does not. An understanding of sovereignty that begins with an essentialized Westphalian metaphor cannot effectively account for change, because the phenomenon that is being described is fixed *ex ante*, unchangeable. It cannot even really describe change. It can show that the conformity of practice to the definition is stronger or weaker, but it has no basis for describing such practices that are orthogonal to the definition.

Nor can such an essentialized approach deal adequately with the question of where sovereignty came from. To begin with an essentialized definition of sovereignty and then argue that practice does not conform to that definition achieves no analytical purpose. And in any case, to describe it via an essentialized definition serves no useful analytical function without a clear argument about why we should care about that particular essence. In other words, such an approach should begin with a clear theoretical discussion that establishes the principled reasoning behind the definition.[50] Most essentializing approaches to defining sovereignty signally fail to do this. Such principled reasoning could, in fact, reasonably lead to an ideal of absolute domestic autonomy for the sovereign in an era of legitimate monarchy and divine right. But that era is long gone, sufficiently so that retaining its essence more than two centuries later seems oddly anachronistic. One could still reasonably ask how an eighteenth-century essence affects contemporary practice, but that is a much more nuanced question than asking the extent to which the eighteenth-century ideal still

---

[50] For a broader discussion of the use of analyticism in the study of international relations, see Jackson 2011.

holds. It is a question that has not been given much prominence in the sovereignty literature.

One could base one's essentializing definition of sovereignty on a historical claim, anchoring the type in a particular context and arguing that the context still to some extent applies. This is fundamentally what scholars do in invoking "Westphalia." But, as noted previously, the Westphalian settlement did not really mark the radical departure from earlier practice that is often portrayed. The practice of international relations that came out of Westphalia is clearly a historical antecedent to the contemporary sovereign states system, but it is not necessarily clear that the middle of the seventeenth century marked a change that distinguishes the practice of international relations afterwards from international politics in other historical state systems. This then suggests the question: why focus on the Peace of Westphalia? Why not Augsburg before it, or Vienna, or Versailles, or Bretton Woods after?[51] Beyond this question, there is the further question about why the degree to which contemporary practice approximates a historical (rather than principled) ideal matters. Such an approach can establish that we do not do things the way they used to be done (although this would require a more accurate definition of the way things used to be done than is usually the case). But it would not tell us how we got from there to here, or where "here" is.

An emphasis on co-constitution, the ways in which norms, practices, and discourses constitute agents while agents simultaneously constitute these norms, marks a key difference between an analysis of sovereignty as a social construction and an analysis that begins with a Westphalian metaphor.[52] To the extent that the latter approach actually examines sovereignty-related practices and discourses, rather than using sovereignty as a background condition, it examines the extent to which behavior conforms to the given definition. Either way, sovereignty is a constant, unchangeable. It can have stronger or weaker effects on the behavior of actors, but this behavior cannot in turn affect the meaning of sovereignty. However, an approach to the study of sovereignty that sees it as a social construct allows that the behavior and discourse of actors in turn can affect what sovereignty means.[53]

---

[51] On changes to the norms of sovereignty as a result of post-war treaty making, see Barkin and Cronin 1994.
[52] Which is not to say this has not been done well elsewhere. See, for example, Burch 2000.
[53] For a more detailed presentation of this argument, see Barkin 2010, chapter 7.

To figure out the contemporary practice of sovereignty, we need to begin with the contemporary practice of sovereignty. But a simple approach to norms, practice, and discourse that sees a linear causal relationship between them and behavior is not in itself sufficient for a discussion of change, either historical or contemporary, in the sovereign states system. Norms constrain agents. Agents respond to norms differently over time, as they find themselves in different political situations. These different responses in turn affect the content of the norms.[54] This third step is the mechanism for understanding change that is missing from Westphalian essentializing approaches to examining sovereignty. Norms exist as social structure only insofar as they affect the behavior of agents. They are, in effect, constituted by this behavior. As such, norms do not exist over time in the absence of behavior that reconstitutes them, and there is no reason to expect that they will be continually reconstituted with precisely the same content over time.[55]

Herein lies the mechanism for studying change in political structures that a co-constitutive approach has access to but a definition-driven approach does not. Looking at ways in which political actors behave toward social structures, rather than just how they behave in response to political structures, lets us follow how those structures are reconstituted in ways that show both continuity with and difference from earlier structures. It allows us, in other words, to see the evolution of norms, practices, and discourses as well as the simple strengthening or weakening of them. It allows us to see how interaction between agents and structures changes both.[56]

In the study of the norms of sovereignty, particularly the propertarian aspects of those norms, there are a number of places one can look to see this process of co-constitution, of agents addressing norms in an attempt, at the same time, to reconstitute and change political structures in ways that in turn lead to changes in the agents themselves. One can look, for example, at the high politics of postwar conferences,

---

[54] For an example of work that studies intentional efforts to change international norms, see Keck and Sikkink 1998.

[55] In Onuf's (1989) language of rules and rule, rules are speech acts that collectively constitute a structure of rule. If they are not spoken and respoken, they cease to be rules, and the structure of rule has changed.

[56] For a detailed methodological discussion of this process and its ontological complications, see Klotz and Lynch 2007.

in which the most powerful sovereigns (i.e., those agents most empowered by the existing social structure of international politics) self-consciously engage in an attempt to update the normative structure of the sovereign states system.[57] One can look at the more gradual deployment of discursive strategies by statespeople.[58] One can look at the seemingly more prosaic world of international law, in which the agents of the state engage in day-to-day activities that have the effect (sometimes by design, sometimes not) of both reinforcing and changing the normative structure of the system.[59] Or one can look at popular political discourse, in which political actors who are not part of the corporate agency of the state both react to political discourses through the lenses of the normative structures by which they are in part constituted and deploy discursive strategies to reconstitute and change those structures.[60]

Before moving on to an actual study of sovereignty, a final note on the general topic of social construction: social constructs in practice are not always neat. The discussion to this point can be read as implying that social constructions are unified entities, that there is, at any given point in time, an identifiable thing that is the social construction of, say, sovereignty. But social constructions are always contested. That is why they change. This contestation means that the boundaries of the social construct are not always clear and that all of the normative elements of the construct are not necessarily mutually compatible. Change, in other words, is messy, and introducing a mechanism for understanding normative change into the study of sovereignty makes sovereignty as a concept messier.

The next two chapters of this book apply a fairly straightforward property rights lens to the study of contemporary sovereignty and ask what this tells us about how contemporary sovereignty is understood and practiced. The following four chapters make this analysis messier, first by introducing different understandings of what property is and then by asking whose property sovereignty is. Both questions, as it turns out, are highly contested.

---

[57] E.g., Barkin and Cronin 1994.   [58] E.g., Goddard 2009.
[59] E.g., Neumann 2007.   [60] E.g., Keck and Sikkink 1998.

3 Sovereign Rights

To speak of a single norm of sovereignty is misplaced. Even at a specific time and place, the variety of discourses and practices associated with the word "sovereignty" is far too varied to be thought of as a specific norm, or even a specific interrelated set of norms. One could instead speak of sovereignty as a norm set, but a more appropriate image might be that of a norm tangle. This image is appropriate even when speaking specifically of state sovereignty. One can speak of state sovereignty as control or as legitimacy, as internal or external, as legal or political, as an empirical observation or as a normative goal. Rather than try to describe this tangle as a whole, or to try to slice it up into smaller knots to be studied individually, this book tries to isolate one specific norm strand from the tangle. This strand is what I call the property rights aspect of sovereignty.[1]

This aspect of sovereignty is best understood as a strand rather than as a slice because it has an internal logic to it. It overlaps significantly with the external/de jure box of Janice Thomson's categorization of sovereignty[2] and the international legal sovereignty box of Stephen Krasner's.[3] But it is different from this category in ways that make it a normative strand (something that, while it may at first appear to wander all over the place, has a clear internal structure to it) rather than a slice (something that, while it may appear compact and neat, is made up of knotty bits that sometimes fail to connect to each other). The first of these ways has to do with the distinction between de jure and de facto. While this distinction is in many ways useful, it is ultimately insupportable in a discussion of rights, particularly in international law. Formal law, as the classical realists agued, cannot be fully separated from the normative structure in which it is embedded.[4]

---

[1] For earlier uses of a property rights lens in this context, see, *inter alia*, Kratochwil 1995 and Burch 1998.
[2] Thomson 1995.   [3] Krasner 1999.   [4] Morgenthau 1940.

Furthermore, rights, including property rights, generally fade when not used. A de jure right that has no de facto presence ceases over time to be accepted as a right. This is particularly true in a legal system such as international law, which is based on the interpretation and codification of practice rather than on legislated statute.[5] And a de facto right, when practiced and accepted consistently, over time becomes de jure.[6]

Similarly, the distinction between external and internal, while useful in many ways, cannot ultimately distinguish between different kinds of behavior associated with the property rights aspect of state sovereignty. Autonomy against interference by the outside world in domestic affairs is, by definition, impossible in a states system – that they are together in a system implies that they interfere with each other, and if this interference did not have any domestic impacts at all, then international relations would be largely irrelevant. This is even more true if, following Bodin, we define sovereignty as the right to appoint magistrates.[7] Property rights sometimes need to be arbitrated; they need magistrates, or some functional equivalent thereof. To the extent that sovereignty is understood as a property right within a sovereign states system, there must then be some mechanism of arbitration, some equivalent of magistrates, at the systemic level. Because there is no higher authority to appoint these magistrates, it must be done by sovereigns collectively rather than individually. Disentangling the domestic aspects of sovereignty from the international in a sovereign states system ultimately cannot be done.

Beginning with a concept such as property rights, rather than with a categorization, for the most part avoids these failures of distinctions because it is based on a core concept rather than on a distinction. There are certainly aspects of sovereignty that can reasonably be discussed both in the context of property rights and in the context of other relevant concepts (such as, perhaps, legitimacy or authority). But there is no need to associate these aspects with one or the other concept exclusively – since this is not a categorization, aspects of sovereignty need not be put in one box or another. As long as an aspect of sovereignty speaks to the logical strand of property rights, it fits here even if it fits elsewhere as well. This is why I refer to the property rights aspect as a lens rather than as a category of sovereignty per se. The utility of the lens rests in whether it allows us to understand

[5] E.g., Henkin 1979. [6] E.g., Bodansky 1995: 105. [7] Bodin 1945: 172.

Property Rights

The term "property right" is used here in the broad sense of the term, to refer to "a socially enforced right to select uses of an economic good."[9] Such select uses might include possession, consumption, or transfer of a good. They might also include the right to earn income from or delegate authority or control over the good. Given this range of uses, property rights are often thought of in the relevant literatures as a bundle of rights, not as a single right that can be specified in the general case.[10] This follows the general use of the term in economics, as well as the neoliberal institutionalist school of international relations theory.[11]

There are several aspects of this understanding of property rights that are worth stressing. The first is that it is quite different from a simple concept of the right to ownership and full control of a thing. A simple concept of ownership would in any case be difficult to apply to the range of economic goods over which one might have a property right. If you own a pen, for example, you can use it or not, keep others from it, take it with you when you go, etc. If you own land, you can still use it or not and keep others from it, but you cannot take it with you when you go. If you own a bond, you can earn income from it, but you cannot use it in an equivalent way because it is an obligation owed to you, rather than a physical thing. If you own the right to use a part of the electromagnetic spectrum, you have use rights, but any concept of physical possession is meaningless.[12]

In other words, it is less about who owns what than it is about who has the right to do what. It is in this sense as much about limitations on absolute rights to ownership as it is about the absence of constraint on ownership. A property right by this usage is one that is fully specified, rather than one that is absolute. And a property right is one that is

---

[8] For a discussion of this epistemological stance (which he calls analyticism), see Jackson 2011, chapter 5.
[9] Alchian 1991: 584.
[10] For a discussion and critique of the "bundle of rights" metaphor, see Klein and Robinson 2011.
[11] See, e.g., Keohane 1984.   [12] Coase 1959.

recognized by all relevant parties. This makes property rights distinct from property claims. A property claim can be purely self-enforced. It belongs to the property holder to the extent that the owner can retain it. But property rights are only such if they are generally recognized. In this sense, property rights fit clearly on the de jure side of a de facto/de jure distinction (although the caveat noted above about the recursive relationship between law and practice, particularly in the context of international law, applies).

Property rights are also not necessarily about what we traditionally think of as property. They can be about any aspect of our relationship with anything that can be considered property. A good example of this is one that is often used in discussions of the Coase Theorem, which argues that the market will allocate the costs of economic externalities efficiently as long as property rights are clear and enforceable, all parties have all the relevant information, and there are no transaction costs to either negotiating or litigating outcomes.[13] The example is of pollution from a factory causing harm to people downwind. In this example, the efficient solution (the one that maximizes aggregate utility) would be mechanisms that reduce the pollution at source. If it is clear who is responsible for the costs of the damage that the pollution is causing, and if the victims of the damage have recourse to enforceable adjudication, then it should be the case that such mechanisms will be installed, because whoever is responsible should be willing to pay the lesser costs of the mechanisms rather than the greater costs of damage to the surrounding businesses. This is true whoever is responsible, be it the polluter or the pollutee (or for that matter a third party). But if it isn't clear who is responsible (or if that responsibility is unenforceable), then it becomes less likely that the mechanisms will be installed. Property rights in this example include the right to pollute or the right to not be polluted, rather than ownership of a particular good per se.

Coase's purpose in discussing property rights was to make an argument about economic efficiency and perfect markets.[14] The purpose in this book is quite different – not to make an argument that norms of sovereignty should aspire to perfectly specified property rights but that much of the normative structure, practice, and discourse of sovereignty

---

[13] Coase 1960. These conditions of course never exist in practice; they are the ideal type of the perfect market.
[14] Coase 1960.

is empirically about the specification of the property rights associated with sovereignty.[15] Sovereign states, in other words, are often willing to recognize that sovereignty creates certain rights as a general rule so that the states themselves might have access to those rights, and to accept that their sovereignty entails certain responsibilities, in order that other states be constrained by the same responsibilities. Because property rights are rights only inasmuch as others recognize them, they are ultimately systemic rather than individual in nature. As such, they are sometimes best defended by defending the system of property rights in which a particular claim is embedded, rather than that claim itself. They are also sometimes best defended preemptively, by defending the broader normative structure when one does not have specific claims pending. This book, then, is about activity that defines and reconstitutes an international system of sovereign property rights, even when a particular sovereign's property rights are not threatened in an immediate sense.

The use of property rights as the lens through which to study sovereignty might seem at first an exercise in neoliberalism, in bringing an economistic perspective to bear on the role of the state in international relations.[16] This is, in fact, not the case, for reasons having to do with the difference between Coase's purpose in discussing property rights and mine. Coase, and those whose use of the concept of property rights are consistent with his, is concerned with efficiency, understood as the maximization of aggregate utility given a level of resource use. He is concerned with using the concept as a way to think about how to allocate rights and responsibilities in a way that maximizes utility.[17] However, not everyone who deals with property rights is concerned with maximizing this particular version of the common good. Actors who are concerned more with their own property rights in practice rather than the general allocation of property rights in theory may well

---

[15] See also Burch 1998.

[16] Which is what Keohane (1982: 325), for example, is explicitly claiming to do in bringing what he calls the "utilitarian social contract tradition," and specifically the Coase Theorem, to bear on international regimes.

[17] For example, the argument in Coase 1960 is cast as a disagreement with Arthur Pigou about whether dealing with economic externalities efficiently requires fiscal intervention by government, or whether it can be dealt with by clear specification of property rights.

be much more concerned about the distributional effects of property rights than their efficiency effects.

This concern with the distributional effects of property rights, and with maintaining or expanding one's own rights even at the expense of economic efficiency, can be seen throughout history, and can be seen well before the precursors of the contemporary discipline of economics developed in the eighteenth century. One can see it in practices such as slavery and feudalism, neither of which is economically efficient but both of which created vested interests. Most premodern societies had political systems that involved some sort of hereditary privilege, which can be seen as a property right to certain forms of political and economic advantage by right of birth.[18] Studying property rights in this light, as something that actors work to establish for their own ends rather than as an efficiency-maximizing public policy tool, is therefore in a way the antithesis of the neoliberal approach.[19] It focuses on the co-optation of property rights by those actors who are able to convince others to accept those rights, rather than the creation of a set of property rights that maximizes the common good.

A skeptical reader might suggest at this point that, having just proposed property rights as the aspect of sovereignty I am discussing, I am perhaps engaging in the sort of definition-driven analysis that I criticized in the previous chapter. But I am not, for two reasons. The first is that I am not claiming that sovereignty must (or should) be studied only as a set of property rights but rather that the lens of property rights provides insights into some practices of sovereignty. Property rights in this sense are an analytic tool to study sovereignty rather than a definition of sovereignty. The second is that I am not making any *ex ante* arguments about what these property rights are. A change in the specific property rights associated with the sovereign state can, in practice, generate major changes in the system. In other words, to begin with a focus on the property rights associated with sovereignty does not assume a particular norm set. Rather, it is a statement of the lens through with norms will be understood.

To this point, I have been discussing both property rights and sovereignty in the abstract, without addressing questions of how

---

[18] On the difference between a system of property rights that maximizes individual advantage (or "rent," as economists would refer to it) and one that is economically efficient, see North and Thomas 1973.

[19] E.g., Burch 1998.

specific agents – be they individual or corporate actors – come to obtain the property rights associated with state sovereignty at any given point in time ("corporate actors" here refers to organizations, including but not limited to states and economic corporations, that have some form of legal personhood and the ability to speak with an identifiable voice[20]). Who decides that states will have these rights? States themselves do. The rest of this chapter and the next will look at aspects of the process by which the society of states arrogates to itself property rights. Later chapters will then problematize this process by asking what counts as a sovereign state and what do we mean by property.

The Recognition Cartel

Property rights are only rights per se if they are socially enforced, which in turn requires that they be recognized by others. Without recognition, property claims can be defended by force, or they can be simply ignored by others rendering them moot; either way, they are not rights in a meaningful sense. But property rights allow the holder some security in the right by virtue of its acceptance by others. Sovereignty in the sovereign states system, by extension, only endows states with property rights to the extent that those rights are recognized by others willing to participate in the enforcement thereof. But who are these others? One answer to this question, not the only one but an important one, is other states. Sovereignty is in this sense a recognition cartel.

There are, of course, other sources of sovereign right, in particular domestic sources. States are only able to govern effectively when their populations accord them the right to govern. Such internal recognition of the rights of the state to govern is part of what empowers states to act effectively with respect to other states. But internal recognition is not the whole story. Both failed states and governments in exile are able to exercise many of the property rights associated with sovereignty even though they often draw on little if any domestic recognition of their right to govern, and they can deploy few if any of the material resources often associated with statehood.[21] How are they then able to act as states? What gives them the rights?

---

[20] See Wendt 2004 for a discussion of the state and corporate actorhood.
[21] For a discussion of sovereignty in the absence of some of the attributes of the state, see, e.g., Jackson 1993. See also Inayatullah 1996.

The short answer to this question is that states that do have domestic legitimacy, and states that have large economies and militaries to bring to bear in support of their foreign policies (an overlapping but distinct group), often choose to act in a way that supports the property rights of sovereignty in general, rather than (or as well as) their own individual rights. This aspect of sovereignty is thus one that must be looked at systemically: the property rights of sovereignty are common to all sovereigns, and for a state to claim a right of sovereignty for itself is to claim it for other sovereigns as well.[22]

State sovereignty in this sense is a system, but it is a self-selected system, a system in which actorhood is endogenous, determined from within the system rather than from without. States are not the only participants in international relations with popular legitimacy or access to resources. It is often noted, for example, that many transnational corporations are not only far richer than many states but also have some negotiating advantages over them.[23] Why then are these corporations excluded from the rights of sovereignty? Because states collectively choose to do so. States collectively choose who will have the rights of sovereignty and what those rights will be. They choose whom to recognize as sovereign, and choose to recognize certain rights in each other that they recognize in no other organizations, rights that then reinforce their centrality in international relations. It is in this sense that sovereignty is a recognition cartel.

Note that, as used here, "stateness" and "sovereignty" are not synonymous. Stateness – whether understood in the Weberian sense of the enforcement of a political order or (per the *Montevideo Convention on the Rights and Duties of States*) as possession of borders, a population, and a government – need not necessarily be sovereign. Organizations can act as states without being recognized by outside actors as being sovereign. Similarly, sovereigns can be recognized as such without having actual effective possession of borders and a population and without governing. In other words, performing stateness is distinct from performing sovereignty. These sets of performances overlap in a sovereign states system, but claims of sovereign right are not reduceable to the practices of domestic governance and national security that stateness entails.

---

[22] D'Amato and Falk 1971.
[23] Nor is this a new argument. See, for example, Vernon 1971.

In general, both the idea of sovereign rights as a principle and the idea of a recognition cartel suggest that all entities recognized within the cartel as sovereign should enjoy the same formal rights. To the extent that these rights constitute the accepted normative structure of the sovereign states system, one would expect that all the sovereign states within the system should enjoy those rights in a similar fashion.[24] However, it is not the case, as some arguments about sovereignty have claimed, that sovereignty must necessarily be a binary condition, in which one is either fully sovereign or one is not.[25] The sovereignty cartel is a group of corporate political actors that works to monopolize certain kinds of rights with respect to international politics. To this end, it chooses to include among its numbers some specific actors and not others, in a system that is self-perpetuating to the extent that the cartel succeeds in maintaining these rights to a significant degree.

A cartel of this sort (as is the case with cartels in general) works best if all international politics can be brought within it, or – to phrase it differently – if no property claims can be made effectively outside of it. This means that the cartel has an incentive to be as inclusive as possible in term of things like territory and population, because the more inclusive it is, the more of international politics that happens within its purview, the easier it is for the cartel to make the rights of membership as exclusive as possible, to prevent nonmembers from successfully claiming those rights. For example, to the extent that one of the rights of sovereignty is the claim to a legitimate monopoly on military force, the claim is more easily maintained if all territories and all populations are represented by sovereigns, leaving no place or people in a vacuum in which there can be no legitimate military force. Complete coverage in this sense would be ideal, but it is not in practice necessary. Several mechanisms exist for dealing with incomplete coverage while maintaining the integrity of the underlying normative principle. Territories without populations can be demilitarized by general consent of the membership of the cartel, obviating the need for a monopoly of force

---

[24] Note that this is not a claim that all peoples or territories should enjoy sovereign representation. Rather, it is a claim that all existing sovereigns be treated equally. The idea that all peoples should enjoy sovereign representation is much newer than the sovereign states system, and remains contested. See, e.g., Grovogui 1996.

[25] E.g., Lake 2003.

there, as is the case in Antarctica.²⁶ The right of a people to sovereignty can be recognized by cartel members in principle but perpetually delayed in practice, as is the case with the Palestinians.²⁷ Too broad an acceptance of exceptions such as these would no doubt eventually undermine the underlying norm, but an occasional acceptance can maintain the universality of the claimed right in principle without requiring universal application of that right in practice.

Similarly, the rights of sovereignty need not be universally applied within the cartel. As is discussed in the next chapter, sovereign right is not absolute and never has been. David Lake claims that even approaches to the study of sovereignty that see it as a social construct rather than a fixed ideal type still "treat it as an absolute condition,"²⁸ but he does not indicate why this is the case or why sovereignty should be seen as a binary attribute. To the extent that assignations of sovereignty are in the hands of a self-selected cartel, and to the extent that the property rights associated with sovereignty are divisible, there is no reason that the cartel cannot grant a particular corporate agent some of the rights and withhold others. Three particular sorts of circumstances in which this sort of granting of partial sovereignty rights happens are (1) those in which there is not widespread agreement within the cartel about whether to include an agent as a member; (2) those in which an entity has historically enjoyed some sovereign rights but does not currently claim to be a fully sovereign member of the states system; and (3) those in which the cartel recognizes the claim of a country to sovereignty in principle but is not willing to grant the associated rights to a particular agent of that sovereignty in practice. Taiwan is a good example of the first group; Hong Kong²⁹ (or Krasner's favorite example, the Knights Templar³⁰) of the second; and Iraq between 1991 and 2003 of the third.

The key to understanding all of these cases of partial sovereignty is that they do not threaten, and sometimes actually reinforce, the

---

[26] See the Antarctic Treaty 1959, Article 1. While it is true that a majority of sovereign states has not signed the treaty, none of the non-signatories has disputed the principle of peaceful use.

[27] See, *inter alia*, United Nations General Assembly 2012.   [28] Lake 2003: 308.

[29] Neither Hong Kong nor Taiwan claim to be separate sovereign states but both are nonetheless members of some intergovernmental organizations. For example, both are members of the World Trade Organization as separate customs territories.

[30] Krasner 1999.

underlying structure of norms of sovereign property rights. In the case of Antarctica, an area of potential conflict over sovereignty is dealt with by mutually agreeing that the norms do not apply there.[31] If sovereignty is essentialized, then this sort of ad hoc exercise can be seen as pulling practice farther away from the definition. But if sovereignty is seen as a set of norms reconstituted through practice, then there is no particular reason why such an exercise is problematic as long as key actors do not see it as problematic. If it sets a norm precedent that can be exploited by actors who seek further norm change, then the exception matters. But to this point Antarctica has proved to be exceptional enough that it does not seem to have been used as precedent for significant norm change (in part because nobody lives there permanently, and all its temporary residents are citizens of an existing sovereignty). The same can be said of the limits placed on the sovereign rights of the Iraqi government from 1991 to 2003. In this case, a clear distinction was made between the notional sovereignty of the Iraqi state and the claim of the Iraqi government to be the agent of that sovereignty.[32] In other words, state practice in this case recognized the exceptional nature of the situation while at the same time discursively reinforcing the underlying norm.

A final note on partial sovereignty is that, as noted in the previous chapter, in matters of normative structure, power matters. Norms empower specific actors at the expense of others, and that power is in turn part of the process of reconstituting norms.[33] In the case of sovereign right, the norms empower states at the expense of other corporate actors, and some states more than others. Those empowered actors (particularly the more empowered states) play a key role in reconstituting the norms of sovereign right. If, say, the United States, the component states of the European Union (EU), and China agree among themselves on an interpretation of sovereign right and act accordingly, this will reinforce those norms rather more than if, say,

---

[31] There are several overlapping claims of sovereignty in Antarctica, but the claimants have agreed by treaty not to pursue those claims. On the creation and evolution of the Antarctic Treaty System, see Peterson 1988.

[32] See, e.g., United Nations (1991) Security Council Resolution 687, which explicitly reaffirms Iraqi sovereignty and territorial integrity while at the same time limiting the right of the Iraqi government to, among other things, certain categories of weapons.

[33] On state power and changing norms of sovereignty, see Barkin and Cronin 1994.

Lichtenstein, Vanuatu, and Eswatini do the same. If a critical mass of the community of states agrees within itself that a particular case of partial sovereignty does not constitute a threat to norms of sovereignty and no actors are able to use that case to affect those norms, then those norms will remain unaffected.

Sovereignty and Hypocrisy

This discussion of the centrality of power, along with much of the rest of the discussion of sovereignty as a recognition cartel, can be read as a straightforward interest-based argument. It is this sort of reading that leads Stephen Krasner to argue that sovereignty is a form of organized hypocrisy.[34] There is of course an element of self-interest involved in any cartel, but such a reading misses much of what is going on in a sovereignty cartel. It misses the role of norms of sovereignty in defining both state interest and, more fundamentally, state identity in the first place. It misses the role of these norms in both constraining and enabling the practices that states, and the people who constitute states as corporate actors, undertake in the conduct of their international relations, and the role of those practices in turn in reconstituting and changing the norms. And it misses the role of state discourse in both defining the bounds of the possible and acting as a mechanism of power in its own right.

To say that there is an interest-based explanation for the sovereignty cartel is of course correct, but it is correct in a way that is ultimately tautological.[35] Being corporate agents, states presumably have reasons for doing things that go beyond the rote following of norms. If one defines these reasons as interests, then any behavior that is other than reactively following norms can be called "interest based," especially if an agent is given latitude to interpret these norms. To argue that any such behavior is interest based tells us nothing.

The claim that behavior is interest based, however, is generally intended to imply that an interest-based narrative rather than a norm-based narrative provides the better explanation of behavior. Arguing that an interest-based explanation for behavior can be made

---

[34] Krasner 1999.
[35] On the ultimate tautology of both interest-based and norms-based assumptions of behavior, see Barkin 2010, chapter 4.

is ultimately banal in itself – the point is rather to make the claim that norms do not matter. This is the argument that Krasner is trying to make – because we can explain state behavior with respect to norms of sovereignty in terms of interest, therefore the norms themselves do not matter. They are epiphenomenal to behavior. Hence the use of the concept of hypocrisy. It implies that states are invoking norms of sovereignty strictly for instrumental reasons. They have no compunctions about breaking these norms when it suits their interests; therefore, the invocation of the norms in the first place, per his argument, is hypocritical.[36]

This approach, norms-as-hypocrisy (which serves here as a stand-in for the broader interest-centric ontology of sovereignty), begs the question of why states bother using the language of sovereignty in the first place. Presumably, if states are both acting purposefully in their own rational interest and using the language of sovereignty, then they must be using that language purposefully to further their own interests.[37] This in turn implies that the language is affecting the behavior of some other actors that the state, as a corporate actor, cares about. But who? Other states? This would imply that there is a class of instrumental states and another of gullible states that have not figured out the real nature of the system despite centuries of experience. But much of the discourse of sovereignty is clearly aimed at an international audience, at other states, rather than internally.[38] And the discourse of sovereignty is also often used by non-state actors to make identity-based, rather than interest-based, claims on states.[39] Krasner speaks of "cognitive scripts" that actors use to legitimize action but then ignore in practice.[40] But why do these scripts succeed in legitimizing norms over time if the underlying norms do not matter?

Beyond the question of why states (or other actors) would bother invoking norms that do not matter, the hypocrisy argument falls short of an adequate explanation of sovereign right in three ways. The first is that norms both set a baseline for expectations and serve to legitimize behavior. The second is that norms of sovereignty are integral to the identity of states as corporate actors in the first place. And the third is that states do in fact concern themselves with reconstituting these

[36] Krasner 1999.
[37] For a discussion of language-as-power in this context, see Krebs and Jackson 2007.
[38] See, e.g., Goddard 2009. [39] E.g., Croucher 2018. [40] Krasner 1999: 66.

norms through practice. In this sense the norms not only affect but also generate specific behaviors in international politics. As such, understanding state behavior requires understanding the process of co-constitution of norms of sovereignty and of states as corporate actors.

The first of these ways in which the hypocrisy argument falls short draws on a well-established argument in the study of both international relations and international law. There are two parts to the argument, that norms set a baseline for behavior and that they legitimize some behaviors and delegitimize others. One of the best-known metaphors for explaining the role of norms and rules as baselines for behavior is the speed limit.[41] Most people do not strictly obey speed limits, so that if one were to look at the effectiveness of speed limits only through the lens of compliance, one would see them as abject failures. However, they do affect driving behavior. Traffic tends to flow at a speed a certain amount above the limit. This amount may vary from place to place according to local driving norms and enforcement practices, but it is generally related to the posted limit. The same can be said of sovereignty norms. Krasner admits that they are often followed, so much so that it is the exceptions that are notable, not situations in which behavior clearly follows norms.[42] Norms, in setting baselines for behavior, define what behaviors will be seen as remarkable and what behaviors are likely to go unremarked.

Unremarked behaviors do not carry reputational costs and do not generate organized opposition (this is true by definition – to oppose something is to remark upon it). More contentious behaviors may well carry such costs and generate such opposition. The norm of not invading other countries, for example, is clearly violated occasionally. But at the same time, the norm is well enough accepted that these violations attract opprobrium in the international community.[43] There are times when a state is willing to accept the opprobrium for what it sees as the benefits of going forward with the use of force. But the violation of the norm does create a real cost. To the extent that norms legitimize certain behaviors and delegitimize others, they affect not

---

[41] E.g., Raustiala 2000.
[42] On studying international rules as normal behavior (and therefore breaches of those rules as exceptional), see Chayes and Chayes 1993.
[43] Although the level of opprobrium can vary widely, from counterinvasion in the case of Iraq to economic sanctions in the case of Russia to mild rebuke in the case of the United States.

only the moral calculations of statespeople, but also calculations of interest.

The second way in which the hypocrisy argument fails is that it cannot address the extent to which the norms of sovereignty create states as corporate agents in the first place, the extent to which state identity is wrapped up in the idea of sovereign rights.[44] The broader question of how states identify themselves, what purpose states as institutions (as opposed to the individuals within them) see themselves as being for, is beyond the scope of this book – indeed, it would be difficult to do the subject justice in only one book. There have nonetheless been notably successful attempts to discuss aspects of this question, ranging from a focus on the moral purpose of the state to the study of the cosmology underlying international relations at any given time.[45]

Having said this, there are ways in which state identity and sovereign right are mutually reinforcing. Take, for example, the idea that sovereignty entails the right to international personhood, which is a core concept in international law. States are formally the individual participants in this realm, and individuals in their own right have no standing. As is the case with other aspects of sovereign property rights, this distinction between states on the one hand and other actors, be they corporate or individual, on the other is maintained by a sovereignty cartel: states monopolize public international law among themselves, leaving little avenue for others to create alternative legal structures.[46] This creates the permissive condition for states to participate in international legal mechanisms, ranging from arbitration to treaty making – they can and others cannot. However, it does not explain why states, particularly states that are less well-established internationally, are so enthusiastic about participating in international legal mechanisms even when the benefits of participating are not clearly greater than the costs.[47] I will discuss this claim about enthusiasm at greater length,

---

[44] For an argument that it is reasonable to speak of identity in the context of the state as a corporate actor, see Wendt 1999.
[45] E.g., Reus-Smit 1999 and Allan 2018, respectively.
[46] That is, states monopolize public international law as a distinct category from private international law, which in turn is still sovereign law but domestic sovereign law applied across borders. For a useful discussion of different categories of international law, see Shaffer 2012.
[47] E.g., Jacobson, Reisinger, and Mathers 1986.

but to the extent that it is true, it suggests that states often participate in international legal mechanisms for the sake of the participation itself. If participating in these mechanisms is part of what sovereign states do, then if an institution identifies itself as a sovereign state, it has a reason to participate, other things being equal, simply for the sake of participating.

The third way in which the hypocrisy argument fails is that it assumes that the norms of sovereignty, Krasner's "cognitive scripts," are fixed and self-perpetuating, or are at least impervious to the effects of constant hypocrisy. In assuming that norms do not particularly constrain practice, in other words, it also assumes that practice in turn has little recursive effect on norms.[48] With respect to sovereign property rights, this assumes that norms that empower states with respect to other actors are held, transmitted, and reconstituted entirely by those other actors, without any need for states to participate in the reconstitution of the norms through practice. If it is indeed the case that the norm structure of the property rights associated with sovereignty is perpetuated entirely despite state practice, then hypocrisy would in fact be a reasonable description. But if it is not the case, then the label of hypocrisy misses the role of states in reconstituting norms.

Even if the hypocrisy label were appropriate, however, it would not in itself mean that we could dismiss the effects of norms on broader patterns of behavior. An example to illustrate this claim can be found in income tax returns. Most people in Western democracies will accept in principle the proposition that some government expenditures are reasonable, and that the government needs to tax to support those expenditures. Yet, even when they are comfortable with overall levels of government spending, many of those same people will attempt to minimize their tax payments, knowing full well that if everyone were successful in minimizing tax payments, government spending could not be supported.[49] Does this make us all hypocrites at tax time? Quite possibly. But to dismiss the combination of the principled belief in taxation and the practice of tax avoidance as hypocrisy cannot explain behavior. Why does taxation sometimes lead to public tax revolts and at other times only to individual tax avoidance? The

---

[48] Krasner 1999. This fits in with a definition-driven approach to studying sovereignty, in which the norms reflect the core definition, which is in turn fixed.

[49] This is, of course, a classic collective action problem, on which see Olson 1965.

question likely cannot be answered without looking at the perceived legitimacy of overall levels of taxation.[50] The beliefs of a population about the legitimacy of levels of taxation affect their political activity in aggregate with respect to taxation, in a way that is not necessarily related to the hypocrisy of individual practice with respect to their own taxes. Focusing on the latter does not allow us to explain the former.

This example works as an analogy to the extent that states benefit from what is, from their perspective, the public good of norms of sovereign property rights. It suggests that when the costs of accepting the sovereign rights of other states are particularly high, states may well engage in hypocritical behavior, claiming rights for themselves but not respecting them in practice in other states (an example might be found in China's acceptance in principle of the rules about maritime boundaries detailed in the United Nations Convention on the Law of the Sea, of which it is a signatory, but its rejection of those same rules with respect to its claims of sovereignty in the South China Sea). But when costs are not particularly high, it makes sense for states to act to reinforce the norms because these norms, for the most part, have the effect of empowering them.[51] In either case, it does not necessarily follow that if states act hypocritically with respect to norms, those norms then have little effect on the general pattern of international politics. Furthermore, this cost-benefit calculation, in which the content of norms remains important, tells at best only half of the story of co-constitution.

The question of whether states act in ways that reconstitute norms of sovereign right, whether intentionally or not, is to an extent an empirical one. The next chapter looks at some examples of states doing this, and more generally looks at the degree to which patterns of international politics can be seen as a process of reconstituting their own normative order. There are, as will be discussed, a variety of ways in which it can be. And this conclusion points to the ultimate weakness in the hypocrisy approach to sovereignty – it cannot explain much of what goes on international politics, much of what states do internationally on a day-to-day basis.

---

[50] E.g., Seligson 2002 and Levi, Sacks, and Tyler 2009.
[51] This may be true for states individually or for small groups of key states. On the latter possibility, see Snidal 1985.

The hypocrisy framing focuses on cases in which states do not act in keeping with accepted norms. The framing is actually quite consistent with a world in which norms of sovereignty do provide a central organizing order for international politics, in that it implies the norms are persistent, and allows that they may, in fact, guide behavior much of the time (inasmuch as breaches of the norms are treated as exceptional). In focusing on the exceptions rather than on the rules, this framing simply does not allow ontological space for an examination of the ways in which, or the extent to which, the norms affect behavior. To use Nick Onuf's terminology, the hypocrisy framing does not allow us to look at extent to which the rules of sovereignty create the rule of the contemporary states system.[52] Looking at the exceptions is in principle neither a more nor a less fruitful way of studying state behavior in international politics. But looking at the exceptions through a frame designed to dismiss the effects of the rules is misleading and unduly constraining.

States do act in their own interests. And states act to undermine the sovereign property rights of other states (and sometimes even their own, when circumstances warrant) when politically necessary or expedient. In this sense, states as corporate actors, and the people acting on behalf of states as individuals, do indeed sometimes act hypocritically, much as individual actors in everyday life do. But to focus on the hypocrisy misses the extent to which the norms underlying sovereign property rights define what the states consider to be in their own interest, what, in fact, states consider themselves to be in the first place. It underestimates the extent to which reinforcing those same rights can be as much in states' interest as is ignoring them when expedient. The sovereignty cartel is in this sense more akin to a political or a drug cartel, in which the focus of cartel activity is to keep outsiders from participating, than it is to a price-fixing cartel in which the greatest difficulty is preventing members from free riding.

Finally, as is generally the case with approaches to the study of sovereignty that are definition driven, the hypocrisy framing is premised on a static understanding of sovereignty, and of norm structures more generally. It assumes a set of norms that are largely fixed, or at least that exist independently of state agency. This does not allow, as already noted, for the necessity for state activity to reconstitute the

---

[52] Onuf 1989.

norms, but it also does not allow for state agency in changing norms. In acting in a manner that is not strictly in accordance with accepted norms, states may simply be prioritizing strategic behavior over appropriate behavior.[53] However, they may be self-consciously undertaking to change norms – practice can reconstitute norms, but it can also shift them.[54] Statespeople, diplomats, and other actors in international relations may act individually to nudge specific norms in one direction or other by emphasizing some practices over others.[55] They may also act in concert, to rewrite norms on a broader scale.[56] As is discussed in Chapter 5 of this book, such rewriting is particularly likely to happen in the aftermath of major systemic wars, when balances of power have been dramatically altered, and when prewar norm structures have been discredited for allowing the war in the first place.

This chapter began with a discussion of the international property rights associated with state sovereignty as a strand of the broader norm complex of sovereignty. The analysis of sovereignty as a property right focuses on what sovereignty allows sovereign states (and for the most part only sovereign states) to do. Looked at in this way, sovereign property rights are as much about the rights of states with respect to other actual or potential actors in international relations as they are about the rights of states with respect to each other. In this sense the property rights of sovereignty are constitutive of international politics as a distinct social structure; as a set of norms, discourses, and practices they ontologically precede, rather than are epiphenomenal to, foreign policy and the day-to-day interactions of states. States (and the people acting on their behalf and with their authority) no doubt act strategically at times in interfering with the property rights of other states. However, it is also in their interest to act strategically to reinforce their own rights with respect to other actors and in doing so reinforce the property rights of sovereignty more broadly. It is this interest that informs the sovereignty cartel. Chapter 4 fleshes out the idea of the sovereignty cartel.

---

[53] On strategic and appropriate behavior and international relations theory, see March and Olsen 1998.
[54] On practice theory in international relations, see Leander 2011.
[55] Or by working to change norms to delegitimize certain practices. See, e.g., Price 1998.
[56] E.g., Barkin and Cronin 1994.

4 The Sovereignty Cartel

A central aspect of the contemporary sovereign states system, to summarize the previous chapter, is what I have labeled the "sovereignty cartel." This refers to a system in which a certain group of corporate actors, sovereign states (or, more accurately, states that identify each other as sovereign), arrogates to itself a set of exclusive property rights and acts to reinforce these property rights against other claimants. This activity can be intended to reinforce this system of rights or it can have that effect without the intention. States do not always act to support these rights, nor are these rights their only core interests. However, by the same token, there are a variety of patterns in state behavior in international politics that do not make sense without recognizing the role of the sovereignty cartel and the role of states in maintaining it.

More fundamentally, looking at some of these patterns reminds us that the contemporary sovereign states system is neither a natural phenomenon nor a necessary expression of politics at a global scale. The system, with its clear legal, normative, and practical distinctions between domestic and international,[1] between inside and outside,[2] and patterns of interactions among sovereigns, is a social construct, and continues because, and only because, the people within the system reconstitute it through practice. Nor is it the case that, having been constructed the way it is, the system provides a coherent political structure for the contemporary world. It is prone to problems ranging from large-scale warfare to mismanagement of the global commons. Even at a more quotidian scale it is prone to internal contradictions, to things that fall into gaps between domestic and international. Chapters 5 through 8 of this book look at these contradictions and into these gaps. This chapter focuses on the ways states act to reconstitute the system despite its contradictions and gaps.

---

[1] On this distinction as foundational of international society, see Bull 1977.
[2] E.g., Walker 1993.

The role of states as agents in reconstituting and reinforcing norms of sovereignty can be seen in a variety of issue areas and specific practices in contemporary international politics. Two sets of these in particular are discussed in the first two sections of this chapter. The first has to do with what was traditionally called "high politics," the politics of state power and of diplomacy. This encompasses issues as varied as rules for the use of force internationally and the propensity for states to participate on an equal legal footing in intergovernmental organizations. The second set is in the realm of "low politics," the politics of the regulation of international economic exchange. This set encompasses issues ranging from multilateral regulation, to the governance of the global commons, to regulatory offshoring.

These issues are all related in some fashion to two of the exclusive sovereign rights noted throughout this book, the right to govern and the right to international personhood. The focus of this chapter is on the reconstitution through practice of these rights. The claim here, in other words, is not that states necessarily want to participate in international fora to accomplish things related to the topic of the particular talks in question, or that states necessarily want the responsibility of regulating yet another aspect of international commerce. Rather, the claim is that they want to reinforce their *right* to do so. In some instances, states in fact want to reinforce their property rights in a way that actually minimizes demands upon their resources and attention.

This somewhat paradoxical outcome, in which states want the right to participate and to regulate but do not necessarily want to do all that much participating and regulating, can be seen in a number of different sorts of outcomes. States may claim that the only legitimate forum for dealing with a particular issue is an intergovernmental one, and then not use that forum for dealing with the issue effectively. This might be a cynical reading, for example, of the 2015 Paris Agreement on climate change.[3] They may claim the right to regulate with respect to an issue, and then delegate that right to other agents such as nongovernmental organizations, as is the case with international accounting standards. Or they may co-opt existing governance structures, in effect imposing the practice of sovereign right onto already existing governance

---

[3] See Dimitrov 2020.

practices, as is (in simplified form) the case with internet addresses.[4] There will be further examples of all of these sorts of outcomes in the course of this chapter.

The first two substantive sections of this chapter are about states doing things that are not in their short-term individual interest in order to reinforce the idea of sovereign right. They do this by reinforcing the idea of the rights of sovereigns in general. The third section is about the responsibilities that come with sovereignty understood as property rights (recalling that property rights are used here to mean clearly specified rules about what one can do with property, rather than as the idea of unfettered rights to one's property). Particular examples come from issues of multilateral participation, human rights, and the governance of the commons. The final substantive section looks at some of the practices through which states as corporate actors reconstitute sovereign norms and discourses. It recognizes that states act ultimately through individual people, and it is the practices and discourses of individuals, both those who act in the name of the state and those who act outside of the state,[5] that reconstitute norms of sovereignty.

Sovereign Right and Power

Perhaps the most obviously propertarian aspect of sovereign right is territoriality, the idea that states have fixed, clearly defined, and linear borders (linear in the sense of there being a line with one state on one side and other on the other, and, with few exceptions,[6] nothing between them).[7] The relationship between states and their territory in the contemporary sovereign states system is in this sense directly analogous to the relationship between individual property owners

---

[4] Not that states will always agree on which route to take. See, e.g., Mueller, Mathiason, and Klein 2007.
[5] Examples of the latter category include efforts by political entrepreneurs to encourage governments to recognize human rights norms or to delegitimize certain categories of weapons, which has the effect of reinforcing the sovereign rights of states to domestic governance and to the exclusive rights to use military force. See Keck and Sikkink 1998 and Price 1998, respectively.
[6] These exceptions include demilitarized zones between the Koreas and between Syria and Israel in the Golan Heights. Neither of these examples, notably, involves recognized sovereign borders; both mark cease-fire lines rather than borders formally accepted by both bordering states.
[7] On territoriality as a core norm of the contemporary sovereign states system, see Ruggie 1993.

and real estate that they own. In both instances, use rights are generally subject to some constraints, such as the use of the property in ways that pollute neighboring properties.[8] In both cases, the owner is a legal person (a state in international law, or individual people or corporations in most contemporary domestic law systems). The property rights of contemporary sovereigns to their territories, in other words, look a lot like a capitalist ownership structure.[9]

This specific sort of sovereign property right to territory is not universal across time. Early definitions of sovereignty in the context of the modern states system were as likely to focus on control of people as they were control of territory. Jean Bodin, as already noted, defined sovereignty as the right to appoint magistrates.[10] Sovereignty in this understanding was ultimately about adjudicating the law with respect to a body of subjects, not about territoriality. Medieval sovereignty was more concerned with rights to labor (whether the agricultural labor of serfs or the military labor of vassals) than rights to territory.[11] Territory in premodern empires was rarely defined by clear borders, except when natural borders such as rivers or mountains impeded traffic. Rather, relations of control and obligation gradually diminished with distance.[12] Both China and Rome serve as examples at the largest of scales, despite building walls in their hinterlands,[13] but the same is true of many imperial structures at smaller scales. Territoriality as a fundamental basis of sovereign power, in other words, exists because the members of the community of contemporary sovereigns chooses to recognize the territorial rights of other members of the community in exchange for their reciprocal recognition.

Another fundamental element of sovereign international power, at least as understood by political realists, is military force. Force has long been understood as central to the idea of a state, most famously by Max Weber, who defined the state by its success in upholding its "claim on the monopoly of the legitimate use of physical force in the

---

[8] See, e.g., Bratspies and Miller 2006.
[9] See the discussion of capitalist ownership in the context of C. B. MacPherson's idea of possessive individualism in the next chapter.
[10] Bodin 1945: 172.   [11] See, e.g., Bloch 1961.
[12] This is, of course, a gross simplification, but reasonable as a generalization. See, e.g., Fairbank 1968.
[13] For a discussion of, for example, Hadrian's Wall, in this context, see, *inter alia*, Everitt 2009.

enforcement of its order"[14] (note that the state is defined here by its order, not its territory). This definition is, however, focused on the use of force domestically, legitimized by a domestic order (meaning, at least in part, legal structure). States do not individually claim a legitimate monopoly of force in the enforcement of the international order. Nor is the claim to use force internationally integral to sovereign statehood – some states do not have effective international military forces but are nonetheless treated as fully sovereign by the community of states.[15] What states do claim is the *collective* and exclusive sovereign right to the legitimate use of force internationally in the enforcement of the international order.

There are two parts to this claim that only sovereign states have the right to legitimately use military force, whether domestically or internationally, and that such force can legitimately be used in the enforcement of the international equivalent of what Weber called an order. This second part of the claim is not the only condition in which states can legitimately use force. They can also use it in self-defense,[16] analogous to the right to individual self-defense in domestic legal systems (such a use of force is not in the enforcement of an order and is sanctioned to more-clearly or less-clearly defined degrees within that order, and so does not contradict Weber's definition). When used beyond self-defense, however, contemporary international norms allow it only in defense of the international order, be that order understood in terms of international[17] or human[18] security. States, in other words, arrogate to themselves the right (and to some extent the responsibility) to use force to defend the norms of the sovereign states system, and deny that right to all other actors or entities.

This particular right is a relatively new development in the norms of sovereignty. The concentration of the right to use force internationally in a set of legally equivalent sovereign entities considerably postdates Westphalia (the last vestiges of feudal rights to force survived into the nineteenth century).[19] And the norms both for collective state responsi-

---

[14] Weber 1968: 54.   [15] For examples, see Barbey 2015.
[16] See United Nations Charter 1945, Article 51.
[17] See, for example, references to "international peace and security" throughout the United Nations Charter, both in the preamble and in various articles.
[18] See, for example, United Nations General Assembly 2005.
[19] The position of Holy Roman Emperor, for example, existed until 1806.

bility for the security of the sovereign states system and against the use of force for territorial expansion developed largely in the twentieth century. Which is to say that, far from being a necessary or original component of a sovereign states system, contemporary norms concerning the right to the use of force internationally are contingent and changeable.

The other part of the claim is that only states have the right to legitimately use military force. The use of force internationally, whether by individuals or corporate actors other than states, is illegitimate. Furthermore, the scope of what counts as state use of force has narrowed. States can still directly subcontract the use of force to private actors[20] but remain responsible for the results (for example, if a private military contractor working for the United States engages in war crimes, the United States government is responsible for those crimes in the same way it would be if they were committed by forces in US military uniform[21]). However, licensing private actors to act in semi-sovereign ways, as was the case before the nineteenth century with privateers[22] and merchant companies,[23] is no longer a legitimate sovereign right.

The flipside of the exclusive right to the use of military force internationally is a set of limitations on not only when but how that force can be used; states trade the right to exclusivity for acceptance of a formal set of rules of war.[24] These rules (among other things) make two sets of distinctions. They distinguish between individuals who are part of the state as a corporate actor and those who, while they may be citizens of the state, are not engaged in using force in its name.[25] And they distinguish between those who use force legitimately and those who do not.[26]

---

[20] Although such actors may have considerable independent influence on international relations discourse. See Leander 2005.
[21] Although there are gaps in this responsibility, akin to those discussed as the interstices of sovereignty in Chapter 6. On these gaps in the context of private military contractors, see Hoppe 2008.
[22] See, e.g., Thomson 1996.   [23] See, e.g., Srivastava forthcoming.
[24] These rules can be found in a variety of places, including the various Geneva Conventions and the Rome Statute of the International Criminal Court.
[25] E.g., Gardam 1993.
[26] The various Geneva Conventions, for example, cover the treatment of members of sovereign armed forces and civilian persons, but not combatants who are not members of sovereign armed forces.

The first distinction, between military and civilian targets, serves to separate states as corporate entities from states as providers of governance. The sovereign right to military force is limited in some ways with respect to other sovereigns understood as corporate actors – for example, by the norm of proportionality[27] and the prohibition of certain classes of weapons.[28] It is limited even more with respect to non-sovereign actors, understood as those not authorized to use military force in the name of the sovereign; states can still blow up civilians within the rules, but only unintentionally, whereas they can blow up soldiers intentionally. This serves to further separate out sovereign states as a distinct category of corporate actor, in which they claim the right to engage in war in exchange for the right to be targeted in war.

The second distinction, between legitimate and illegitimate users of force internationally, serves to protect, rather than allow the targeting of, sovereign actors. Put simply, states generally do not target sovereigns, understood as individuals authorized by the state to speak with the sovereign's voice, such as national leaders and diplomats. The individuals who make the sovereign decisions to use force internationally are thereby protected from the threat of that violence against their persons (a protection that does not, of course, extend to those individuals who directly engage in the use of force under their orders). But states do target illegitimate users of force as individuals. Such targets, furthermore, are not protected by the sorts of due process rules that in most countries govern state actions against illegitimate users of force domestically.

As an example, Bashir al-Assad, as the internationally recognized president of the sovereign state of Syria, was not (to public knowledge) targeted by any of the several other states operating militarily in his country in the 2010s, despite almost certainly having engaged in war crimes and despite widespread international opprobrium.[29] Leaders of the Islamic State, which has claimed sovereignty but not had that claim accepted by the community of sovereigns (which is to say, the

---

[27] E.g., Hurka 2005. [28] E.g., Price 1997.
[29] And when sovereign leaders are targeted, such as Fidel Castro by the United States, it tends to be covertly, with an attempt at deniability. See, *inter alia*, Holland 1994.

sovereignty cartel), however, are fair targets as individuals.[30] Illegitimate users of international force are in this sense in a category by themselves as individuals afforded no protection by international law, as particular threats to sovereign right to the monopoly of international force.

A third way in which states are empowered by the sovereignty cartel is through the right to participate internationally. A key development in the normative structure of the contemporary sovereign states system and the resulting practices of international politics is the evolution of multilateralism, mostly since World War II.[31] Earlier practices of international politics involved sovereign recognition and diplomatic exchange, but these practices did not require, and often did not display, full formal legal equality among sovereigns. This can be seen, among other places, in displays of formal diplomatic rank in the Westphalian era,[32] and in relations of, in essence, vassalage between European and many non-European polities from the beginning of the era of European imperialism until well into the twentieth century.[33]

Multilateralism, however, requires a much clearer delineation of the relative formal status of sovereigns, because international organizations (IOs) need clear, and clearly delineated, decision rules.[34] These rules, for a large majority of IOs, are variations of one sovereign/one vote, with no formal voting power at all for non-sovereigns. Voting in this context is a property right: it is based on ownership of property (in the sense of territoriality), it is heritable by successor states, and particular votes can even be sold to other actors (see Chapter 6 for a discussion of the selling of sovereign rights). Many IOs are trying to become more transparent and to create mechanisms for non-state actors to have their voices heard in multilateral fora.[35] However, full formal participation in most IOs remains reserved for sovereign states. Territorial political organizations that function as states, even when they function as states more effectively than the

---

[30] By some measures, forty-three of forty-four original senior leaders of the Islamic State are dead, although not all were assassinated by sovereign military forces. See Chulov 2018.
[31] For a general discussion of the phenomenon of multilateralism and its development, see Ruggie 1992.
[32] See Osiander 2001.
[33] For a related discussion in the language of sovereignty, see Strang 1996.
[34] Or, more precisely, they need such rules if they are to have votes or legal outputs.
[35] Grigorescu 2007.

recognized sovereignty of which they are a part, such as Somaliland, get neither votes nor other benefits of IO membership.

There are, of course, exceptions, in two categories. The first category is representation for non-sovereigns. Some hybrid organizations, such as the International Union for the Conservation of Nature, have parallel voting structures for sovereign and non-sovereign members. A very few organizations, most notably the International Committee of the Red Cross, have a formal role in international politics despite not being intergovernmental at all.[36] Finally, some IOs give votes on an exceptional basis to members that are not fully sovereign, such as trade or functional organizations in which Taiwan or the European Union (or both) have a vote,[37] or the few organizations in which Palestine is represented.[38] These exceptions, however, all developed for historically specific reasons that do not set broader precedents of non-sovereign participation. The large majority of votes in a large majority of IOs are owned by sovereign states.

The other category of exceptions is IOs in which only sovereign states have votes, but these votes are not distributed equally. There are few such organizations, but some of them, particularly the United Nations Security Council and the international financial institutions,[39] are quite important. These exceptions are not only historically contingent, but all began during World War II,[40] not a time of international politics as usual.[41] While these particular exceptions have a real impact on core issues of international security and finance, and while they are unlikely to disappear in the near future (because that would require that the few states empowered with greater votes agree to be

---

[36] The International Committee of the Red Cross is written into the Geneva Conventions as a neutral party. It appears, e.g., in eleven articles of the *Geneva Convention Relative to the Treatment of Prisoners of War of 12 August 1949*.

[37] The EU acts as member in lieu of its constituent states in those areas in which it has primary competence, such as trade.

[38] Primarily the United Nations Educational, Scientific, and Cultural Organization at the global level, as well as several institutions, such as the Arab League and the Organization of Islamic Cooperation, at the regional level.

[39] The international financial institutions include the International Monetary Fund, the World Bank Group, and the regional development banks.

[40] Several international development banks have been created with subscription-based voting structures since 1945, but these have all been modeled on the World Bank, and that model has not migrated to any other kind of institution.

[41] On the fluidity of the normative structure of sovereignty during great power war, see Barkin and Cronin 1994.

disempowered[42]), they are unlikely to set precedents for new multilateral fora going forward, outside of the specific institution-type of development banks.

The predominance of the one country/one vote system in contemporary multilateralism is relevant in the context of a discussion of the sovereignty cartel because it has significant empowering effects for a majority of sovereigns.[43] It seems a natural system to many contemporary observers because it mirrors the one person/one vote system of (an idealized) representative democracy. This analogy in turn suggests a normative assumption of equal legal sovereign right for all states, no matter their size or level of effective participation in international relations. This assumption gives states a say in IOs and other international legal mechanisms even when they do not have the material resources to participate fully in negotiations or to have a direct impact at an international scale on the issue at hand. The assumption also represents a willingness by the states most able to bring diplomatic resources to bear to allow other states a greater voice than they might otherwise have. The great powers of the world, in other words, are willing to give the sovereign minnows of the world their own vote in order to support the principle of sovereign equality and exclusivity.

This principle, in the context of IOs and multilateralism, is important in the practical conduct of international politics because the right to sovereign exclusivity is the mechanism through which states claim a monopoly on international regulatory authority, and IOs are often the vehicles through with this authority is used. Exclusive regulatory authority in turn is often practiced through the sovereignty cartel.

Sovereign Right and Regulation

To note that states claim the exclusive right to regulate the activities of individuals and non-state corporate actors domestically is not novel. It is, for example, implicit in Weber's definition of the state quoted in the previous section; the "order" that only the state can use force to enforce includes a regulatory order. Political authorities have always claimed the right to tax (because, really, what's the fun of being a

---

[42] For a more detailed version of this argument, see Barkin 2013, chapter 2.
[43] Barkin 2013.

political authority without the right to tax?), and taxation is after all a form of economic regulation. When sovereigns have been able to maintain an exclusive ability, as well as right, to tax, they have likely been able to lay effective claim to the exclusive right to regulate as well.

What is more novel in the contemporary sovereign states system is the mutual recognition of the exclusive right of states as a category of actor to regulate, and the underlying assumption that this mutual recognition cartel is regulatorily universal, that all economic activity globally should fall within it. This assumption is a twentieth-century (and arguably a late-twentieth-century) development.[44] Earlier states, whether "Westphalian" (in the sense of being European states in the eighteenth and nineteenth centuries) or polities elsewhere and in other eras, neither recognized the international legitimacy of foreign regulation nor developed a concept of a global regulatory order.[45] Neither imperial China nor Rome (to return to examples used previously), both of which developed extensive regulatory states domestically,[46] recognized economic regulation by neighboring polities as formally equivalent to their own. Nor did they much care about regulation in regions outside their areas of political activity. Regulatory cooperation across legally equivalent sovereigns was, at most, rare.

Two aspects of this universality assumption in the context of the sovereignty cartel that are relevant here are its multilateralism and its comprehensiveness.[47] Multilateralism, as noted above, means that states see the right to regulate as a collective, as well as individual, sovereign right and have developed institutional mechanisms through which to implement this right collectively. These mechanisms generally operate on a one country/one vote basis. Furthermore, states are sufficiently committed to the claim to this collective right that the states that have the economic wherewithal to enforce their own regulatory vision

---

[44] The regulatory state itself can be seen as a late-twentieth-century development. See, *inter alia*, Moran 2002 and Glaeser and Shleifer 2001.

[45] It can be useful to think of the concept of a global regulatory order in the context of Michel Foucault's idea of governmentality. It is the concept that we need the regulatory forms of government even outside of the geographical scope of individual governments; government beyond governments. See, e.g., Burchell, Gordon, and Miller 1991.

[46] To the extent that one can delineate the domestic from the international in imperial systems of government.

[47] For another take on multilateralism and regulatory universality, see Burley 1993.

recognize the right of multilateral participation of states that do not have such wherewithal.

This is not to argue that such wherewithal does not matter to outcomes. Clearly it does; bigger states (and even more so the biggest) are better able to navigate multilateral negotiations than small ones, and they have a credible threat to nonparticipation that small ones do not have (because multilateral regulation can move forward without the latter but not effectively without the former).[48] Having said this, however, multilateralism matters.[49] The institutional mechanisms, and the formal equality of states within them, give states with fewer economic resources a greater voice and institutional power than they would otherwise have. And states with greater economic resources get little out of this granting of voice and institutional power beyond the reinforcement of the norm of sovereign right.

The other aspect is comprehensiveness. There are many elements of international nongovernmental activity that states in the contemporary international political economy require be regulated somewhere by a recognized sovereign. Two examples of this phenomenon (both of which are discussed at greater length in Chapter 6) are banking and shipping. Both banks and ships that operate internationally need to be registered with a national (sovereign) authority and be subject in their international operations to the relevant regulatory authority of that state.[50] They need not operate in a meaningful way in their state of primary registry, but they cannot operate internationally at all without a state home.

This regulatory comprehensiveness is the source of a variety of related phenomena in the international political economy including financial offshoring, tax havens, and flags of convenience. It is the reason that some of the biggest financial centers in the world are in small islands in the Caribbean and that fully a third of Ireland's gross domestic product (GDP) appears to be phantom profits of transnational corporations that do little business in the country but use it as a tax dodge.[51] It is the reason that some of the biggest shipping fleets in the world are registered in places where they are not owned and do not visit. For example, the second biggest flag state for international

---

[48] E.g., Gruber 2000.   [49] E.g., Ruggie 1993.
[50] On international financial regulation, see Drezner 2007. On flags of convenience, see DeSombre 2006.
[51] Boland 2017.

shipping by some measures is Liberia, not generally known for its regulatory acumen. The registry is not even run from Liberia – it is primarily run from an office in Reston, Virginia, and the Liberian government has little involvement in it beyond authorizing the office as its sovereign agent and receiving in exchange an occasional check with the registration fees, less expenses.[52]

This does not mean, of course, that states are powerless to exclude internationally regulated banks or ships from their territory, or to pressure regulatory havens into tightening their regulatory standards.[53] A sovereign regulatory home is not necessarily sufficient for participation in the international economy, but it is necessary. International economic actors cannot legally operate without a sovereign regulatory home. This system complicates regulation and taxation in individual states. At the same time, however, it can be a lucrative property right for smaller states that find a regulatory niche in the international economy from which they can profit. In other words, it presents a cost for states that could effectively enforce their regulatory standards without it, and a benefit for a set of smaller states that have no basis to claim those benefits other than the sovereign property right to regulate. In the case of any particular regulatory regime one can generally argue that one of the world's major economies has an interest in the regulatory pattern (in the case of flags of convenience, for example, the pattern was developed by the United States to keep international shipping cheap as US labor standards increased[54]). But taken as a whole, the system has some clear empowering effects for smaller states and is built on the use of force in enforcing a collective and universal sovereign order.

An example of the sovereignty cartel treating sovereigns as categorically distinct from other actors can be found in the Basel Accords on banking supervision. These accords, now in their third iteration (known as Basel III), are voluntary standards for banking regulation agreed to under the auspices of the Basel Committee on Banking Supervision, which is located in the Bank for International Settlements (BIS).[55] The membership of the BIS is central banks rather than governmental executive branches per se, but in this context it is reasonable to think of central banks as components of governments.

---

[52] DeSombre 2006: 216.   [53] Drezner 2007; Barkin 2015b.
[54] DeSombre 2006: 72–77.   [55] Basel Committee on Banking Supervision 2010.

One aspect of the Basel Accords is the creation of minimal capital requirements for banks. Capital in this context is weighted both for riskiness and liquidity – a million dollars of junk bonds from an obscure company counts less than a million dollars of bonds from a large company with a strong credit rating. In these weightings, sovereign debt is counted categorically differently from other debt. It is counted as low risk and liquid, even when market conditions suggest otherwise.[56] States have agreed to count themselves as more financially reliable than other organizations, not because empirical evidence supports such a claim but because it is states setting the rules.

The regulatory universality of the sovereignty cartel has been expanding over the course of the past half century or more from the transnational to the international, from covering economic activity between states to covering economic activity even outside of states. The cartel now claims governance of the entire global commons. This began with governance of specific resources in the high seas with the International Convention for the Regulation of Whaling in 1946, and the governance of specific non-state spaces with the Antarctic Treaty in 1961. While these two treaties can (and probably should) be read as efforts primarily to preserve rather than co-opt the commons,[57] later developments can more easily be read as cartel behavior.

Over the course of the 1970s, states collectively arrogated to themselves not only the right to manage but also the right to profit from what had previously been a true commons. Two particular moves illustrate this observation. The first is the creation of the International Seabed Authority, which among its tasks distributes royalties from mining the seabed under the high seas to member states. This task is based on the explicit claim that it is sovereign states as an exclusive collective that own the rights to economic exploitation of those parts of the planet outside of individual members of the collective.[58] The second move is the general acceptance by states of exclusive economic zones (EEZs), areas extending up to 200 nautical miles from shore in which the closest state has the exclusive right to regulate (and tax)

---

[56] Gros 2013.
[57] For details, see Friedheim 2001 and Peterson 1988, respectively.
[58] The United Nations Convention on the Law of the Sea (Part XI) speaks of rights to resources "vested in mankind as a whole," but defines the International Seabed Authority as acting in the interests of and being responsible to member states, eliding the difference between states and mankind.

economic activity. EEZs in some cases improved the regulation of marine resources; in other cases they failed spectacularly.[59] The point here is that they represent an agreement within the sovereignty cartel to take resources that had previously been the global commons (which is to say, outside the direct regulatory control of states collectively) and make them effectively the property of states.

One response to the argument in this section is that there has been a major expansion in the past half century of private as well as public international regulation. The literature on the regulatory state is as much about states subcontracting regulation to quasi-state and non-state actors as it is about the expansion of direct state control.[60] Examples of private regulation include industry self-regulation[61] and the creation of certification standards for products.[62] However, this expansion of the practice of private international regulation does not actually contradict the claim by states of the universality of the sovereign right to regulate. Private international regulation is voluntary, in the sense that it is not legitimate to use force in the enforcement of a private regulatory order. Private regulation also tends to happen when private actors try to preempt public regulation (meaning that the private actors know that sovereigns have the authority to regulate), when states cannot agree among themselves on how to regulate, or when states prefer to subcontract regulation. In all these cases, private regulation responds to, rather than undermines, the sovereign right to regulate.

One final aspect of the universality of the sovereignty cartel in the context of regulation that warrants discussion is citizenship. In the contemporary international political economy, people, as well as banks and ships, need to be registered somewhere. States will not accept individuals as legitimate economic actors unless they are vouched for by a sovereign state.[63] Some citizenships, of course, afford much greater access to the international political economy than others – as with other forms of regulation, state registry is a necessary condition for international activity but not a sufficient one. For the small proportion of the world's people who are unlucky enough to not have citizenship (generally because they were born in the wrong place at the wrong time),

---

[59] E.g., Barkin and DeSombre 2013: 139–141.
[60] E.g., Moran 2002 and Glaeser and Shleifer 2001. [61] E.g., Haufler 2001.
[62] E.g., Gulbrandsen 2010. [63] E.g., Brysk and Shafir 2004.

there are some mechanisms agreed to by the sovereignty cartel to partially ameliorate the problems of lack of citizenship, such as refugee papers or Palestinian Authority passports. These exceptions illustrate the rule that the sovereignty cartel decides who is a legitimate person in the contemporary international system and who is not. The Universal Declaration of Human Rights tells us that all people have the right to a nationality, which contemporary legal scholarship interprets as the right to citizenship.[64] The flipside of this right, however, is that legitimation by a national authority is an integral part of being a rights-bearing person in the contemporary international system. Sovereigns are supposed to collectively include everyone in citizenship, but by the same token they monopolize the granting of citizenship.

Sovereign Right and Sovereign Responsibility

The responsibility of sovereign states as a group to grant the right of nationality to all people suggests an aspect of the property rights of sovereignty that has not been highlighted to this point. Property rights often include limitations and responsibilities. These can include the responsibility to not use one's property to negatively affect others' property, or the responsibility to participate collectively in maintaining property (as in a homeowners' or condominium association). The same is true of sovereignty understood as property. Sovereign right comes with a set of limitations on the abuse of, and responsibilities to protect, both people and, increasingly, the global commons.

The development of sovereign responsibility to people as individuals (and this is to people in general, rather than to citizens specifically), usually expressed in the contemporary international system as respect for human rights, is discussed in some detail in Chapter 5. The short version of the story is that all members of the contemporary sovereignty cartel have accepted in principle a commitment to respect and protect human rights. Since this commitment is written into the rules of the United Nations, as well as being expressed in a variety of supplementary treaties,[65] a state cannot be recognized as fully sovereign by the community of sovereign states without accepting the commitment.

---

[64] E.g., Benhabib 2005.
[65] Calls for faith in, respect for, realization of, observance of, and promotion of human rights appear in six places in the Charter of the United Nations (in the Preamble and in Articles 1.3, 13.1b, 55, 68, and 76).

It is certainly the case that not all states respect this commitment in practice, and some clearly miss the mark egregiously. Looked at from a different angle, however, one can make the case that this commitment has a significant impact on both international discourse and on state practice. The discourse can be used by states to legitimate foreign policy that might otherwise look like direct interference in the domestic affairs of other states. Examples range from human rights conditions on foreign aid[66] to the decision by a majority of governments in both North and South America to recognize Juan Guaidó rather than Nicolás Maduro as president of Venezuela in January 2019.[67] Because the discourse can be used in this way to legitimate intrusive foreign policy, it can also have the effect of constraining state practice that might invite rights-based criticisms. The existence of the commitment at the international level can also affect state practice through domestic legal systems, because the normative commitment is also formally a legal obligation.[68]

The idea of a sovereign responsibility to the global commons has also developed in the last half century or so, following and in parallel to the development of the sovereign claim to the right to govern the commons.[69] Until well after the middle of the twentieth century, multilateral regulation of the commons was voluntary: for example, states could participate in agreements to limit fishing efforts by their nationals but could also free ride on those agreements without penalty.[70] Over time, however, norms of sovereignty with respect to the commons evolved to include an element of constraint as well as enablement. This can be seen, for example, in the norm of the nonmilitary use of Antarctica and outer space, which was first introduced in formal agreements by subsets of states that chose to sign on but has since become a generally accepted element of customary international law.[71]

This evolution can also be seen with respect to the exploitation of marine living resources (i.e., fish) across borders and on the high seas. Early agreements to manage these resources sustainably were plagued by free-riding issues, and they were conceptually as well as practically

[66] E.g., Nielsen 2013.   [67] Associated Press 2019.   [68] Simmons 2009.
[69] Sand 2004.
[70] On the development of multilateral governance of international fisheries, see Barkin and DeSombre 2013.
[71] E.g., Scott and Carr 1996.

undermined by these issues.[72] Negotiations in the 1970s toward the United Nations Convention on the Law of the Sea led to an acceptance of the general principle of state responsibility to participate in sustainable management but did little to operationalize that principle. By 1995, however, the United Nations Straddling Stocks agreement, an implementing agreement to the Law of the Sea Convention, spoke of a "duty to participate," authorizing cooperating states to act against free riders.[73] Participation had become a responsibility as well as a right. Or, more specifically, the right to participate had come to include the responsibility of participating.

The expansion of the regulatory universality of sovereign right in the contemporary international system to include responsibility for the commons is a development that is important for two reasons that will become clearer in coming chapters. The first is that it helps to highlight the observation that the contemporary sovereign states system is increasingly being universalized, bringing within it the authority to regulate everything everywhere, and the implied responsibility to do so effectively. This is a relatively new development, being contingent on the norm that all people should have a nationality, should be citizens of a sovereign (because if not all people are citizens of a sovereign, sovereignty cannot be universal).[74]

The second reason is that it helps to highlight the extent to which the sovereignty cartel is a participatory enterprise, in that it involves active participation by sovereigns in the collective enterprise of global governance, rather than just an agreement among a class of actor to leave each other alone with respect to their internal affairs. The sovereign states system really is, in this sense, a system that is distinct from the sum of its parts, which has increased its level of what John Gerard Ruggie, following Emile Durkheim, has called its "social dynamic density."[75] This participatory enterprise aspect of sovereignty, however, can come to be in tension with the autarchic, inasmuch as they represent two different ways of thinking about property and property rights. This tension is the topic of the next chapter.

---

[72] Barkin and DeSombre 2013.
[73] The "duty to cooperate" is listed as a general principle in Article 5 of the agreement (United Nations General Assembly 1995).
[74] Relatively new and unevenly applied. See, e.g., Grovogui 1996.
[75] Ruggie 1983.

The Reconstitution of Sovereignty

Before getting to the discussion of this tension and questions of how norms of sovereignty change, however, the final task of this chapter is to look at how the norms of sovereignty are reconstituted. States are corporate actors, meaning that they have a voice and corporate personality of their own that is distinct from the individual people acting in the name of the state at any one point in time, and that they have legal personhood. And while we often speak of states as if they were people, state sovereignty in the contemporary international system is as likely to be vested in a constitutional structure of a state as it is in an identifiable individual. Who then acts to reconstitute the norms of sovereignty?

At the most general level, individuals who act internationally or who participate in the international political economy reconstitute the norms of sovereignty habitually, through practice. They do so by using their passports or by claiming protected status under international law if they do not have access to passports.[76] They do so by working for transnational corporate actors that recognize and accede to both comparative national and international regulatory standards. They do so by checking the time on an electronic device that uses coordinated universal time as defined by the (intergovernmental) International Telecommunications Union.[77] In all these activities they are implicitly accepting the regulatory universality of the sovereignty cartel. There are, at the same time, individuals who act to circumvent or undermine the authority of the cartel, whether for economic (e.g., smuggling) or political (e.g., terrorism) reasons. When these actions threaten the norms of sovereignty, members of the cartel are often willing to use significant force to enforce the international order.

Individuals who are not part of the state as a corporate actor (i.e., who are speaking for themselves, not for the state) participate through the reiteration of the discourse of sovereignty in ways that, while they may not be intended to do so, enable the sovereignty cartel by engaging in speech acts that frame the sovereign state as the central actor in global politics. This may be done by as simple a verbal expedient as anthropomorphizing the state, for instance, speaking of Canada or China or Cameroon as one would of a person, as an individual

[76] Salter 2008.   [77] Burdick 2017.

intentional and motivated actor. This practice is a commonplace. One can look to the international news section of just about any major newspaper on any given day for examples.[78] The practice is in a way analogical to the recognition of states, and not of people, as legal people in international law; it makes the sovereign state the default unit of discourse, and it makes it difficult to even speak about international politics or law without reference to the state.[79] Furthermore, it trains people broadly to think about the international in terms of a set of discrete sovereignties.

The reiteration of the discourse of sovereignty also happens through more intentional claims on the language of sovereignty for political purposes. Arguments for greater autonomy of particular countries from international interference are often phrased in the language of sovereignty. Examples range from arguments against participation in international organizations in developed countries (such as arguments for Brexit in in the United Kingdom)[80] to arguments in favor of domestic decision-making autonomy from European and/or from neo-colonial international norms in developing countries.[81] Whether the audience for the discourse is internal or external to the country in question, claims on the language of sovereignty are attempts to use norms of sovereignty to circumscribe the terms of political discourse with respect to international politics.[82]

In these examples the language of sovereignty is being used (whether or not the claimants would understand it in these particular terms) to deny the language of sovereignty to political arguments in favor of reinforcing the institutional structure of multilateralism.[83] As such, this use has a complicated relationship with the sovereignty cartel; it reproduces the discursive centrality of sovereignty, but a sovereignty that is focused on autonomy rather than on universality. Other discourses have a countervailing effect, however, directly supporting the idea of

---

[78] I say this primarily in reference to newspapers in English. I have not found a study of this phenomenon across languages, but I suspect that it holds across most of them.
[79] For an interesting take on this, see Luoma-Aho 2009.
[80] For a discussion of such arguments in the context of political discourse in the United States, see Patrick 2018.
[81] E.g., Vorhölter 2012.
[82] On this sort of use of discourse for power-political purposes, see Krebs and Jackson 2007.
[83] Gee and Young 2016.

sovereign universality by expressing popular claims for the necessity of multilateral action, in realms ranging from international security[84] to climate change.

At a narrower, more concrete scale, the norms of sovereignty in general, and the rights claims that are constitutive of the sovereignty cartel more specifically, are reconstituted by the quotidian practices of the individuals who collectively animate the state as a corporate actor. By this I mean individuals who work for the state and are empowered in some way to speak for the state as a sovereign actor; in this context, those who speak to a primarily international audience. This category includes politicians and legislators who deploy the language of sovereignty for explicitly power-political purposes. More importantly, however, it includes professional and clerical staff whose job is to cross the t's and dot the i's of the state's international regulatory functions. Most importantly, it includes the people who negotiate for states at the international level, particularly in multilateral fora.

Inhabitants of this category of professional are generally both trained and paid to represent the state as a corporate actor and as an international legal person, whether that training be in diplomacy, negotiation, international law, or a cognate field (this is in part a tautology – people who regularly act in a diplomatic capacity for states have a background in diplomacy, because that is what they do regularly). While their jobs are in part to represent the positions of their particular states to representatives of other states, they are also in part to enact sovereignty through practice, because sovereignty is what allows their practice of statecraft.[85] In claiming that they represent states as the legitimate voices of sovereign international personhood, they are reconstituting the norm of sovereign international personhood. They could not but do otherwise and still be doing their jobs.

They are reconstituting the norm of sovereign international personhood through practice, but what of the sovereignty cartel more specifically? At a basic level the cartel is actually implicit in the combination of the norms of sovereign personhood and multilateralism. If states are the only legitimate international legal people and are expected to act collaboratively to address international issues, then to remain legitimate states must act multilaterally, and to retain the norm of

---

[84] E.g., Barkin and Weitsman 2019.
[85] For a more complicating version, see Sending, Pouliot, and Neumann 2011.

intergovernmental multilateralism, states must retain the claim of exclusive legitimate international actorhood (because absent this claim why should it be representatives of states, rather than of other corporate actors, who have a voice and a vote?).

The trend over the course of the past century or so toward claims of regulatory universality in the context of the sovereignty cartel might be in part a result of members of this professional class representing organizational interests. A bureaucratic politics model of foreign policy would suggest that policy outcomes at the national level are the result of participants in the decision process acting to maximize the position and resources of their specific bureaucracy relative to others in the government.[86] In multilateral negotiations, members of equivalent bureaucracies across governments are well placed to maximize the positions of their organizations with respect both to other parts of their own governments and other potential sources of international regulation by colluding to expand the scope of claims both to regulatory domain and to regulatory universality.[87]

Even absent such collusion, however, state claims to sovereign universality are a feature of the contemporary international system, and it is (part of) the job of members of this class of state employees to make these claims concrete through practice. The system need not necessarily have developed in this way, but for various historically contingent reasons it has, and multilateral practice reflects this. The sovereignty cartel has in this sense become institutionally embedded as appropriate behavior in the quotidian practice of multilateralism, as state diplomats interact with other state diplomats as sovereign peers, and with representatives of other organizations as categorically different.

A final category of people that must be noted in this section consists of those who either profit from or are protected by individual claims to represent state sovereignty. As a property right, sovereignty comes with claims to benefit economically from economic resources, be those resources natural or regulatory. States have the right to royalties from the extraction of resources from their soil or their seas. They also have the right to proceeds from regulatory charges like corporate registry. In aggregate these rights are worth trillions of dollars. Who exactly is the state in this context, though? Often these royalties or charges go into transparent fiscal budgeting processes. But sometimes they do not;

---

[86] E.g., Allison and Halperin 1972.   [87] See, for example, Finnemore 1996.

sometimes the state seems more like an absentee landlord than an actor for the common national good. In either case, the state in this context is generally whoever the community of sovereigns recognizes as the legitimate sovereign.

When, for example, the EU pays nonmember states for the right to fish in their EEZs, it does not pay actors because they have physical control over these seas (often the relevant states do not), nor does it ensure that the money goes to coastal communities, or even more broadly that it is well spent. It simply pays the money to the relevant sovereign authority.[88] Being that authority, therefore, can be lucrative, and as such one's sovereign right to state property is worth defending. However, that right only exists in the context of a sovereign states system that operates as a recognition cartel and that supports the norm that the property rights adhering to sovereignty include the exclusive right to define the conditions of extraction of physical property and to provide regulative legitimation. The individuals who control this right have a vested interest in maintaining not only their individual claim to sovereignty but also the system that enables that claim, particularly when those individuals profit directly from the claim.

Conclusions

The key takeaway from this chapter is that the property rights that are an aspect of contemporary state sovereignty are not a natural given. In terms of content they are historically specific and have become both regulatorily and geographically more universal in scope over time. As with any property rights, if they are not exercised they can be lost.[89] States, in making propertarian claims based on sovereign right (whether these claims are about access to resources or the authority to regulate) are making specific claims about the proximate issue at hand, but they are also making broader claims about sovereign right in the contemporary international system. This process of claims making is integrated into the everyday practices of multilateral diplomacy and helps to explain the extent to which the more powerful states in the system (however one wants to understand power) accord to weaker

[88] Kaczynski and Fluharty 2002.
[89] Examples include the right to use categories of weapons such as chemical weapons and the right to free access to resources in and under the high seas. Both rights were delegitimized before they were formally constrained by treaty.

states the right to claims both to regulatory equality and to the resources of the global commons.

All of this begs two question, though. The first is who is sovereign in the first place? If sovereignty can be understood as a property right of the state, who then owns the state, or, more specifically, to which individuals do sovereign property rights accrue? The second question is what do we mean by property in the first place? Regulatory universality is a specific property right associated with norms of contemporary sovereignty. But, as was noted above with respect to the use of the language of sovereignty to make popular claims for greater national autonomy, this specific right is not necessarily normatively consistent with other property rights associate with sovereignty. The next chapter looks at the question of whose property, while the following one discusses different understandings of property underlying contemporary norms of sovereign right.

5 | The Sovereign

Sovereign states actively participate in the process of reconstituting their property rights with respect to international politics through the everyday practices of their foreign policies. This observation helps to establish the proposition that a study of the property rights aspect of state sovereignty is relevant to an understanding of contemporary international relations. But it also begs several questions, such as who counts as sovereign in the first place and what precisely we understand property to be. This chapter begins to address these questions by looking at historical ideas about who can be sovereign and what the limits of sovereignty are.

One might question the decision to look at processes of reconstituting sovereignty through practice before addressing what seem to be ontologically prior questions of who is sovereign in the first place. To a certain extent, this is a chicken-and-egg problem – in an examination of the co-constitution of structure and agent, one must begin with one or the other, and the choice in this book was to begin with agents constituting and reconstituting structure. To begin with agents emphasizes that sovereign statehood is a cartel and that the membership is self-selected. It is, however, self-selected within the social structure of a set of norms about who or what is a legitimate participant in the cartel. And it is these norms that are the focus of this chapter.

The answer to the question "to whom do sovereign rights accrue?" might at first seem straightforward – the state. But this answer only begs further questions. When we say "state" in this context, we generally mean the corporate agent that acts as sovereign, making the answer tautological. Not all corporate actors that specialize in governance are sovereign states: neither rebel groups, however firmly in control of their territories, nor subnational governments possess sovereign property rights in the contemporary sovereign states system. When control of the state as a corporate actor is disputed, it may well not be clear which individual actors legitimately constitute the state;

determining the sovereign is therefore a different matter from determining the state.[1] Furthermore, there are some sovereign states (corporate actors endowed by the international community with the property rights of sovereignty) that do not meaningfully govern – failed states still, for example, usually get a seat at international negotiations and can still sell flags of convenience. Sovereign property rights, recognized as such by the community of sovereigns,[2] accrue to whomever that community recognizes as the sovereign, whether with respect to new or existing states.

Several factors might affect this grant of recognition. It is, in historical institutionalist terms, both historically contingent and sticky,[3] meaning that, other things being equal, the actors (corporate or individual) that have been recognized by the cartel as representing a state's sovereignty will generally continue to be so recognized. Physical control of a recognized sovereign territory matters, but is not determinative (recognized governments in absentia, for example, are rare but not unheard of[4]). Geopolitics can intrude, particularly when there are viable alternatives as holders of the rights of sovereignty.[5]

Nonetheless, legitimate sovereignty has been seen by the community of sovereign states, first in the context of the European states system and over the course of the past two centuries or so more broadly as the system globalized, to require a certain constitutional structure.[6] By this I mean a certain relationship between the state and the constituency that the state is seen as governing, be that constituency territorial or

---

[1] The Montevideo Convention on the Rights and Duties of States, for example, notes that states "should possess" a permanent population, defined territory, and government, and that the "political existence of the state is independent of recognition by the other states" (Montevideo Convention Articles 1 and 3, respectively). But the Convention says nothing about sovereignty, about the question of to whom accrue the listed rights and duties.

[2] "Community" is being used here following Cronin (1999: 5), who uses the term in this context to mean a "collectivity of political actors organized on the basis of a common good and a shared sense of self, giving its members a positive stake in building and maintaining internal relationships." I use the term here as more specific and agentive than "international society" as used in the English School of international relations theory.

[3] Capoccia and Kelemen 2007.   [4] E.g., Talmon 1999.

[5] E.g., Coggins 2014.

[6] On the concept of legitimacy in international relations and the role of normative societal consensus in determining legitimacy, see Clark 2005.

societal.[7] The norm structure represented by these required constitutional relationships is enabling of sovereign rights, but it can also be constraining; the preference for a particular form of relationship between governors and governed prevents some categories of action by the state, even when this action is entirely domestic in nature.[8] Furthermore, these relationships change over time. A prospective sovereign's place in this relationship provides the normative basis for claims to be the holder of sovereign property rights.

This relationship has gone through four major permutations since the middle of the seventeenth century.[9] In the era following the Westphalian settlement, religion was a key element of the relationship considered to be constitutional of the authority of the state and thus outside of its authority to change. Following the Vienna conference, monarchical solidarity, the idea that a polity could not fully participate in international relations without a legitimate monarch, was a required constitutional element of legitimate sovereignty. Through the course of the late nineteenth and early twentieth centuries, the focus of the constitutional basis of sovereignty shifted from the monarchy to the nation, understood as an independent entity. Following World War II, it again shifted, and the norm of territorial legitimation evolved: a state was legitimated by control of a previously defined piece of territory, which was itself fixed.

The collective understanding by the community of states as to the legitimate constitutional relationship between sovereign and governed shifted somewhat in the aftermath of the Cold War. The territorial legitimation of the Cold War weakened somewhat. Meanwhile, the idea of the individual citizen, represented by a set of formal political rights, as the constitutional basis of sovereignty (already present in the founding documents of the United Nations in the 1940s) became increasingly embedded in international discourse. This new norm has not displaced earlier norms of the legitimate constitutional structure of

---

[7] This is not to argue that contemporary sovereignty is something invented in Europe and exported. See, e.g., Branch 2012.
[8] Stephen Krasner (1995) discusses the relationship between "rulers" and "ruled" in a manner that is compatible with the discussion here. His terminology is too limiting, however, as it implies a much narrower set of relationships than is historically the case.
[9] This is one version of the history; there are, of course, other reasonable periodizations and interpretations of norms of legitimacy in those periods. See, e.g., Clark 2005.

sovereignty and is by no means uncontested in contemporary international politics. At the same time, however, it remains relevant to those politics.

The Legitimated Constitution of Sovereignty

This constitutional structure can be thought of in terms of legitimated sovereignty – the community of states recognizes the sovereign rights of those actors it considers to be legitimately sovereign (keeping in mind that legitimacy, like sovereign rights, need not be dichotomous – a state, or a sovereign, can be more or less legitimate). The use of the term "international legitimacy" here can be defined, following Martin Wight in his essay titled "International Legitimacy," as "the collective judgement of international society about rightful membership of the family of nations; how sovereignty may be transferred; and how state succession is to be regulated."[10] States' need for certain institutional structures to legitimate themselves can act as a significant constraint on their final authority over their internal affairs. It is in part through this sort of constraint that religion was deeply embedded in the social construction of seventeenth-century governance in Europe,[11] and that human rights have become embedded in the contemporary construction of state sovereignty.

There are a number of different aspects of the way in which sovereignty is understood that can change over time, one of which is the legitimation of the sovereign, that which is seen by the international community as required by an actor in order to be considered properly sovereign.[12] Since the (gradual) inception of the European sovereign states system, legitimated sovereignty has been understood to be associated with particular constitutional arrangements within the state, be those arrangements reflective of religious, national, constitutional, or territorial constituencies. These constituencies have in turn been reflected by particular institutions required of the state. "Constitutional arrangements" refers here to any institutions that are central, core features of the political structure of a state. They need not be written or even formally articulated. They do, however, need

---

[10] Wight 1977: 153. For a discussion of political legitimation more generally, see Weber 1968, especially part I chapters 1 and 3, and part II chapter 10.
[11] E.g., Onnekink 2016.
[12] Other aspects include those discussed in Wight 1972 and Bartelson 1995.

to be seen as ontologically prior to the political function of the state, and as being beyond the legitimate authority of the state to fundamentally change.[13]

When public authority within a domain has not possessed these constitutional arrangements, recognized by the community of sovereigns as integral to legitimate sovereignty, that authority has generally not been recognized by that community as properly sovereign and has not been accorded full sovereign rights in international relations.[14] This is not to say that the international community will necessarily take decisive and immediate action against an illegitimate sovereign. When dealing with revolutionary France, for example, the European monarchies clearly had to take France's military power into account as well as its legitimacy. Illegitimate claimants to sovereignty are, however, generally treated as different and apart from legitimate ones, and this different treatment can affect the course of international relations.[15]

Not only do accepted understandings of the proper constitutional arrangements affect conceptions of what legitimate sovereignty is, but these understandings change over time. Exogenous evolutions in ideas, in political philosophies, play a fundamental generative role in such change. New ideas that evolve in the domestic political realm and are brought into the international realm affect conceptions of what sovereignty means and what functions a state should serve. For example, the Rousseauvian idea of a general will and the Hegelian notion of a universal nation had a profound and independent impact on nineteenth-century European politics by helping to create the modern idea of a "nation" as a thing worth fighting for. However, power, in the traditional realist sense of the term, matters as well; it is usually the conceptions of legitimacy and sovereignty of the existing powerful states in international relations that become the international norm. The powerful are sometimes in a position to impose their ideas of legitimacy on the less powerful; therefore, it is the ideas of the most powerful states that matter most.[16] Furthermore, the issue of whether a state is adhering to international norms is at least a partially subjective judgement, and it is the judgements of powerful states that are of the greatest import in conferring sovereign legitimacy. Yet once

---

[13] On the relationship between domestic and international legitimacy, see Clark 2005.
[14] E.g., Strang 1991. [15] Kocs 1994. [16] E.g., Lumsdaine 1993.

created, international norms of legitimation both constrain state behavior, including the behavior of the powerful, and help to define the very interests that states pursue. In John Ruggie's terminology, the international normative structure defines states' legitimate social purpose.[17]

Change in the accepted constitutional arrangements of legitimated sovereignty is most likely in the aftermath of major international events such as systemic wars, events so cataclysmic that they significantly alter the distribution of capabilities in the international system, while at the same time highlighting new ideas about the role of politics and the state.[18] The defeat of the previously powerful in systemic wars allows the winning coalition to impose whatever norms it holds in common on the losers. The ends of systemic wars are often therefore watersheds for international governance structures, including norms of legitimated sovereignty.[19] At the same time, the demands of prosecuting the war often accelerate processes of political diffusion, as new forms of economic relations broaden the base of political participation and new ideas are co-opted in efforts to marshal the resources necessary to win the war.[20]

This process of economic advance and political diffusion can be seen in systemic wars from the Thirty Years War through the Cold War. Thus the aftermaths of systemic wars provide both incentive and opportunity for change in the accepted constitution of legitimate sovereignty. Such changes can be deliberate attempts by the powers that be to restore as much as possible of an old order, as was the case with the norm of monarchical legitimacy created at the Congress of Vienna, or less deliberate and more radical shifts in the sources of international legitimacy, as was the case with the rise of nationalist ideas to international acceptance in the second half of the nineteenth century. It should be noted here as well that predominant norms in international relations are rarely universally accepted. They are often contested either by those still sympathetic to older norms or those wishing to

---

[17] Ruggie 1982. In a sense, because the international normative structure reflects the social purpose of the powerful, it is the great powers who are most constrained by it.
[18] Barkin and Cronin 1994. For an argument for seeing change as more gradual, see Allan 2018.
[19] Gilpin 1981, chapter 5.
[20] Tilly 1992, chapter 4, and North 1981: 208–209.

encourage new ones. Such contestations can come from either state or non-state actors and can, if sufficiently widespread, undermine norms of legitimation. It is this potential for contestation that makes it necessary for sovereigns to act as a cartel to protect the norms underpinning their property rights.

Sovereignty claimants who do not honor or do not conform to dominant constitutional norms, and as a result are not seen as fully legitimate by the community of states, are likely to be excluded to some degree from regular patterns of discourse within this community.[21] At the same time, states that do honor and conform to these norms can use them to legitimize behavior to this community, particularly aggressive forms of behavior that might otherwise trigger a more negative international response. This process of discursive legitimation of action is likely to affect outcomes of state interaction. Clues to legitimizing norms in international relations can thus be found in patterns of exclusion and inclusion in international discourse and in discursive attempts by both individual states and supranational organizations to legitimize action that might otherwise be seen as affecting the sovereign rights of the objects of said action. Actors that conform to these norms are more likely to be recognized by the community of sovereigns as legitimate full members of the cartel; as a result, they are more likely to be accorded the full property rights of sovereignty.

The rest of this chapter will examine briefly international norms of the legitimate constitutional structure of the sovereign state, in five sections, highlighting five different sets of norms since the seventeenth century. These norms constitute only one part of the international normative structure, including norms related to the legitimate constitutional structure of sovereignty; those identified here had a significant impact on international relations, but not to the exclusion of other norms, legitimating or otherwise. This historical account is intended to be illustrative rather than determinative; it suggests some examples of norms of sovereign legitimation at various points in time rather than offering a general account of the evolution of the international normative structure. The account does nonetheless suggest how the normative structure came to be as messy as is currently the case.

[21] It must be stressed again that while the "community of states" may be formally democratic, some states are far more central to this community, for reasons either of power or history, than others, and it is the judgments of these states on matters of international legitimacy that matter most.

Absolutism, Religion, and the Westphalian System

Although the role of the Peace of Westphalia in the genesis of the modern sovereign states system is generally overstated, as we saw in Chapter 2, it did mark the end of a devastating, generational war that affected most of the European polity. The Peace itself was to a large extent an attempt by the signatories to create a system of public authority in Europe that would avoid the sort of widespread violence and destruction that had plagued Europe throughout the period of the religious wars.[22] There were two particular aspects of the Westphalian settlement that can be thought of as the legitimate constitutional basis of sovereignty in that era. The first aspect was religious. The primary proximate cause of the Thirty Years War, and much of the warfare in Europe in the previous century, was religion: conflict over who had religious authority within a given territory. It made sense, then, that a core of the treaty was an agreement on religious authority. Earlier practice, as codified in the Treaty of Augsburg in 1555, was that the religion of the prince was the religion of the state. This had signally failed to contain religious war in northern Europe, however, and the Peace of Westphalia introduced a wide range of restrictions on the religious freedom of the prince and of religious protections for subjects. Princes, for example, could not convert, and in many principalities the rights of religious minorities were explicitly made a matter for international concern.[23] In other words, legitimate sovereignty did not authorize rulers to breach the religious settlement of the Peace, which was self-consciously constitutional of the new Westphalian European international system.

This religious settlement formed the basis of and greatest exception to the broader legitimizing principle of the treaty, the idea that the sovereignty of the state was legitimized in the person of the ruler.[24] In other words, from the point of view of international relations, the person of the prince was seen as being the absolute functional embodiment of the state. The ruler, in other words, owned the state. Louis XIV's infamous aphorism, *L'état c'est Moi*, was in this sense meant

---

[22] Tilly 1992: 165–166. See also Croxton 2015. [23] Krasner 1993: 242–244.
[24] Again, this does not necessarily mean that princes had complete freedom of action domestically, but rather that it was they personally who were considered as the state for the purposes of international relations. It should be noted that this form of legitimation did not depart radically from late feudal practice.

Absolutism, Religion, and the Westphalian System   87

literally: the state, from the point of view of the international community, was defined not by its territory or its population but by its ruler. Thus the second aspect of the Westphalian settlement that formed the legitimate constitutional basis of sovereignty was the identification of state with ruler, and a corollary separation of populations from a similar identification and, as a result, from active participation in the conduct of international relations. The property rights of sovereignty were vested in the person of the ruler, rather than in the institution of the state.

This second aspect of sovereign legitimation helps to illuminate many of the patterns of the practice of international relations in Europe in the late seventeenth and early eighteenth centuries, such as the malleability of territorial borders to political adjustments, and the professionalization of warfare and its separation from state populations. When it is the ruler that legitimizes the state, then territorial adjustments, regardless of the desires of the inhabitants, are legitimate as long as the ruler agrees to them. Thus minor territorial adjustments could be, and were, used as mechanisms for conflict resolution in ways that were no longer practicable in later eras, when states came to be legitimated by broader sets of institutions. And when the ruler is, for the purposes of international relations, the state, then warfare becomes the concern of the ruler only, rather than the concern of the population more broadly. This identity of the state with the ruler helps to explain why warfare in this period was more a sport of kings, fought by professionals, rather than the much broader and more devastating warfare that was the norm before and after.[25]

The first major attempt to end the religious wars was the Treaty of Augsburg in 1555. The Westphalian settlement was not that different in content, which suggests that the ideal basis of the Westphalian system had been in place for the better part of a century by 1648.[26] A major difference between the two treaties, however, was the balance

---

[25] William McNeill (1982: 139–140) notes this pattern and dates it to start in 1650, although he ascribes the cause to evolution in European patterns of taxation.

[26] Perhaps the most important difference from an international systemic perspective was that under the Treaty of Augsburg, sovereigns had greater religious freedom. In this sense, the Peace of Westphalia, which succeeded in creating a system of sovereign states, placed greater restrictions on the internal authority of princes than the Treaty of Augsburg, which failed. This contrast suggests that constraints on sovereign autonomy, far from being antithetical to a

of power in Europe that each faced. The end of the Thirty Years War saw France and Sweden militarily predominant in the territories of the Holy Roman Empire. Two interests these powers shared in common were a desire for autonomy from pan-European political institutions, and a preference for small, militarily weak polities in what is now Germany. Both interests could be fulfilled by a system of legitimation that promoted the independence of the German princes from the Empire, which absolutist legitimation accomplished quite effectively. The congruence of the ideas contained in these settlements and the interests of the most powerful political entities in Europe helps to explain why Augsburg failed while Westphalia endured.

Monarchicalism and the Congress System

The ideal of the ruler as the absolute embodiment of the legitimate state, already weak by the latter half of the eighteenth century, was weakened further by the French Revolution and its language of republicanism. It was not immediately replaced; norms of international behavior remained strongly contested through the course of the French Revolutionary and Napoleonic Wars.[27] The end of the wars saw the victors, primarily Britain, Prussia, Austria, and Russia, in something of a dilemma. Their goals were essentially conservative; the common denominator of the Grand Coalition was a desire to defeat revolutionary change.[28] Yet the demands of the war, the need for extensive popular participation in the war effort if it was to succeed in defeating a France that was very successful at mobilizing popular support for war, created a much broader degree of popular participation in international affairs than had been the case in the Westphalian system.[29] This process served to encourage and exacerbate the strains that had already begun to affect the ideological basis of the system of absolutist legitimation in the latter half of the eighteenth century. The Great Powers, meeting in Vienna after the wars in an attempt to reconstitute an international order, were faced with the task of reconstituting as much as possible of the old order while facing the new domestic political realities created by the war.

system of sovereign states, may in fact be necessary for such a system to function effectively.
[27] Schroeder 1994.   [28] Kissinger 1958: 56.   [29] E.g., Lyons 1994.

In the compromise that was eventually reached at Vienna, norms of sovereign legitimation were grounded in the institution of the monarchy. Countries were considered legitimate in the Congress system if they had monarchies, preferably led by members of one of Europe's traditional royal families.[30] This differed markedly from the Westphalian system, in which the ruler, from the perspective of the international system, owned the state. In the Vienna system, the country was recognized as an entity in and of itself, but one that was embodied by a monarch and thus required a monarch to be granted full sovereign rights. The monarchy was constitutionally necessary as a representative of the state, but states were no longer necessarily the absolute property of their rulers.[31] This dualist form of legitimation provided a compromise between traditional ruling classes wanting to retain their status and an emergent body politic beginning to demand inclusion in the institutions of the state.

The introduction of a more limited monarchical legitimation into international politics led to a change in many of the patterns of international relations from what had been the case before the French Revolution. Heads of state went from being the sole legitimate actors, in and of themselves, in international relations, to being legitimators of countries. This meant that transfers of territory as mechanisms of conflict resolution among rulers were no longer as common or as easy as had previously been the case.[32] Territory was now part of a country rather than simply being the rulers' to do with as they pleased, which gave state boundaries significantly more permanence than in the Westphalian system.

Another crucial difference between the two systems lay in the nature of the limits of the domestic authority of the sovereign. Sovereignty tends to convey upon the state the authority to do as it sees fit internally, except when such action compromises the legitimating constitutional features of sovereign statehood. In the case of the

---

[30] E.g., Ferrero 1941 and Cronin 1999.
[31] For a discussion of the process of reaching this compromise form of legitimation at Vienna, see Cronin 1999, chapter 3.
[32] Once the system had been put into place. At the conference itself there was a significant amount of bartering of territory and calculation of balance, but once the treaty borders had been settled upon they became fairly static. For a discussion of the process of negotiating the Treaty of Vienna, see Webster 1931 and Webster 1934.

Westphalian system, one such feature was religion: rulers had the authority to do pretty much as they pleased within their states and little authority to intervene within the domain of other rulers, except with respect to breaches of the religious settlement. In the Vienna system, an equivalent feature was legitimate monarchy. If domestic political developments threatened to undermine a legitimate monarch, other states could legitimately intervene to support the old regime, or to reinstate it if it had already been overthrown by a liberal revolution.[33] In other words, legitimate intervention in the Westphalian system was triggered by an act of the ruler; in the Vienna system, by acts against the ruler. This helps to explain a pattern of Great Power intervention in the domestic politics of European countries throughout the first half of the nineteenth century.

Patterns of conflict in this system tended often to revolve around those countries without or with threatened monarchies. One of the primary roles of the Great Powers in the concert system was to intervene in these states to reimpose legitimate monarchies in order to reduce the risk of revolution that might emanate from these states and spread throughout the system. Examples of this sort of Great Power behavior include interventions in clearly domestic disputes in Naples, Piedmont, and Spain to support beleaguered monarchs.[34] Arguments for supporting either side of the Greek revolt of 1821–1829 addressed legitimist concerns, and part of the final settlement to the revolt involved the Great Powers, rather than any indigenous Greek political process, electing a new king. A condition of Belgian independence in 1831 was the installation of a king from a legitimate royal family, in this case that of Saxe-Coburg. In the meantime, a series of revolutions and secessionist movements that were successfully dealt with by monarchical governments in Italy, Germany, and Poland attracted little international attention.[35]

This system of European sovereign legitimation, as with any such system, could not last beyond the time when the major powers in the international system were willing to support it. A number of forces acted to weaken the norm of monarchical legitimation, including the

---

[33] Holsti 1992: 28.

[34] Britain, traditionally less enthusiastic about the conservatism of the concert system than the other powers, did not support these interventions. At the same time, however, it neither acted strongly to oppose them nor denied their legitimacy.

[35] Craig 1971, especially chapter 1.

increasing relevance of non-European countries, particularly in the Americas, that had never been governed by it.[36] The most important proximate factor in its demise was the wave of popular unrest, which peaked in the revolutions of 1848, that contested the ideas upon which monarchical legitimation was based and made it clear that they were no longer acceptable to an increasingly politicized European bourgeoisie.[37]

Norms of monarchical legitimation had also, however, ceased serving the interests of the Great Power coalition that had created it in the first place. One Great Power, France, ceased to be a monarchy; another, Great Britain, came to use its foreign policy to pursue both imperial and marketizing rather than monarchical norms; a third, Austria, became too weak internally to continue to act as the focus of the concert system; and a fourth, Prussia, came to decide in time that other ideas, particularly those of nationalism, were more conducive to its foreign policy aims than ideas of monarchical solidarity.[38] Yet it is interesting to note that the discourse of legitimate monarchy had been so strongly reinforced in international practice by the series of interventions in the early part of the nineteenth century that it remained an element of international practice into the twentieth; the last clear example of this norm playing a constitutive role was with Norway's independence from Sweden in 1905. Despite perhaps the most democratic political constitution in Europe, the Norwegians felt it necessary to import a king from an established royal family (Denmark's) as the ceremonial head of a constitutional monarchy.[39]

Nationalism and the Two World Wars

Nationalism had motivated a series of popular revolutions across Europe in 1848. While these had for the most part not succeeded in forcing regime change in the short term, nationalism become an accepted and legitimate element in the practice of international relations in Europe by the early 1860s. However, it was not codified as a core part of a definitive international agreement until after World War I. With the acceptance of Wilson's Fourteen Points as the foundation of

---

[36] Temperley 1966.
[37] "The revolutions of 1848 signaled the end of respect and established order, both at home and in foreign affairs." Taylor 1954: xxii.
[38] Pflanze 1963.   [39] Craig 1971: 307–308.

the Versailles settlement, however, the "nation" came formally to be seen by the international community as a fundamental source of legitimacy for the state.[40] The gradualness of this transition, and the lack of formal codification until well after the norm was established, may have contributed to the relative lack of clarity of the normative structure of international legitimacy in this period. For example, Bismarck's idea of the nation's role in politics was notably different from President Wilson's.[41] In turn, this lack of clarity may well have been a significant contributing factor to the levels of international violence experienced in the latter part of this period.

The common denominator of the idea of the nation, in this context, is that it is to be understood as an entity unto itself, something apart from the simple cumulation of like-identifying people. Analogies can be found in the general will in Rousseau's terms or a universal entity in Hegel's. Nationalism as a legitimating norm thus requires of states neither democracy nor a respect for liberal rights. It requires of them only that they represent nations. In a nationally legitimated international system, states can only interfere in the domestic affairs of other states for nationalist reasons, particularly if these involve members of the national group represented by the intervenor. A state is considered legitimate by the international community if it represents a given national group, and all members of that national group are a legitimate concern of the state.[42] For this reason nationalist norms of sovereignty, as suggested previously, are relatively destabilizing. Because state boundaries will rarely conform perfectly to national groups, and because national affiliations are themselves changeable, the scope for legitimate causes for interstate conflict are potentially quite high. At the same time, because nationalism as a philosophy is particularly successful at mobilizing popular participation and antagonisms, conflicts are prone to being large-scale and nasty. Thus an

---

[40] For discussions of the process whereby Wilson's ideas on national self-determination became a foundational concept of the League of Nations system see, *inter alia*, Ferrel 1985; Baker 1922; Ambrosius 1991; and Mee 1980.

[41] Bismarck's idea would have been close to the Hegelian notion of a nation universally embodied by a monarch, whereas Wilson's would have been closer to a liberal notion of popular participation in governance.

[42] For further discussions of nationalism and its development, see Gellner 1983; Hobsbawm 1990; Anderson 1983; and Smith 1983.

international system of nationally legitimized states is potentially prone both to large numbers of conflicts and to particularly costly ones.

There are two particular sources of instability in an interstate system in which nations constitute a legitimate source of sovereignty. The first is states that do not represent nations. The second is legitimate states that do represent nations but that either contain a significant minority of a national group represented by another state, or have a significant number of their nationals resident in states representing other nations. Classic examples of the first type of destabilizing state were the Hapsburg and Ottoman empires. Both, in the decades leading up to the First World War, put much of their diplomatic effort into finding ways to shore up increasingly tenuous domestic political structures.[43] These efforts were a significant contributing factor to many of the international crises of the late nineteenth and early twentieth centuries, including the crisis that precipitated World War I. This dynamic was recognized at Versailles; the breaking up of both empires was intended by the victorious powers to a large degree to eliminate nationalist claims against multinational empires as a major source of conflict in Europe.[44]

The second source of instability in a nationally legitimated state system is the potential for conflict arising from national minorities. Territorial claims based upon concentrations of nationals abroad did have a certain legitimacy in the eyes of the international community in this system. The classic example of this dynamic is the series of German expansions that preceded World War II. The remilitarization of the Rhineland, the Anschluss with Austria, and the annexation of the Sudetenland from Czechoslovakia were all seen by the international community as having a certain element of legitimacy, as they were all cases of the German state coming into greater conformity with the German nation.[45] National populations, however, rarely live exclusively in neatly defined geographical territories, and disputes over territory containing elements of more than one national group can thus not necessarily be solved based purely on legitimate claims. Disputes over territory with more than one national claim are as a

---

[43] In Austria's case, its efforts to isolate Serbia, which instigated a series of international crises and ultimately sparked World War I, can be seen primarily as an attempt to diffuse its internal nationalist problem. See Kann 1950.
[44] Barkin and Cronin 1994: note 4.
[45] Taylor 1961: 54–55, 134–135, and 155.

result a significant source of risk when nations are a major source of state legitimacy.

Precisely this sort of dispute, German nationalist territorial demands gone awry, was widely and popularly seen as a primary cause of World War II. The tendency of the system of nationalist legitimation of states to generate conflict spirals created a reaction against nationalism as the main organizing idea of the international community. Furthermore, a proliferation of self-identified nations threatened to overwhelm a nationally legitimated state system. This reaction does not mean that nationalist ideas no longer affected international relations, or that they ceased to have appeal or to serve as organizing features of many popular movements; clearly, they still do. What it does mean is that the nationalist logic was no longer seen as the core legitimate source of claims by some states against others, either to territorial adjustment or to the right to interfere in the domestic affairs of other states for purposes of promoting the position of a particular national minority.[46] This significantly changed patterns of international relations and of international conflict.

Territorial Control and the Cold War

The end of World War II saw international relations dominated by two superpowers that viewed the world in very different ways, different enough that in many respects two distinct international systems were created after the war, with a wide range of economic, security, and social institutions duplicated on both sides of the Iron Curtain.[47] The superpowers, however, did have some things in common. Both defined themselves in ideological, rather than nationalist, terms. And both superpowers were averse enough to renewed world war and later to nuclear war that norms of state legitimation developed around such common denominators as were available. Both superpowers were interested in a world in which regional conflicts were containable, and in which weapons of mass destruction would not be used. At the

---

[46] Again, this is not to suggest that it was never done, rather that it could not be done legitimately, as had been the case in the interwar period. As a result, it was done much less frequently.

[47] Examples include the General Agreement on Tariffs and Trade and Comecon, and the North Atlantic Treaty Organization and the Warsaw Pact, each with its own rules of legitimacy.

same time, norms of self-determination had become firmly enough a part of the ideal structure of international society that they could not be entirely ignored.[48] The compromise between the needs of the powerful and predominant ideas of legitimate government was the norm of territorial legitimation.[49]

The basis of this norm is the reification of defined territories. National borders in this system, as agreed upon in the immediate postwar settlement, came to be sacrosanct in and of themselves, to be taken as prior to the operation of international politics.[50] Except under the most extreme of circumstances, they could not be altered.[51] In other words, the constitutional structure of the sovereign state in this system was based on a relationship between state and territory, rather than between state and people. This tended to reduce legitimate sovereignty to a question of control. The ability of a state structure to provide government within a defined territory requires that it maintain a functional control over that territory. If it could not do so, it might be replaced by a different state structure. If the new government gained territorial control, it then generally became, in the eyes of the international community, the legitimate state. While some version of territoriality has always been an element of modern state sovereignty, the constitutional nature of territorial control has not; governments "in absentia" have often been recognized by the international community, while governments with adequate territorial control but without legitimate institutions have not.

Territorial legitimation contributed to the tendency of violent conflict during the Cold War to be within countries rather than between

---

[48] Although the idea of self-determination does not generate a straightforward norm of legitimacy. "On the surface it seems reasonable: let the people decide. It was in fact ridiculous because the people cannot decide until someone decides who are the people" – Sir Ivor Jennings, quoted in Buchheit 1978: 9.

[49] It is in this context interesting to compare the League of Nations' stipulation that the "Members of the League reserve to themselves the right to take such action as they shall consider necessary for the maintenance of right and justice," in its covenant, Article 15, Paragraph 7, with the emphasis of the charter of the United Nations on the maintenance of international security, understood as the prevention of the violation of established borders, in Article 1, Paragraph 1; Article 2, Paragraph 4; and Article 51. The former emphasizes the justice of nations, the latter the inviolability of borders.

[50] This is codified as such in the Charter of the United Nations.

[51] Examples of border changes include Pakistan, which was exceptional in being made up of two noncontiguous parts, and Vietnam, which eventually reunited.

them.[52] This pattern of conflict served the interests of the Cold War superpowers by helping to contain international conflict and prevent escalation to major power war. Conflicts were usually about who would end up in control within a previously defined set of national borders, almost never about where those borders would be. If a government proved unable to maintain control domestically, it became legitimate, tacitly if not formally, for the major powers to intervene domestically on behalf of one of the domestic factions vying for control. This led to the pattern of civil and proxy wars that characterized the Cold War period. Two observations suggest that the norm of territorial legitimation did in fact come to provide the baseline for expectations in this period. The first is that, with very few exceptions, changes in previously defined borders were not looked to as solutions to international crises. The second is that new governments, including those that came to power through violent means, were usually recognized by institutions such as the United Nations without difficulty. That control within set geographic boundaries led to international recognition of a government as the legitimate state suggests that territory was ontologically prior to state legitimacy in the eyes of the international community.

Exceptions to the normal pattern of Cold War politics arose from territories that were not clearly defined by the international community *ex ante* as being within a particular state. If the ownership of such a territory was claimed by more than one state, it tended to generate protracted and intractable conflict, because the settling of the claim one way or the other in a system of territorial legitimation is likely to be irreversible, creating a zero-sum dynamic. Such territories were rare in the Cold War, but those that did exist, such as the West Bank and Gaza, parts of Kashmir, and stretches of the Sino-Soviet border, often generated major and long-lasting conflicts.

Most violent conflicts in the system of territorial legitimation, however, were generated in states that were not in reasonable control within their own borders. Since the ability to provide government within a defined territory was an element of state legitimacy in this system, states that did not have physical control, and thus could not

[52] Small and Singer (1982: 59–60, 222) identify forty-four civil wars in the period from 1945 to 1980 and eighteen interstate wars. Of the eighteen, at least eight were interventions in civil conflict, and seven involved territory that had not been clearly allocated to a sovereign state in the postwar settlement.

provide government, throughout their territories were functionally less than fully legitimate. Such states ran the risk of attracting the involvement of outside powers in domestic conflicts, potentially escalating both the level of violence and the intractability of the conflict. The list of domestic conflicts that attracted superpower involvement in this way during the Cold War is extensive.[53]

The sorts of foreign policies that territorial norms of legitimation encouraged had generated opposition from elements within the Western democracies for decades. The idea that societies that saw their own states as being legitimated by political institutions that emphasized norms of liberal democracy should, for *raisons d'état*, not oppose (and often support) regimes abroad that clearly failed to respect these norms was a consistent source of criticism of Western foreign policies from within those democracies. Furthermore, as the ideological underpinnings of the Cold War confrontation between East and West faded, the postwar economic systems of embedded liberalism in the West[54] and central planning in the East started to give way to an international economic system more congruently liberal in its domestic and interstate dimensions.[55] The spread of economic globalism and interdependence became increasingly at odds with norms of state legitimation focused on exclusivist state structures. Yet the international system continued to recognize territorial norms, largely because the West could not force fundamental international normative change on its own.

Citizenship Rights and the Post-Cold War State

The proximate cause of the weakening of the norm of territorial legitimation was the end of the Cold War. Although the norm had been coming into disrepute among many in the West for decades, ideological conflict and the fear of superpower confrontation sufficed to keep it intact as a core source of legitimation in international relations. Since no way of changing norms could be found that would

---

[53] Of Small and Singer's (1982) list of civil wars in the period 1945–1980, more than half attracted involvement by outside powers.
[54] Ruggie 1982: 209–214.
[55] McNamara (1998) provides an example of this evolution when she traces the evolution from embedded liberalism to the new economic orthodoxy, which she calls competitive liberalism, in the context of European monetary cooperation.

not threaten stability, existing norms were reconstituted through Cold War practice. The strength of the belief in the stabilizing influence of this norm is suggested by the reaction of the American government to the breakup of the Soviet Union in 1990. The initial response of the first Bush administration was to oppose the disintegration of its rival, fearing that it would be too destabilizing. However, with the end of the Cold War the threat of superpower confrontation that had helped keep the norm of territorial legitimation in place seemed to disappear. It was replaced with a discourse of a new era in international relations,[56] one in which there was some talk of unipolarity, and in which the major powers were, for a short time, almost exclusively Western liberal democracies. This is not to say that territoriality per se necessarily weakened as an element of the legitimation of sovereignty. Rather, what weakened was the idea that borders are necessarily fixed and ontologically prior to the states that govern within them.

A norm that began to replace territorial legitimation as a defining feature of the constitution of legitimate sovereignty in international relations was the norm of human rights. This norm includes civil and political rights, a set of relations between the state and each of its individual citizens that guarantees to each citizen certain political rights against the state, but not economic, social, and collective rights.[57] The priority of this set of rights is itself a socially constructed idea; it is not objectively obvious, for example, that the right to vote is more important than the right to eat. This set of human rights has become accepted throughout the West, though, as the defining characteristic of contemporary liberal (or market) democracy. In the immediate post-Cold War world in which the states that dominated the practice and the discourse of international relations mostly claimed to be liberal democracies, a state to a significant degree was legitimated in the eyes of the international community insofar as it guaranteed these rights. If it failed to do so then other states could limit their recognition of its sovereign rights. This in turn resulted (inconsistently) both in exclusion from participation in the society of states and a greater tendency for intervention in domestic affairs to promote human rights.

---

[56] This is suggested by the almost universal acceptance in the literature on international relations that the post-Cold War period is historiographically distinct from the Cold War period.

[57] Vincent 1986: 11–13.

Such intervention occurred only in cases of clear and gross violation (and often not then), but even in these cases, intervention would not have been deemed legitimate prior to 1990. Clear early examples are the UN Security Council-sanctioned interventions in Yugoslavia in 1992 and Haiti in 1994, but interesting examples are also to be found in the increased intrusiveness of international organizations in countries such as Guatemala and El Salvador,[58] the trend toward international monitoring of domestic elections,[59] and in the increased emphasis of intergovernmental organizations such as the United Nations Development Programme (UNDP) on concepts such as "good governance," which would not have been possible during the Cold War.[60] The evolution of the norm of human rights as constitutive of sovereignty culminated in the discourse (and, in Libya, the application) of the responsibility to protect.[61]

The norm of human rights as an element of state legitimacy in international relations was of course not new to the post-Cold War period; it has been developing within the West for some time. It has, for example, been accepted as an informal but binding precondition for entry into the European Union since the EU began expanding and has been an increasingly significant part of the foreign policy discourse, both in the West and elsewhere, for decades.[62] It was even accepted formally by the international community in the midst of the Cold War in the form of the Helsinki Accords.[63] It was only with the demise of the Soviet Union, however, that the most powerful site of contestation of the liberal/capitalist constitutional model ceased to actively resist the imposition of this model on the international community as a whole in a more functional way. In this sense, the end of the Cold War was an equivalent of the end of a systemic war in that it marked a radical and sudden change in the international distribution of power, of the kind that has historically accompanied many major shifts in the normative structure of international relations.

An interesting and illustrative example of the relationship between sovereign right and human rights in the contemporary international

---

[58] Burgerman 2001. [59] Kelley 2008.
[60] For a history of the development of ideas within the UNDP, see Murphy 2006.
[61] E.g., Morris 2013.
[62] Two examples of how the discourse of human rights significantly affected patterns of international relations in specific issue areas in the 1980s can be found in Klotz 1995 and Sikkink 1993.
[63] Thomas 2001.

system is to be found in the rules of the International Criminal Court (ICC). These rules clearly give signatory states the authority to try their own nationals in the first instance. It is only if the ICC judges find that states have not lived up to their responsibility to enforce international law with respect to war crimes and crimes against humanity that the ICC gains jurisdiction over individuals.[64] States, in other words, retain the legitimate right to legal authority over their citizens, but this right is contingent upon its own exercise in the case of certain categories of crimes against human rights. The state retains full sovereign rights in a key domain of governance, but that right remains subject to the constitutional structure of the norms of sovereignty.

The effect of human rights legitimation on international discourse was to make it easier to intervene in the domestic affairs of states that fail to guarantee these rights. This does not suggest an increase in levels of altruism in the making of foreign policy. It does mean, however, that norms of nonintervention apply less to states that fail to guarantee the human rights of their citizens than to those states that do. The normative costs of intervention in these cases are lower, so that when state interest might suggest such an action, it is more likely to be carried out. Only the more egregious violators are delegitimized, and even in these cases, significant action is only undertaken when it is in the interest of a major power. It does mean, however, that the international political costs of intervening in these states is lower than for more legitimate sovereigns; therefore, there is a greater chance of it happening. Furthermore, even when the discourse of human rights is used to mask *raison d'état*, this discourse itself can still lead to different outcomes than would otherwise have resulted. An invasion of Iraq under the guise of democratization, for example, yields a different occupation strategy than an invasion designed to protect legitimate monarchy.

The discourse of human rights legitimation in international relations will only remain institutionalized within the international system to the extent that it continues to be reconstituted through state practice. The continuing strength of this new norm structure therefore depends on agency, on continuing policy choices made by participants in international affairs. This means that to the extent that actors in international politics wish to reinforce norms of human rights as constitutive of legitimate sovereignty, they must continue to actively

[64] United Nations General Assembly 1998.

engage them discursively. It also means that new, or newly powerful, actors that wish to undermine these norms can look to new forms of practice to change the constitutional structure of sovereign right in a way that minimizes the role of human rights.

Conclusions

The expansion of the role of human rights in legitimating claims to sovereignty may already have peaked, given, among other things, the decline of the discourse of responsibility to protect and the increasing international assertiveness of China. This leaves the contemporary sovereign states system with a set of historically developed, overlapping, and often mutually contradictory sources of sovereign legitimacy claims. Some are weaker than others; for example, monarchical claims by Gulf Cooperation Council rulers help to legitimate their claims to legitimate sovereignty against a backdrop of weak human rights provision, but it seems unlikely that claims to a right of absolute monarchy would be accepted by the international community with respect to a newly created state. Meanwhile, nationalist and territorial claims are still used by sovereign claimants to legitimate their rule, but the role of political rights as expressed in elections in supporting claims to be a legitimate sovereign have expanded greatly in the past three decades.

These multiple discourses of sovereign legitimacy can yield contesting claims to sovereign right. To a significant extent these claims are international, inasmuch as it is the sovereignty cartel that needs to recognize the rights to make them valuable in the international political economy. When such contestations occur, be they the result of civil conflict, questionable election results, coups d'état, or other domestic political events, different players can bring different discourses to bear with respect to different audiences. The norms structure of sovereignty claims, in other words, is messy and not directly determinative of outcomes. But it does provide the language in which those claims are made.

6 Sovereign Property

The messiness of the norms structure is to be found not only in the question of what the property rights of sovereignty are, but also in the logically prior questions of what we mean by property in the first place and of whose property sovereignty is. This chapter argues that property can be understood in different ways and suggests two particular philosophies of property that inform contemporary sovereign rights. These philosophies are in tension with each other, and the tensions are not reduceable to what Stephen Krasner calls organized hypocrisy.[1] The two philosophies both have deep roots in the practice of state sovereignty; they are sincerely held, not only by sovereigns but by the populations they represent. However, contemporary practices and discourses of sovereignty do not work out the tensions between them in an organized way. Contemporary state sovereignty, in this sense, is disorganized sincerity rather than organized hypocrisy.

The constitutional structure of sovereignty sets some of the background conditions underlying sovereign property rights, and addresses the question of who owns those rights. Studying this structure illustrates that the property rights that states work to reconstitute and reinforce in the conduct of their foreign relations are limited and conditional. States at the same time work to reinforce their rights as legitimated sovereigns and work within a system in which claiming too much right can undermine their legitimacy as sovereigns. In other words, in a regulatory sense this constitutional structure places constraints on the actions of sovereign agents. However, the structure is also constitutive, in that it defines who the sovereigns are, what they are enabled to do, and how they think about the rights that they have. In turn, the way in which sovereign agents think about the property rights that they have is further conditioned by the prior question of how they think about property.

[1] Krasner 1999.

Take, as an example, the international system in most of northern and western Europe in the immediate aftermath of the Peace of Westphalia. In this system, populations are objects of property rights, rather than holders of them, in the context of international politics. However, religion is not a property right of sovereignty in this system. This represented a change from the constitutional structure of the political system within the Holy Roman Empire following the Treaty of Augsburg in 1555, in which populations were also the objects of sovereign property rights, but those rights included religion. The change in structure was a conscious attempt to limit religion as a cause of war. It was at least partially successful in doing so, because the withdrawal of recognition that religious conversion of subject populations was a legitimate sovereign right made any attempt to do so less legitimate and therefore normatively easier to oppose, both by the populations in question and by other sovereigns.[2]

Similarly, the Cold War system of territorial legitimation had the effect of associating sovereign right with predefined and reified territory. In such a system rulers could be deposed without undermining national sovereignty, which was then vested in the subsequent ruler. But territorial adjustment did constitute a far greater affront to sovereignty. In significant ways, this pattern is the opposite of that to be found in the absolutist system of the late seventeenth century, despite both being modern sovereign states systems.[3] Constitutional structure does not in this sense determine absolute limits to what can be done within a particular international system, but it does tend to draw the outlines within which actors in international politics think about political activity.

In this sense, norms concerning questions of what property means and of who is sovereign affect patterns of international politics by affecting what actors consider to be within the realm of the possible. This chapter is primarily devoted to addressing these questions. In keeping with the arguments of previous chapters, these questions are approached intersubjectively, not definitionally. In other words, in this chapter I will look at different understandings of what property means

---

[2] E.g., Straumann 2008.
[3] On the distinction between state and nation in the legitimation of sovereignty, see Barkin and Cronin 1994.

and different understandings of where sovereignty is vested, at different points in time, and processes of change from one to the other.

The chapter proceeds in two stages. The first part looks at the evolution of understandings of the form of sovereign right and the ownership of sovereignty within the context of the modern sovereign states system, beginning with the Westphalian settlement and continuing to the present. It looks first at the question of what property is understood to mean and then at the question of who owns (or, more precisely, who is recognized as having the property rights of) sovereignty. The second part examines in more detail contemporary understandings of what property means in the context of sovereign right in the current sovereign states system. More specifically, it argues that there is at present no clearly predominant intersubjective understanding of what the propertarian basis of sovereign right is. Rather, there are two competing understandings.

These draw on different legal traditions, one Roman and the other English. The understanding that draws on the Roman tradition sees property in terms of absolute control and in terms of exclusion. Property in this sense means excluding others from having control over that which one owns. The understanding that draws on the English tradition sees property more in terms of use rights than in terms of control. This understanding is based in the idea of contract rather than the idea of exclusion. One can agree through the mechanism of contract to forego control of one's property, either completely or conditionally, in exchange for some other value, as one sees fit, and still retain ownership.

As metaphors for these two different understandings of property, think of a Wyoming rancher and a New York investment banker. The archetypical Wyoming rancher[4] builds a fence around his ranch and shoots anyone who crosses that fence, be they cattle rustlers or government inspectors. This is the Roman idea of property, as a tangible, material thing from which all others can be excluded.[5] The New York banker, on the other hand, securitizes her assets in a way that maximizes financial return. This is property as contract, not property as physical control. Property in this sense may represent a material thing

---

[4] I am not making any claim here that actual contemporary ranchers in the American West think this way – this is an archetype or a metaphor (take your pick).
[5] For a more nuanced discussion in the context of sovereignty, see Holland 2010.

like a piece of land, or it may represent a purely financial commitment such as a bond. And property in this sense is infinitely divisible – an asset can be carved up into different segments representing different risk profiles and distributed accordingly. Property in this sense is as much conceptual as tangible – the banker likely cares less about what the underlying asset is than about the contractual commitments that have been attached to it.

The Wyoming metaphor translates fairly straightforwardly to the realm of the sovereign states system. In this metaphor, states guard their borders and try to prevent outsiders from having control over what happens within those borders. The international relations equivalent of the New York metaphor is one in which sovereign states act to maximize utility by contracting with other sovereigns to assure the most efficient allocation of available assets and resources. The term "utility" is used here in an economistic sense – it can be understood as GDP, as collective security, or as any other thing that has a use value and that is positive sum in nature. But it cannot be understood as control for the sake of control, or as something that is inherently zero-sum.

The ultimate argument of this chapter is that in the context of the practice of international relations, these two understandings of property are both legally and practically mutually incompatible. As commercial law they are incompatible in that the Wyoming metaphor does not allow for some of the core institutions of contemporary capitalism, such as incorporation and shareholding. As international norms, the Wyoming metaphor corresponds with an understanding of sovereignty as autonomy, as the right to noninterference. But the sort of cooperation on issues of international governance that comes from the New York model is directly antithetical to autonomy – it is about binding oneself to a set of rules that one agrees to but that are in part created by others. In other words, it is about ceding some control to authorities beyond one's borders.[6]

The second part of this chapter makes the case for this incompatibility from a different but related perspective. It relates norms of

---

[6] Cooley and Spruyt (2009) argue that this sort of contracting is a compromise between political utility and formal sovereignty. However, the ability for sovereigns to contract in this way is an aspect of their international legal personhood, and is therefore, I argue, a part of, rather than a compromise of, their sovereignty.

property to norms of governance, which is in itself in important ways a propertarian relationship. Chapter 7 fleshes out this norm conflict empirically, and Chapter 8 will discuss some of the potential ramifications of this incompatibility.

Property and Contract

International law in Europe in the seventeenth century, the law of sovereigns as it was then constituted, saw the relationship between sovereign and sovereign territory as one of property, following Roman definitions of property as interpreted in late-medieval and early-modern legal texts.[7] This differs from many contemporary ideas of property, particularly in the English legal tradition, in that it was far more exclusionary.[8] Under Roman law, the owner of property had absolute rights both to exclude others from and to use said property. Furthermore, property was seen as indivisible; it could be bought and sold in its entirety, but the extent to which owners could allow specific use rights was highly limited.[9] In this sense absolute ownership was a major hindrance to contractual relationships between owners and potential users. In fact, under Roman law the relationship between landlord and tenant/laborer was as much one of personal obligation as contractual or monetary obligation, reinforcing the degree to which both sides of this relationship were constrained from contracting as they saw fit. Furthermore, both contract and property law applied only among private individuals; property owners had no rights against expropriation by public authorities.[10] The laws of contract and purchase and sale on the one hand and of real property on the other were seen as being in different categories in Roman legal practice.[11] In other words, the idea of contracting existed, but it was not fundamental to understandings of property in the way that it has become in contemporary practice.

The feudal understanding of property was much more conditional than the Roman.[12] It was rather more complicated in that it allowed

---

[7] Kratochwil 1995.
[8] This late-medieval and early-modern interpretation of Roman legal texts may well have born little resemblance to ancient Roman understandings of their own law and should not be taken as an accurate statement of Roman law per se. See, for example, Berman 1983.
[9] Holland 2010.   [10] Kratochwil 1995: 25–28.   [11] Berman 1983: 136.
[12] The phrase "conditional property" is taken from Teschke 1998: 338.

the inhabitants of the land some vested rights of use, meaning that there was usually no clear individual ownership. There was at the same time, however, little room for contracting; property rights were largely traditional, and therefore could not be easily changed by the decision of individuals.[13] Although relations of force in medieval Europe were of course such that in practice lords could often do as they pleased with respect to the peasantry, tradition governed most property relations. One could make the argument that most actual property relations in mid-seventeenth-century Europe reflected medieval as much as Roman notions of property. As early as the sixteenth century, though, continental legal scholarship, particularly on the subject of states and sovereignty, referred mostly to Roman rather than feudal antecedents.[14] Some scholars have argued that sixteenth-century theorists of the state used Roman precedent specifically to eliminate feudal notions of conditional property because these notions allowed for opposition to a centralizing state that Roman law did not.[15] In any case, early modern legal scholarship tended to relate sovereignty to understandings of property based on the Roman written tradition, as seen through the lens of late medieval practice, that were not based on the premise of the right of owners to contract with their property as they see fit.

The seminal text introducing the idea of contract into political theory and discourse was Thomas Hobbes's *Leviathan*, published in 1651.[16] It is interesting to note that though the Hobbesian metaphor is so often used to describe the situation of the Westphalian state system,[17] it comes from a work published after the Peace was signed; those negotiating the Peace likely knew nothing of Hobbes or, more to the point, his ideas. Late-medieval and early-modern legal practice, following the Roman tradition as interpreted from recovered texts, allowed for contracts, but placed contracting in a different category from property. Real property (meaning primarily land) was governed by a normative and legal structure distinct from that governing commercial contract, the purchase and sale of goods.[18] Political

---

[13] Ruggie 1983.
[14] See, for example, Bodin 1945. Even in his earlier works, when he was still arguing for a more limited, more feudal sovereignty, Bodin's literary and legal references were almost entirely Roman.
[15] Franklin 1973. [16] Hobbes 1991. See also Holland 2010.
[17] E.g., Ahrensdorf 2000. [18] Berman 1983.

relationships in general, and hence practices of sovereignty in particular, were normatively related to the former rather than the latter. It was not until the time of John Locke that the idea of contract as the legitimate source of governance became widely accepted in England, and not until after Rousseau, more than a century later, that this idea began to have a significant impact on Continental politics. Furthermore, the idea of politics as contract came to international relations through changes in thinking about domestic political structures and legitimation, rather than the other way around.

The introduction of this idea into political discourse can be understood as reflecting a change in popular understandings of the notion of property in the most basic sense, the property relation of the individual self. The medieval self was not an autonomous entity but was part of a divine chain of being that was ontologically prior to the individual.[19] Inasmuch as feudal property relations were themselves legitimated through reference to this same ontology, the rights of individuals to their selves and their labor was formally subordinate to the social hierarchy. In Roman law, an individual could be the absolute property of another individual; there were no restrictions on the rights of owners against slaves, and slaves held no individual rights to their labor, or for that matter their bodies.[20] Perhaps the greatest philosophical novelty of Hobbes' work, and an element that can be found in most expressions of the idea of contract in modern political theory, is the placing of ontological priority on the autonomous individual. In order to be in a position to contract for an appropriate government, individuals must first be able to claim to be the legitimate ultimate source of political authority. In order to do so, they must first be sovereign unto themselves. In other words, they must be the property of none other than themselves. This idea – that individuals are, corporeally and politically, their own property and that they can therefore contract out their bodies (as wage labor) and their political legitimacy (through political or social contract) – is referred to by C. B. Macpherson as "possessive individualism."[21]

To the extent that state sovereignty reflects a propertarian relationship, a change from Roman to contractarian understandings of

---

[19] Reus-Smit 1999 and Allan 2018.
[20] This is the case for republican Rome. The rights of slaves did increase over the course of the later empire. Harper 2011.
[21] Macpherson 1962.

property can have a significant impact on the practice of international relations. The Roman understanding of property suggests a sovereign that can expect full autonomy in its dealing with its population and territory, beyond the conditions of the constitutional structure of the system, because its ownership of these is absolute. It is quite limited, however, in the extent to which it can bind itself by creating restraints on its autonomy by contracting with other states. Statespeople may be willing to enter into agreements, such as military alliances requiring the state to come to the defense of other states, that obligate their states to take external actions. But they are less likely to think in terms of agreements that delimit the scope of the state's internal actions, both because it is discordant with their ideas of what states should do, and because it threatens to undermine respect for the state in a population that is conditioned to these same ideas. The state thus has broad freedom of action with respect to the domestic polity but much less freedom of action in its ability to achieve such goals that are best achieved through cooperation.

The contractarian understanding of property yields a state with the opposite strengths and weaknesses. It has less freedom of action in its interactions with its domestic polity, which has become conditioned to think in terms of their contractual rights against the state, and its territory, to which its claim is no longer absolute. However, it has a much broader freedom of action to achieve its interests through contractual cooperation. One can, in some sense, see this contractarian state as the weaker of the two forms, but, as is discussed in the next section, one can just as easily see it as the more capable, in that it has a range of international behaviors open to it that the state based on the more absolute Roman understanding of property is denied.

Ownership and Contract

These two understandings of what property means – the Roman understanding of property as indivisible and the contractual understanding of it as divisible – do not speak directly to the question of whose property sovereignty is. This question is distinct from the question discussed in Chapter 5, of how claims to sovereign right are legitimated. That discussion is about proximate claims – given an existing sovereign state recognized as such by the sovereignty cartel, who gets to exercise sovereign right? The question here is a prior one – in whose name can sovereign right be claimed? What is the ultimate normative source of sovereignty? The answers to these question help to connect norms of property right with conflict over norms of sovereignty.

Both the Roman and contractual understandings of property are compatible with an understanding of sovereignty that vests sovereign right in the person of the head of state. In fact, the change from absolutist to monarchical legitimation over the course of the eighteenth and nineteenth centuries reflects at least some acceptance of the idea of political contract in the legitimation of sovereign rulership, to the extent that monarchical legitimation left space for the development of constitutional monarchy, a practice in which the idea of contract is implicit.[22] The period of change from absolutist to monarchical legitimation, however, also saw the development of a new norm of the ownership of sovereignty: the norm of popular sovereignty.[23]

The change in the European states system in the century surrounding the French Revolutionary Wars from one of princely sovereignty, in which the state was legitimated largely through medieval ideas, of the divine chain of being and of feudal obligation, to one of popular sovereignty, in which the state is legitimated through its representation of the people or the nation, has been well chronicled.[24] The preeminent nineteenth-century theorist of international law and sovereignty, for example, argued that sovereigns represented nations and that it is the natural law of nations that legitimates the positive law of sovereigns.[25]

The change from princely to popular sovereignty would seem at first to yield a straightforward answer to the question of whose property is sovereignty – the property of the people. But the general acceptance of the idea of popular sovereignty has in fact yielded two types of answer to this question, one evolving from the English political tradition and the other from the continental European tradition. The answer yielded by the English political tradition has tended to be that the state is the property of the individuals who comprise it, those who by implication contract for it or those who are subject to its actions.[26] The answer yielded by the Continental tradition has varied from a relatively

---

[22] For a critique of this use of contract theory, see Baumgold 2005.
[23] E.g., Jackson 2007.
[24] See, for example, Bull 1977; Wight 1977; Osiander 1994: 317–318; and Hall 1998.
[25] Vattel 2001.   [26] Macpherson 1962.

individualist perspective to a much more communitarian or nationalist perspective. Even at its most contractual, however, the Continental tradition has tended to see the national polity as in some way different from the simple cumulation of individuals within it. This difference ranges from the Rousseauvian "general will" to the Hegelian notions of civil society as the universal family and the state as representative of the universal will. Thus to this tradition the sovereign state is the property not of the individuals who comprise it, but of the nation as a whole, the nation as a distinct entity.[27] Representations of sovereignty in early US political science, following the German legal tradition, reflected the idea that sovereignty is the property of a collective agent, rather than of a collectivity of individuals.[28]

This leaves us with two different answers to the question of whose property is sovereignty. Both answers, the nationalist and the individualist, have been internalized to varying degrees in the past two centuries; both have been subjectified as a fundamental element of popular political ontology. At times the nationalist answer has been the more potent of the two. The Continental tradition, that the sovereign state is the property of the nation, is perfectly compatible with Roman understandings of property underlying seventeenth-century sovereignty.[29] Instead of a subject owing a personal obligation to the person of the sovereign ruler, a citizen owes a personal obligation to the entity of the sovereign nation. To the extent that participants in contemporary nationalist conflict genuinely believe that the mechanisms of state power legitimately exist to serve the interests of "the nation" understood as something other than the cumulation of nationals, the idea of the state as property of the sovereign nation will continue to impact international politics and global governance.

The English tradition's answer to the question of whose property sovereignty is, the autonomous individuals who comprise the citizenry, is less compatible with the understanding of property underlying seventeenth-century sovereignty. Because it sees the legitimacy of the

---

[27] This construction is in reference primarily to the Hegelian tradition in which the modern state is seen as a synthesis in which a universalized concept/actuality of nation is antithesis to the particularities of individual intent. Hegel 1974: 283–306. Even Rousseau's discussion of social contract, however, might be better understood as a social compact and is presented in a language of personal obligation, e.g., Rousseau 1984: 147–150.
[28] See, for example, Burgess 1890: 52–57.   [29] E.g., Lee 2008.

state in the implicit contract with its citizenry, this tradition is more compatible with contractual ideas of property, specifically the more market-oriented understandings of contract. In other words, within the English tradition property tends to be understood in the possessive individualist and market capitalist sense; that individuals can contract to do with their property and their selves (their labor) as they see fit, subject (to greatly varying degrees in different parts of the English tradition) to generally agreed constraints and to the stricture that it not interfere with the ability of others to do the same.[30]

As should be clear from the discussion to this point, norms of what property means in the context of sovereign right need not covary with norms of whose property sovereignty is. While the era of absolutist sovereignty was absolutist both in the sense that sovereignty was the individual property of the ruler and in the sense that the property right was itself understood as absolute, subject to the constitutional constraints of the system, the passing of the ownership norm does not necessarily imply the passing of the concurrent norm of how property was understood. Popular sovereignty is fully compatible with either Roman or contractarian norms of property. It is this Roman idea of property, filtered through certain strands of German political philosophy, and associated with both corporate and exclusive definitions of who the "people" are, that gave rise to some of the twentieth century's most virulent nationalisms.

The norm of popular sovereignty, the idea that sovereignty is the property of the people, has by the beginning of the twenty-first century mostly displaced the norm of princely sovereignty, the idea that sovereignty is the property of the ruler (however defined).[31] There are a few legal exceptions to the demise of princely sovereignty, but these have limited effect both on relevant intersubjective understandings of the state and on the conduct of politics. For example, the British monarch remains the titular sovereign, but in practice is likely to remain so only insofar as she makes no attempt to make use of her sovereign right in that capacity without having been asked to do so by the government.[32] There are also some practical exceptions to the demise, such as Saudi Arabia, and to lesser degrees the other Persian Gulf monarchies, in which the state is both practically and formally associated with the

---

[30] Macpherson 1962.   [31] Jackson 2007.   [32] Bogdanor 1997.

ruling family.³³ But these exceptions are limited to the west coast of the Gulf. Saudi Arabia is, in this context, different from, say, North Korea or Turkmenistan in that the rulers of those countries claim to be ruling in the name of the nation, not in the name of the ruler's family. While the claims in both cases clearly contain a strong element of hypocrisy, the claim nonetheless makes a clear difference to the conduct of politics, and to patterns of rulership, within the country.

The norm of popular sovereignty being thus well established in contemporary international relations, there remains the question of what property rights sovereignty brings, and the understanding of property associated with those rights. This question in turn affects the issue of the ownership of sovereignty. Popular sovereignty means that the people are sovereign but does not specify who the people are. The question of who constitutes the people, whether they are a collection of individuals or a collective entity, is in turn related to ideas of governance. Intersubjective understandings of what constitutes sovereign property in international politics are therefore related to understandings in domestic politics via this question of ownership. This relationship in turn suggests that norms of property and norms of governance at the domestic level are related to those at the international level. In particular, the relationship between Roman ideas of property and modern ideas of nationalism on the one hand, and English ideas of contractual property and modern ideas of political contract on the other, can illuminate some of the key tensions in contemporary practices of sovereignty.

Social Contracts and Nationalism

The norm underlying nationalism is that each self-identified group has the right to rule itself as it sees fit, without outside interference. The norm underlying most concepts of the social contract is that government should be by common consent, to the common good of the governed. Both of these norms have been central to the development of popular sovereignty, and the two are in fact perfectly compatible, even mutually reinforcing, in the realm of the development of popular sovereignty.³⁴ The very idea of popular sovereignty implies both: that

---

[33] Although in the case of Saudi Arabia this may be a form of religious rather than monarchical legitimation narrowly understood, e.g., Al-Atawneh 2009.
[34] On which, see Wight 1977.

the people (the nation) have the right to decide for themselves (social contract).[35] The two norms do not necessarily overlap, however. There can be nationalist governance in the absence of norms of social contract, as is the case in the more virulent cases of nationalism, particularly its national socialist variants. And there can be social contract without nationalism. Locke's social contract was not inherently limited to national groups, whereas Rousseau's social contract was in ways designed subnationally, being best suited to politics of civic, rather than national, scope.[36]

But there is clear potential for overlap between the two norms, particularly between what Ernst Haas calls "liberal nationalism"[37] and what might be called the liberal democracy approach to social contracting, with its emphasis on property, the rule of law, and representative democracy. It is these two variants of the respective ideas that provide much of the normative structure for contemporary sovereignty. Statements of this normative structure can be found, among other places, in the various human rights treaties that a large majority of the world's states have signed.[38] These generally include both the right to self-determination and to the components of liberal democracy as mentioned previously. As long as nationalist norms allow for the protection of the social contract rights of minorities, as liberal nationalism does, and social contract norms allow for the expression of group self-determination, as liberal democracy does, the two norms are not only mutually compatible, they can be mutually reinforcing.

This mutual compatibility, however, only works within individual states. When the same norms are applied to international relations, the two norm sets come into conflict, because they treat the distinction between the domestic and the international differently. Nationalist norms see a clear principled distinction between the domestic and the international. However big a practical difference there may be between politics in the two realms, though, the principled distinction between these realms is much less clear for social contract theory.

---

[35] Buchheit (1978: 13–16) sees these two norms as integral parts of the norm of self-determination; he labels them "external" and "internal" self-determination, respectively.
[36] E.g., Mumford 1961: 261.   [37] Haas 1997: 19–21.
[38] The seminal treaty statement of this structure can be found in the Universal Declaration of Human Rights, Articles 6–11, 17, and 21 (United Nations General Assembly 1948).

While in Chapter 2 the distinction between the domestic and the international was rejected as definitional to sovereignty, the distinction between inside and outside[39] can still be analytically useful in understanding certain aspects of sovereignty. "Internal sovereignty," as I am using the term, refers to the authority of the prince or the state to manage its domestic affairs without the interference or imposition of outside authority. This is often referred to as autonomy. "External sovereignty" refers to the acceptance of the prince or the state as sovereign by the community of sovereigns. In other words, external sovereignty means membership in an international system, in a sovereignty cartel, in which only sovereign states can participate, a system in which sovereigns recognize their own kind and no others as legitimate participants in relations among various territorial political authorities. This distinction between internal and external sovereignty is often discussed in the literature.[40] It need be further noted here only that they will not necessarily covary; a state with full external sovereignty may have only tenuous authority in much of its territory,[41] and a political authority that has full physical control of a territory may not be recognized as sovereign over that territory by the community of states.

Definitions of the term "sovereignty" with respect to politics in the period immediately before Westphalia often focused on autonomy, although it was originally meant as far more limited than the way in which it is currently used. As noted above, for example, one of the seminal theorists of the modern state, Jean Bodin, defined the principal attribute of sovereignty in terms of the authority to appoint the most senior magistrates.[42] The term "autonomy" itself is open to a variety of definitions and interpretations. When we speak of the sovereign state system, however, we often refer to it as "Westphalian." To the extent that the Peace of Westphalia was important in the development of the modern states system, it was for helping to codify the concept of external sovereignty, the idea that a certain form of secular authority, the principality or kingdom, can legitimately engage in diplomatic relations with other principalities or kingdoms.[43] The Peace had relatively little impact on the internal sovereignty of the territorial authorities in

---

[39] On which, see Walker 1993.   [40] A good example is Thomson 1995.
[41] See, e.g., Jackson 1993.   [42] Bodin 1945: 172.
[43] Although this right at the time did not grant exclusive international legal personhood solely to that level of governance, as is currently the case.

question with respect to other internal political entities. To the extent that it had an impact, it was as likely to delimit as to expand internal sovereignty, by setting explicit limits on the authority of certain sovereigns to constrain the religious freedoms of their subjects.

In many principalities, particularly in Central Europe, princes did indeed have supreme domestic authority and could treat both the land of their principalities and its inhabitants as if they were personal property. This authority, though, predates Westphalia and was as much a relic of late-medieval practice as a result of encroaching modernity.[44] Elsewhere in Europe, sovereigns had little internal domestic authority, and the Peace did little to increase it. In the Netherlands, for example, the sovereign did not have the authority to rule on matters of commerce or money, had very little authority to legislate, and had limited ability to raise either armies or navies on his own.[45] In short, he had little of the internal authority we think of as being a function of sovereignty. The development of a modern state system in the seventeenth century may have given the Dutch sovereign some extra political leverage domestically by making him the only person authorized to enter into treaties with other sovereigns, but did very little to affect the patterns of overlapping authority that were Dutch politics at the time. From the perspective of the other states in Europe at the time, he was nonetheless sovereign; his voice was the voice of the United Provinces.

By the eighteenth century discussions of sovereignty were much more likely to focus on external sovereignty, on the idea of an international law of states that was more than specific treaties among sovereigns.[46] The distinction between internal and external sovereignty, between the domestic and the international, is thus both historically and normatively complicated. Historically the two sovereignties do not covary, and external sovereignty has yielded different patterns of domestic authority in different polities. Normatively the two sovereignties draw on different sets of philosophical arguments that often do not speak to each other.

The distinction between the realm of the domestic and the realm of the international is nonetheless relatively easily maintained with respect to applications of the norm of nationalism. After all, nationalism is all about making distinctions between the us-group and the

---

[44] Osiander 2001. [45] Wilson 1967; Weber 1968; Boxer 1974.
[46] Vattel 2001.

them-group. It has in fact been the historical pattern that these two normative realms be separate, that legitimate behavior with respect to the in-group be different from legitimate behavior with respect to the out-group. Even liberal nationalism, with its protections for minorities from the national majority, is still premised on a distinction between those within the national group and those outside it.[47]

The distinction between the realm of the domestic and the realm of the international can be more problematic with respect to social contract theory. It is somewhat sustainable with respect to some approaches to social contract theory, particularly those of the modern continental theorists. Rousseau's social contract, for example, is viable only insofar as the contractors have a common general will.[48] This does not require an out-group, in the way that nationalism does, but suggests a relatively small polity, and hence the need for many separate polities.

The distinction is much less sustainable, however, with respect to the English, or Lockean, tradition of social contract theory, the variant of social contract theory most compatible with liberal nationalism.[49] In this tradition, the barriers among countries are practical ones rather than philosophical ones. This tradition assumes the centrality of the autonomous individual, what C. B. Macpherson called the "possessive individual,"[50] to political life, and sees the role of the state as protecting that autonomy to the greatest extent possible that is compatible with the autonomy of others. There is in this tradition no group, no nation, no general will that is politically prior to the autonomous individual. As such, there are no inherent philosophical barriers to the social contract operating at the level of the global polity. There are practical barriers, both technological and social. However, as these barriers are lowered, limiting social-contract groups to national boundaries makes less and less sense. When individual liberty is best maintained, or individual utility maximized, by governance at the global level, then that is the level at which the social contract should be put into effect.

In short, then, the potential for compatibility between the two norms of governance at the domestic level is clear, although this is only the case with nationalism to the extent that the state matches the nation.

---

[47] E.g., Haas 1997: chapter 2.   [48] Rousseau 1986: 25.
[49] Haas 1997: 42–49.   [50] Macpherson 1962.

But the idea of the social contract, at least in its English variant, can also be applied to the international polity, whereas the idea of nationalism does not make sense applied to an international polity (it would argue for breaking it up into national polities). In other words, the one norm mitigates toward the creation of effective international governance as barriers to such governance on a global scale are overcome and as the number and severity of inherently global issues of governance increases. The other norm mitigates toward the maintenance of separate and mutually exclusive political units, and is therefore a barrier to the creation of mechanisms for effective international governance.

Property Norms and International Politics

The distinction between these two norms, these two understandings of where the ownership of sovereignty ultimately resides, became increasingly relevant in the half-century after World War II, because the English tradition of social contract theory provides the philosophical underpinning of neoliberal globalization.[51] By neoliberal globalization I mean the pattern of what has been called "competitive liberalism,"[52] in which policies and regulations are harmonized across countries to reduce as much as possible barriers to market exchange. This is in contrast to the Bretton Woods era pattern of embedded liberalism, in which international infrastructure was provided multilaterally but much more scope was allowed for state interference in markets for the purpose of social welfare.[53] The diffusion of neoliberal norms and neoliberal globalization since World War II, and especially in the period between the demise of Bretton Woods and the Great Recession of 2008, goes hand in hand with the diffusion of English social contract norms (note that I am not making a cause-and-effect argument here; rather, I am making a co-constitution argument). It also, not coincidentally, mirrored the rise of the practice (lagged several years behind the norm) of multilateralism.

The norm of multilateralism can be read as the English version of social contract theory in which it is states, rather than individuals, who

---

[51] For the argument that what we refer to as globalization is in fact a particularly neoliberal form of globalization, see McNamara 1997. The predominant form of neoliberal globalization in the 1990s was often referred to as the "Washington consensus." See, e.g., Gore 2000.

[52] McNamara 1998.   [53] Ruggie 1982.

are the participants in the contract. Neoliberal globalization is the process of regulating international interchange through an analogue to the social contract in which it is corporate actors that are the primary participants in the political process. In some instances of harmonization, these corporate actors are either private firms or non-governmental organizations (NGOs), but in the most celebrated instances of regulatory globalization, the actors are sovereign states.[54] In a way, social contract theory fits better at the interstate than domestic level, because it is a system of actual, rather than implied, contracts. Social contract theorists generally accept that individuals cannot for practical reasons all participate in the continued negotiation and renegotiation of the social contract. It is thus an implied contract, one that citizens agree to implicitly rather than explicitly. However, with some exceptions,[55] states actually can opt out of individual bits of the multilateral contract; they can choose which aspects of the social contract to accept and which to reject, and still remain within the system.

The World Trade Organization (WTO), and the General Agreement on Tariffs and Trade (GATT) that preceded and was incorporated into it, provides a useful illustration of multilateralism as social contract. It began as an agreement to not discriminate among trading partners, driven by a largely defensive logic, defensive both against the beggar-thy-neighbor trade policies of the Great Depression and against the security effects of the exclusive economic blocs that preceded World War II.[56] It was multilateral, but it was a fairly basic multilateralism, more at the level of principle associated with embedded liberalism than at the level of regulatory detail associated with neoliberal globalization. It was not until the tail end of the Bretton Woods period, with the Tokyo Round agreement, that the GATT began to be an exercise in neoliberal globalization. Since then, both the regulatory scope of the GATT/WTO and the degree of specific regulatory harmonization called for by its rules have consistently expanded.[57] However, they have expanded in ways explicitly agreed to by member

---

[54] Drezner 2007; Kahler and Lake 2003.
[55] These exceptions being primarily customary international law and those issues of international security that fall under the purview of authoritative collective security organizations.
[56] Barkin 2003, chapter 6.   [57] E.g., Barton et al. 2006.

countries in multilateral negotiations, and member countries retain the right to withdraw from all of, or in some contexts from specific instances of, the rules. And when member states ceased to agree after the mid-1990s, the expansion ceased.

The GATT/WTO, a set of rules for international trade, is a good illustrative case because social contract theory, at least in its English variant, is designed to create a market society. Individuals within the society are thus committed to participate in a market society; social contract theory presupposes that they want to participate, as an assumption about human nature. An example of this assumption can be found in John Locke's definition of a state of perfect freedom as the ability to "dispose of their Possessions, and Persons as they think fit."[58] Social contract theory at the international level similarly involves states in, and presupposes that they want to participate in, a global market. In other words, it presupposes collective decision-making about a collective (global) economy rather than individual decision-making about distinct national economies. This allows for the benefits at the international level that social contract theorists ascribe to government. But it undermines nationalism.

The nationalist norm allows national governments to make political and executive decisions about domestic policy. The social contract norm allows the national government to participate in the international legislative process, but not, within those areas governed by the international social contract, to take political action that is incompatible with the legislative result. (This applies to those governments that choose to participate in the contract. Some choose to not participate, but very few.) In other words, the social contract norm applied internationally leads to state participation in global rules that states must then obey, while the nationalist norm suggests a state not bound by common regulation, not bound in its internal behavior by international law. The norm of government by social contract, applied, as it logically should be, at the international level, is one of consensual multilateralism. The norm of national self-government is one of national autonomy. This incompatibility leads to what I call normative dissonance, an idea that is developed further in Chapter 8.

---

[58] Locke 1960: 309.

Conclusions

This brief survey suggests a number of different understandings of the nature of property relations that have underpinned ideas of governance and the state over the course of the past half millennium or so, and their effects on the possibilities within which an international system can be constructed. The medieval state, such as it was, reflected medieval property: it was governed by tradition and concepts of personal obligation, and allowed for a right of dissent by force. The renascent classicism of the middle of the millennium was similarly reflected in state structures and the sovereign states system, mixing concepts of autonomy with a politics of personal obligation. The growing subjectification over the past two centuries of contractarian understandings of property has in turn increasingly come to be reflected in an international system in which the state may (or may not) be losing its ability to control, but is gaining an ability to contract.[59] This evolution is expressive of the way individuals identify themselves at least partially by their accepted notions of property, from someone defined by their position in an extended system of personal obligations to someone defined by their contractual relationships with other autonomous individuals.

An intermediate stage in the evolution of the relationship between sovereignty and property can be seen in the change from princely to popular sovereignty roughly two centuries ago. This stage marked a change in the answer to the question "whose property?" rather than the answer to the question "property understood how?" It is at around that time that the concept of the autonomous sovereign gradually came to be replaced by the concept of the nation-state.[60] The sovereignty of the prince, of the autonomous ruler, was undermined by the growing relationship between state and nation, by the idea of the state as representative of the body politic rather than the person of the prince. At the same time, the change marked a rapid expansion in the role of the state, in the extent to which European states became involved in the

---

[59] Kratochwil (1994) argues that the idea of contract is in fact limited in its ability to describe interstate cooperation. We are, however, speaking of different things: he is talking about the idea of contract as an analytic tool, whereas I am talking about it as a subjectified norm. Its usefulness for the former is not necessarily relevant to its adoption as the latter.

[60] Cronin 1999.

everyday lives of most individuals, and in the breadth of issues that states came to regulate. In other words, states as institutions of governance became more powerful as the sovereignty of princes eroded. Within these empowered states, the answer to the second question, that of "property understood how?" has gradually drifted from norms of mutual obligation to norms of possessive individualism.

What does this mean for our understanding of contemporary sovereignty? Two trends stand out, one at the national level and one at the international level. At the national level, an understanding of the sovereign as the anthropomorphization of the possessive individual, rather than as a political representation of property relationships based on personal obligation, changes the perception of national interest from a focus on autonomy to a focus on utility. In a politics of personal obligation, one improves one's situation by minimizing obligation owed to others, while maximizing obligation owed to oneself. As a sovereign, this can be interpreted as minimizing obligations owed to other sovereigns and to superior authorities, while maximizing obligations owed to the sovereign from those within the state. Thus the emphasis on autonomy in traditional understandings of what constituted the national interest. In a politics of possessive individualism, one improves one's situation by contracting in a way that maximizes benefits while minimizing costs. Absolute autonomy in such a politics can be seen as a benefit but need not necessarily be. In the possessive individualist state, the focus of definitions of national interest should therefore shift from autonomy per se to something closer to efficiency in dealing with other states.[61]

At the international level the most visible related trend is the phenomenon of states as collective, rather than individual, decision-makers. This is not entirely new; reconstructions of international politics from Westphalia to Versailles to San Francisco were examples of collective efforts to define and redefine the intersubjective understandings through which international politics operated. Those efforts, however, focused on constitutive rules, the basic structures without which an international system as such could not operate, and were clearly major historical events rather than the everyday practice of international politics. Contemporary collective decision-making, on the other hand, is mostly about regulative rules, of the sort that before

[61] A similar point is made in Slaughter 1997.

Conclusions

this century were made at the state level, if at all. One could argue that the rapid contemporary proliferation of collective decision-making by states is a response to new issues, such as managing the global environment, that simply did not confront earlier decision-makers. But there are other issues, such as international commerce and communications, that have drawn the attention of governments for millennia. The contemporary proliferation of global issues could thus explain an increase in international consensual regulative rulemaking but not the qualitative change seen in the twentieth century. The trend to collective decision-making is thus reflective of change in the way both statespeople and populations understand the meaning and role of sovereignty and the state, as well as exogenously increasing globalization.

All this is the case to the extent that the idea of a possessive individualist sovereign, as a normative reflection of a contractual understanding of property, replaces the ideas of both a sovereignty informed by Roman understandings of property and nationalist norms of state legitimation. But the process of neoliberalization of multilateralism that was an institutional expression of the possessive individualist sovereign appears to have lost much momentum in the early twenty-first century, reflecting among other things the effects of the Great Recession and of China's development into an effective superpower. This leaves us with two understandings of property underlying property rights claims in contemporary state sovereignty that are in practice mutually incompatible. Where does that leave contemporary norms of sovereignty?

7 The Interstices of Sovereignty

The previous two chapters have complicated the norms of sovereignty and have suggested that not all norms of sovereignty generally, and not all understandings of property informing norms of sovereign right specifically, are mutually compatible. This chapter looks at the tension between the two different conceptualizations of sovereign property, and at international economic activity that falls into the cracks between them. It argues that the contradictions between the different understandings not only allow for but necessitate spaces, or interstices, in the sovereign states system where illicit economic activity can thrive and where otherwise legal economic behavior becomes illicit.

Much of the illicit economic activity in the world today can be explained by the failure of individual states to govern effectively, or even by benign neglect by states. But not all. In essence, while some illicit activity can be traced to the failure of states to live up to some ideal of perfect sovereignty, other such activity can be traced back to contradictions between the two understandings of property that inform the practice of the contemporary sovereign states system. This behavior, in other words, falls into the interstices of the sovereign states system. Faced with these contradictions, states in the sovereignty cartel are forced to give up some of their ability to govern in practice, in order to support sovereign right in principle. This trade-off is not something that can be obviated by better governance within the context of a sovereign states system; rather, it is inherent to that system. Recognizing that there are interstices in the system that cannot be eliminated is a necessary part of creating global governance mechanisms to deal with many forms of illicit international economic activity.

What I have been calling the Roman conceptualization of property suggests an international political economy of trade (or not) among a set of distinct and autonomously regulated sovereign states. The contractual conceptualization of property suggests a more unified international political economy regulated multilaterally and as a whole. In the former case the role of global governance is to address only transnational issues, those that arise between rather than within states. It is, in other words, to lubricate the interactions of a set of distinct regulatory systems. In the latter case, the role of global governance is to provide the template for domestic governance and regulation on a much broader range of issues. It is to provide a forum for creating a common set of regulatory systems. There is an ensuing tension and contradiction between the right of sovereigns to govern individually and their right to govern collectively.

This argument builds on the works of other scholars looking at interstitial economic activity. Ronen Palan, for example, develops the argument that "offshore" economic activities, best categorized as semi-licit international activity, are a necessary safety-valve for a globalized economy operating in a sovereign states system.[1] Daniel Drezner notes that legal sovereignty can be a useful economic resource for small and/or poor countries, many of which are willing to rent out their sovereignty to the highest bidder.[2] Elizabeth DeSombre argues, in the context of flags of convenience in the international shipping industry, that powerful states could regulate the "offshore" world if they wanted to but often find it in their interest not to do so.[3] Aida Hozic, in the context of cigarette smuggling in the Balkans, suggests that illicit international economic activity both reflects historical context and provides opportunities to relatively weak states in a globalized world.[4] What this chapter adds to this body of work is the observation that states are complicit in interstitial economic activities not only for reasons of convenience or to promote economic growth, but also (and self-consciously) to reinforce the cartelized position of the sovereign state as the functional and legal core of the international system. States, in other words, are dealing with the contradictions between different understandings of sovereignty in a globalizing economy by prioritizing sovereign right, however understood, against the logic of globalization.

To make this argument, I begin by discussing what the term "illicit" refers to in this context, noting that it covers a range of activities, including but not limited to those that are illegal. This is followed by an examination of the interstices of sovereignty, the holes in the international regulatory system that provide a home for much illicit

[1] Palan 2003.   [2] Drezner 2001.   [3] DeSombre 2006.   [4] Hozic 2004.

economic activity. These interstices are where states are often forced to make the choice between enforcing their sovereignty in practice, or reinforcing their sovereignty in principle. The need to choose between the two helps to explain why states, even powerful and rich states, are often willing to legitimize the role of weaker states in illicit economic activity, even when the more powerful states could prevent such behavior if they so chose. I then look at the phenomenon of sovereignty as a marketable good, of states renting out their right to regulate to non-state economic actors.

Illicit International Economic Activity

The term "illicit activity" suggests activity that is in contravention of the rules, whatever those rules may be. It can mean illegal activity, but suggests a broader category, also including activity that, while perhaps legal in a literal interpretation of the rules, is nonetheless designed to contravene the spirit of those rules.[5] Illicit economic activity, then, is activity undertaken in contravention of the letter or spirit of a set of rules in order to make money. Illicit international economic activity is such activity undertaken across national borders.[6]

But it isn't that easy. Defining illicit economic activity domestically can be relatively straightforward, because there is (ideally) one set of laws against which to measure behavior. Internationally, however, there are different sets of laws in different countries. An economic activity that is perfectly legal in one country can be illegal in another country. If the activity impacts both countries, is it illicit? A good example of this question could be found along the Canadian–US border during the Prohibition era. One of Canada's largest fortunes of the twentieth century, that of the Bronfman family, was made from prohibition. The family's distillery company, Seagrams, made and sold liquor in Canada, a perfectly legal activity. The company did not sell its products in the United States, which would have been illegal, nor did it attempt itself to smuggle its products across the Canadian–US border. However, the company did sell large quantities of its product very close to poorly guarded portions of the border, knowing full well that it would then be smuggled. It made quantities of its product that only

---

[5] E.g., Abraham and van Schendel 2005. [6] Naim 2005; Andreas 2004.

made business sense if it assumed that a large proportion would be smuggled.[7]

So, even though the company did not knowingly break any laws, did it engage in illicit international economic activity? For the purposes of this book, the answer to this question is yes. Illicit international economic activity, as the phrase is used here, includes not only activity that is illegal in all of the countries in which it is undertaken, it also includes activity conducted within the laws of one country where that activity is legal, when the ultimate target of the activity is another country, where that activity is illegal or differently regulated.

There is a wide range of activities that fall under this heading. At one end of the range is activities that are illegal in all countries in which they are practiced. Examples include international narcotics trafficking and trafficking in people. Much smuggling outside of the narcotics industry does not fit into this category, particularly when the products being smuggled are legal in both countries. Some smuggling involves products that are legal in the country of export but illegal (either in general or when unregulated) in the country of import and therefore break the laws of only the receiving country. But some smuggling involves products that are not illegal in either country; in these cases it is only the "international" part of the exchange, the fact of crossing national borders, that accounts for illicitness. An example is smuggling of endangered species of flora and fauna, in which it is specifically the international trade that is illegal.[8]

At the other end of the range of illicitness are activities that are not illegal in principle in any of the countries in which they are practiced but are regulated differently in various countries. The illicitness here results from attempts by economic actors to arbitrage regulations in order to minimize costs of compliance. Many of these behaviors are discussed in the overlapping literatures on offshoring and regulatory havens.[9] Examples of this sort of behavior include offshore banking, flag-of-convenience shipping, tax havens, and pollution havens.[10] In each of these examples, a state will intentionally offer lower labor or environmental regulatory standards or lower taxes to a specific

---

[7] Newman 1978.
[8] In countries that have ratified the Convention on International Trade in Endangered Species of Flora and Fauna, currently numbering 183.
[9] Palan 2003 and DeSombre 2006, respectively.   [10] Palan 2003; Barkin 2015b.

industry in order to attract investment or income.[11] Not all offshoring is an example of illicit behavior – it is only illicit when economic actors (in this case companies) relocate specifically to circumvent the costs of complying with laws in their primary place of business.

Three examples serve to illustrate the difference between licit and illicit offshoring or regulatory haven activity. The migration of back-office computer work to India is not in any way illicit – Indian technology workers are not doing anything that would be illegal in the United States or Western Europe, they are just doing it in a more cost-effective way (or, phrased differently, for lower wages and with less institutional power[12]). But the migration of private banking from the United States and Western Europe to small island nations in the Caribbean or Mediterranean Seas is illicit, because the comparative advantage of the banks in these more lightly regulated locations is specifically that they help people from richer countries avoid their taxes.[13] In other words, part of the income base of offshore banking is derived specifically from abetting individuals in breaking the tax laws of their home countries.

Similarly, the practice of flagging (registering) ships in countries with which they have no connection, such as Liberia, official home to the world's largest tanker fleet even though it neither produces nor consumes enough petroleum to fill even a tiny fraction of the fleet, is also illicit. Tanker owners flag in places such as Liberia so that they can pay lower taxes than they would in the countries in which they actually pick up or deliver their oil and so that they will face lower labor and environmental regulatory standards. But they do not operate in Liberia – they operate specifically in those countries whose taxes and standards they are trying to avoid. Thus a Liberian-registered tanker operating in US waters can pay its sailors a fraction of what they would be paid on a US-registered ship in the same place, and provide them with lower labor and safety protections.[14] Flags of convenience are illicit by the definition used here because they are designed to excuse ship owners from obeying the laws of the places where they operate.

These two categories of behavior, smuggling and offshoring, are not necessarily mutually distinct. An example of overlap can be found in a

[11] E.g., Palan, Murphy, and Chavagneux 2013.
[12] E.g., Ravishankar, Pan, and Myers 2013.
[13] E.g., Palan, Murphy, and Chavagneux 2013.   [14] DeSombre 2006.

case of cigarette smuggling from Albania to Western Europe. Tobacco companies were exporting to Albania far more cigarettes than Albanians were likely to smoke. The Albanian government bonded the cigarettes, benefiting from extra tax revenues in the process, and the cigarettes were then smuggled to Western Europe. Because they were bonded by a government recognized by the European Union, the cigarettes were legal there, and therefore fetched a higher price than unbonded cigarettes could (but were still much cheaper than cigarettes bonded by the EU). Albania in this case was acting as a tax haven. However, the tax advantage of using this haven could only be realized if combined with smuggling to get the cigarettes to the EU without being taxed again.[15] Interestingly, the EU decided that this pattern was sufficiently illicit that it needed to be stopped, but the attempt to stop it was targeted only at the tobacco companies (against which the EU launched lawsuits, settling with Philip Morris for $1.25 billion).[16] The Albanian government, even though it was self-consciously abetting cigarette smuggling in order to increase its revenues, was acting within its sovereign rights.

The Interstices of Sovereignty

This idea of sovereign right provides a link between the discussions of sovereignty and of illicit international economic activity. As has been noted already, much of the illicit economic activity in question happens in what might be called the interstices of sovereignty. In other words, it falls in the cracks between sovereignties, and between practices of sovereignty: in some cases, it self-consciously arbitrages sovereignties.[17] As such, it does not fit in neatly to the sovereign states system in general. Sovereign entities, states, are faced with decisions when confronted with this sort of interstitial activity. They must prioritize among various understandings of sovereign right. States often make claims of individual right, but at other times they focus on collective and contractual rights, prioritizing the maintenance of the sovereignty cartel over immediate regulatory or political needs.

The case can be made that all illicit international economic activity can be seen as interstitial to sovereignty to some extent. Even at the end

[15] Hozic 2004.   [16] Geitner 2004.
[17] On regulatory arbitrage, see Barkin 2015b.

of the spectrum of illicitness involving activity that is illegal everywhere it is conducted, economic activity does not so much fall through the cracks of the sovereign state system as point to the impossibility of a state maintaining complete social and economic control. Even here, however, international cooperation can be undermined by sovereign right. A good example is the trade in illegal narcotics. The international trade in these drugs is at one level fundamentally similar to the domestic narcotics industry. Governments try to stop it, and fail.[18] But this trade is abetted by discontinuities in sovereignty. International law enforcement, which builds on a contractual understanding of sovereign property, is hampered by more nationalist understandings of sovereignty that, *pace* both Bodin and Weber,[19] see law enforcement as both the central right and central duty of the state.[20] And in some countries, parts of the state are themselves involved in the drug trade, giving it sovereign protection.[21] This involvement, the use of sovereign right to protect illicit economic activity, does not undermine sovereign property rights in principle, although egregious failure by a state to stop exports can undermine claims to sovereign right by governments, by exhibiting a failure to govern. By the same token, effective interdiction of production and export of narcotics can reinforce an otherwise weak claim to sovereignty, as was the case with the Taliban in late 2000 and early 2001.[22]

Toward the other end of the spectrum is activity that is legal in some countries but not, as practiced, in others. This end is best exemplified by offshoring for the purpose of finding regulatory havens, particularly in industries such as finance and shipping.[23] This activity is best seen as interstitial, in that its practitioners are engaged in regulatory arbitrage to take advantage of economic activities that are regulated nationally but that are inherently global in character. The sort of outright illegality seen in the narcotics example and the interstitial arbitrage seen in the offshoring example are probably best seen as poles of a range of behavior rather than as a dichotomy. Many instances of smuggling, for example, involve goods that are legal in all countries involved but taxed differently. Government reaction to smuggling can range from active opposition to tacit acquiescence.

---

[18] E.g., Caulkins et al. 2005. [19] Bodin 1945: 172; and Weber 1968: 54.
[20] E.g., Friedrichs 2007. [21] E.g., Reno 2000. [22] Farrell and Thorne 2005.
[23] For a discussion, see Barkin 2015b.

Such illicit activity generally has the effect of weakening states' ability to govern effectively (this is the case whether they are combating the illicit activity or participating in it). States' reactions to illicit international economic activity can vary significantly, based both on the interest of the government in and its capabilities to combat the activity. However, sovereigns will usually engage the behavior in some fashion, either by combating it, finding ways of regulating it, or finding ways of profiting from it. Combating it represents one kind of assertion of sovereign right, profiting from it another. Nonetheless, states are often unable to make much headway against illicit activity even when they try. The United States' "war on drugs" is a good example both of a state committing itself to an assertion of control and of a state failing to fully assert control.[24]

Finding ways to regulate illicit international economic activity represents a trade-off between the Roman and contractual understandings of sovereign rights, between autonomous control within borders and collective control of the global economy. It represents, in other words, an acceptance by states that the sovereign states system does have interstices, and an attempt to contain them rather than eliminate them. The contractual understanding underpins economic globalization, but at the same time undermines state control. Eschewing the contractual understanding means both withdrawing from the economic benefits of globalization and from the normative legitimation of participating in the multilateral system.[25] It would undermine both external legitimacy, by distancing the state from the community of sovereigns, and internal legitimacy, because it would likely be economically disastrous. However, too much focus on the contractual understanding of sovereign right can threaten the domestic legitimation of sovereignty, to the extent that it depends on norms of nationalism and a distinct national political order.

Discussions of illicit international economic activity often focus on whether it weakens sovereignty, and the answer to the question posed as such is generally yes: states may try to make the best of the sovereignty/globalization contradiction by minimizing the loss of

---

[24] For a discussion, see Caulkins et al. 2005.
[25] In Ruggie's (1992) terminology, a withdrawal from globalizing forces would almost by definition mean a withdrawal from multilateralist international politics, and multilateralism is a predominant contemporary legitimating norm in international relations.

sovereignty, but some loss is inevitable.[26] These discussions, however, understand sovereignty as control. States' responses to illicit activity, even when they accept a loss of control, are often designed to reinforce sovereignty understood as sovereign right. This leads to the observation that legitimate sovereignty, the concept of the sovereign right of states, is a valuable commodity. It is valuable both in a sociological or legal and an economic sense. Sociologically, it is valuable in that it provides the normative and legal underpinning of sovereignty, the legitimacy without which the state would be just one more example of a protection racket, of organized crime, among many.[27] This sociological value, combined with the position of the sovereign state as the anthropomorphized individual of international law, in turn makes sovereignty an economically valuable commodity – states can sell or, more precisely, rent out their legitimacy, their legal personality, to economic actors who want some control over legitimate international regulatory structures.

Some states take advantage of the economic value of sovereignty (in order of decreasing licitness) by becoming regulatory havens,[28] by taxing activities they know to be implicated in illegal economic activity in other countries[29], and sometimes by direct participation in illegal activity.[30] The states that do so are usually, but not always, smaller or poorer states, or states with weak domestic legitimacy (making it more difficult to raise revenue domestically).[31] When revenue from these activities makes it into national budgets in states for which the profits generated by illicit activity are great enough, relative to national budgets, to make a difference, the states in question generally see themselves as too insignificant on the international stage to need to worry about the systemic implications of their activities. When revenue is pocketed by the person of the sovereign (be that an individual person or several people who claim sovereign rights) it is generally in states with domestic institutional structures that are too weak to prevent state capture. Either way, this sort of activity has been discussed in the international relations literature (and will be discussed further in the following sections), and is well captured by phrases such as "sovereignty for sale."[32]

[26] E.g., Andreas 2000.　[27] The organized crime analogy is from Tilly 1985.
[28] Barkin 2015b.　[29] Palan, Murphy, and Chavagneux 2013.
[30] E.g., Reno 2000.　[31] E.g., Moore 2004 and Gilley 2006.
[32] Drezner 2001.

But why do other states, particularly those that see themselves as important enough on the international stage to have to worry about the systemic implications of their actions, allow the sale of sovereignty? Because of the sociological value of sovereignty. The normative structures of sovereignty are not exogenous conditions. They need to be regularly reconstituted and reinforced through the practices of actors.[33] States, then, need to act to reinforce norms of sovereign right if they are to continue to benefit from them; this is the logic of the sovereignty cartel. And it is those states that worry about the systemic implications of their actions that are most likely to self-consciously act in a manner designed to reinforce the norms of sovereign right, that it is states rather than any other institutions that have the right to govern. There is a strong parallel here with international law. Customary international law reflects practice, and changes with changing practice. States recognize the effects of practice on law, and much of the hortatory content of international diplomacy can be explained by self-conscious attempts to affect custom.

Legitimizing Illicitness

To recap, states respond to some kinds of illicit international economic behavior by combating it, and to other kinds by legitimating it. A good example of this sort of legitimating response is provided by flags of convenience. This is the practice of registering ships that operate internationally in states, usually small and relatively poor, that are neither a destination for the ships nor home to the owners of the ships. Ship owners register their ships with flags of convenience because registering in these countries involves lower taxes and regulatory standards than registering in the states in which they operate or from which they are owned. This practice is illicit for three reasons. The first and most general reason is that ships generally reflag so that they can act in a way that would be illegal elsewhere. The second reason is that there is a generally accepted principle in international maritime law, called cabotage, according to which ships must be registered in states with which they have a clear operational or ownership connection. The third reason that this practice is illicit is that it allows ships and ship owners to behave within a country's national waters in a way that is

---

[33] E.g., Reus-Smit 1999.

illegal in that country. For example, a ship that is owned by an American and spends a majority of its time in American waters can pay its crew much less than the US minimum wage because it is subject to the regulations of the state in which it is registered, not the states in which it operates.[34]

The states whose laws are circumvented in this way prioritize contractual sovereignty, the idea of the sovereign right of states as a category to regulate, over the loss of regulatory control implicit in allowing ships to be regulated by microstates or landlocked states. States need not necessarily accept this loss of control. Most states, for example, actively enforce the cabotage rules in air transport that they ignore in sea transport.[35] States have not always ignored them in sea transport either – Great Britain enforced a set of cabotage rules collectively called the Navigation Acts rigorously in the eighteenth century, and it was these rules that made them the world's preeminent maritime commercial power.[36] Furthermore, states retain the right within their territorial waters to enforce regulations on ships selectively as they see fit. In other words, the loss of regulatory control by states is not inherent to the nature of international shipping but rather is largely voluntary.

Why then do states accept the practice of reflagging? International shipping is in some ways inherently interstitial to the sovereign state system. Eighteenth-century Britain dealt with this problem by using its maritime power to capture monopoly rents from international shipping through the Navigation Laws, which reinforced British sovereign control at the expense of its trading partners, not a difficult task because those partners were often colonial possessions. But it created a zero-sum game in international shipping, a game that other countries often chose not to participate in and which therefore acted as a brake on the growth of international commerce. Britain eventually revoked these rules in the interest of promoting international trade.[37] The interstitial aspects of international air transport, meanwhile, are dealt with through a patchwork of bilateral agreements mediated by multilateral rules negotiated at the International Civil Aviation Organization. These rules have the effect of Balkanizing international

[34] DeSombre 2006   [35] E.g., Bliss 1994: 382.
[36] E.g., Mathias 1983; Ekelund and Tollison 1981.
[37] E.g., Barkin 2003, chapter 4.

air transport and making it less efficient than it could be without the resulting restrictions on who can fly where.[38]

The practice of reflagging allows international maritime shipping to work with much lower direct costs than would be the case with either equivalents of the Navigation Laws or an international air transport model. At the same time, it allows states to enforce those regulations they care most about. The same effect could be had, however, without the requirement that all ships be registered with a sovereign authority. This requirement is not about efficiency; it is about legitimacy. The fact that states require ships to be registered with a state, any state, in order to enter their waters is a mechanism for enforcing the principle not only that states have the sovereign right to regulate, but that that right is exclusive to sovereigns. Only states can legitimately regulate, and therefore a ship without a state registry, without a sovereign flag, is illegitimate even if it is registered with a slew of respectable non-state bodies whose de facto function is to regulate its standards.[39]

Reflagging is thus an example of reacting to illicit economic behavior in the interstices of sovereignty by regulating it only as much as necessary and allowing it to function in as low-cost a manner as possible. But this economic efficiency is tempered by a process of mutually legitimating both the behavior and sovereign right by only allowing the behavior when the economic actors are authorized by a state that is a member of the sovereignty cartel.[40] An interesting aside here is the practice by some states of second registries. Some states with first ship registries with high (and therefore internationally uncompetitive) standards have second registries with lower standards that are open only to vessels that do not operate on a domestic basis. This is an example of a sort of intentional offshoring of sovereignty, of claiming the sovereign right to participate in international regulation in a way that is explicitly extraterritorial.[41]

---

[38] Nayar 1995.
[39] And there is indeed a slew of respectable non-state bodies, from labor unions to insurance consortia, whose function is to regulate ship standards in lieu of effective flag-state regulation. See DeSombre 2006.
[40] Membership in the cartel for purposes of regulatory authorization is in fact a little fuzzy, inasmuch as some overseas possessions, mostly of the United Kingdom and France, that are not independent sovereigns are nonetheless accepted as flag states. The home countries could, however, end this practice if they saw fit.
[41] DeSombre 2006.

Similar examples can be found in the offshore financial industry, which the developed world has shown a consistent ability but an inconsistent desire to regulate effectively.[42] Even the world of cigarette smuggling is lubricated by sovereignty. Nor need this sovereignty be that of fully sovereign states – cigarette smuggling between the United States and Canada is partially enabled by the complicated semi-sovereign status of transborder Indigenous Canadian and American communities[43] (complicated in this context because it involves recognition of some of the property rights of sovereignty by both the states involved and the international community but does not result in membership of the sovereignty cartel[44]). The governments involved could as a practical matter easily put a stop to the bulk of the cigarette-smuggling business but are unwilling to undermine Indigenous sovereignty sufficiently to do so.

There are many areas of illicit international economic activity in which governments are not as willing to engage in cartel behavior, in a process of mutual recognition and legitimation of economic practices and norms of sovereignty. These include issues with respect to which states do not care about economic efficiency because they oppose the primary activity in the first place, such as narcotics trafficking (although claims of sovereign right can still protect sovereign participants in the drug trade). They can also include issues with respect to which states prioritize other interests, such as revenue generation or national security, over economic efficiency.[45] Finally, they include issues that have developed other regulatory patterns for particularistic historical reasons (the civil aviation example fits partially into this category). But where economic activity in the interstices of the sovereign state system does not threaten core state values or interests, the process of mutual legitimation can often be found.

Sovereignty for Sale

The discussion of the interaction of norms of sovereign property rights and the international political economy to this point has focused on

---

[42] E.g., Drezner 2007.
[43] Of course, the language of "smuggling" is itself grounded in a discourse of the rights of the sovereignty cartel. For a different language of the same events, see Simpson 2008.
[44] E.g., Wiessner 2008.
[45] Although even on these issues there is a tension between efficiency and sovereignty, e.g., Palan, Murphy, and Chavagneux 2013; Drezner 2007.

non-state actors arbitraging the sovereignty cartel for economic gain. But, as has been noted a few times already, sovereigns themselves also use claims of sovereign right directly for economic benefit. That this phenomenon has been called "sovereignty for sale"[46] underlines the property rights aspect of contemporary sovereignty. The phenomenon navigates the tensions between different understandings of sovereign property by making claims both on assertions of sovereign regulatory universality that build on contractual interpretations of sovereignty, and assertions of exclusive ownership of the state as an economic good that build on more absolute interpretations of sovereignty. In other words, in selling (or, more accurately, leasing) the regulatory prerogatives of sovereignty, sovereigns are claiming ownership of their own right to regulate in a market for regulation that is created by the universalist regulatory claims of the sovereignty cartel.

What, then, do sovereigns sell? The answers can be put in three categories of economic goods: regulatory legitimacy, citizenship, and physical goods. The first of these categories includes many of the subjects of regulation already discussed in this chapter, such as shipping, banking and corporate registration, the bonding of goods, etc. What these have in common is that they are created as goods by the sovereignty cartel, without which they would have less economic value, if any. Corporations, for example, need a sovereign tax home because other states will not let them operate in their territories without it.[47] A ship in international waters without a national flag is, by international law, a pirate, but a ship in international waters with a flag bought online from a sovereign that then makes little if any meaningful effort to effectively regulate that ship is nonetheless a legal participant in the international political economy.[48]

The right of states to sell (or lease) their regulatory sovereignty, and the willingness of the sovereignty cartel to support that right, is extensive but not limitless. Other states retain the right to prevent the purchasers of sovereign regulatory authorization from operating within their territory if the economic entities that are the purchasers fail to conform to domestic regulation. States can, for example, prohibit ships or banks that do not meet domestic standards from docking

---

[46] Drezner 2001.
[47] On the advantage that sovereign right gives small states in tax competition, see Rawlings 2007.
[48] DeSombre 2006.

in their ports or taking domestic deposits.⁴⁹ But this does not derogate from the ability to operate between sovereignties (even in the cigarette-smuggling example noted previously, the EU saw Albania as operating within its sovereign rights). And norms of collective sovereign responsibility for international property can trump the sovereign right to regulatory authorization in some instances. For example, states can act as flags of convenience for vessels fishing in international waters, but those vessels are still subject to interdiction if they operate in contravention of multilateral fishing regulations⁵⁰ (the precedent for this sort of interdiction can be traced back two centuries, with claims of international customary law against the transport of slaves on the high seas⁵¹).

The sale of citizenship (in which category I include the sale of lesser forms of domestic legal personhood, such as permanent residency or even permission to work) is in some ways a subcategory of the sale of regulatory legitimacy. Citizenship is sold by many states on a retail basis, generally to wealthy individuals to attract investment. Often this is done with clear and transparent rules and processes, although there is a substantial industry devoted to buying citizenships for wealthy clients who are not satisfied with their current legal home, a sort of citizenship laundering.⁵² It is, however, also sometimes sold wholesale, such as when the Comorros sold passports in batch lots to the United Arab Emirates for people who were born in the UAE, but to whom the government did not wish to grant citizenship rights.⁵³

Citizenship can be seen as a form of regulatory legitimation of individuals by the state. It is a phenomenon of the sovereignty cartel; people need it because states collectively require it of people, require that all people belong, in a regulatory sense, to a specific sovereign authority. However, citizenship is different from other forms of sovereign regulatory legitimation in important ways. People have a right to citizenship in international law;⁵⁴ economic entities have no equivalent right to a regulatory home. Revoking citizenship is therefore a much more normatively fraught exercise than granting it in the first place. And citizenship exists in a recursive relationship with contemporary sovereignty. To the extent that contemporary sovereignty is popular,

---

⁴⁹ Barkin 2015b   ⁵⁰ DeSombre 2005.   ⁵¹ E.g., Guilfoyle 2009.
⁵² Abrahamian 2015.   ⁵³ Abrahamian 2015.
⁵⁴ Often referred to as a right to nationality; see the Universal Declaration of Human Rights, Article 15 (United Nations General Assembly 1945).

legitimated by or, indeed, an expression of the people that the state represents, citizenship is an integral part of sovereignty and is the normative source of sovereign right. When a state sells citizenship it is changing who are the people of popular sovereignty. And because revoking citizenship is a rarer event than selling it, the redefinition is likely to be permanent. The property rights of the sovereign can in this way be used to redefine whose property sovereignty is.

The third category of economic goods that sovereigns sell comprises physical goods. These are primarily natural resources, ranging from oil, to minerals, to trees, to fish. Natural resources located within a country's territory or exclusive economic zone are, from the perspective of the international community, the sovereign property of the state. This gives the state (or whomever is empowered by the sovereignty cartel to act on behalf of the state) the right to sell, sell rights to, or charge royalties on its resources.[55] This process is in many ways a straightforward expression of a Roman exclusivist understanding of property: the state owns the physical economic goods within its territory and can sell those goods as it sees fit.

It is also, unlike the sale of regulatory sovereignty, not necessarily either an illicit or interstitial activity, making it a less clear fit in this chapter than the other two categories. However, it can be affected by the sovereignty cartel in ways that introduce both illicitness and interstitiality. This is the case because the sovereign right to sell resources in a given territory does not necessarily require actual physical control of that territory. The sovereignty cartel decides who has sovereign ownership of national resources and therefore who profits from their sale, which can create a disjuncture between sovereign profit from natural resources and the actual governance of the extraction of those resources.[56] For example, in 2019 some Libyan oilfields were controlled by the UN-recognized government but the majority were physically controlled by a different political organization, the (self-styled) Libyan National Army. The latter organization, not being a recognized member of the cartel, could only sell its oil either illicitly at a substantial discount or by paying royalties to the recognized sovereign government that it was actively fighting.[57]

---

[55] E.g., the United Nations Convention on Biological Diversity, Article 3 ("States have, in accordance with the Charter of the United Nations and the principles of international law, the sovereign right to exploit their own resources").

[56] E.g., Kaczynski and Fluharty 2002.   [57] Economist 2019.

Furthermore, the cartel can legitimate the sale of sovereign property even when the conditions of such sale are not within the sovereign's domestic law, whether the illegality stems from corruption or from a failure to enforce domestic regulatory standards and property law.[58] For example, the EU pays several West African states for the right to allow EU vessels to fish in their waters. Little if any of this money goes to the adjacent coastal communities (often in contravention of local laws), and much of it disappears to corruption.[59] Nor does anyone end up effectively regulating the actual fishing; the coastal states often lack the capability to do so, and the EU lacks the motive (since it is not the EU's resources being overfished). From the EU's perspective this is a straightforward commercial arrangement – it pays for the right to fish. From the perspective of the relevant West African sovereigns it is a lucrative arrangement. Other local actors, however, are frozen out of any benefits from the fishing activity by the cartel behavior of the sovereigns.

The phenomenon of sovereignty for sale can be looked at in a number of ways in an analysis of the norms of sovereignty. It is a clear indication that, in significant ways, sovereignty is a traditional property right in that it gives sovereigns the right to sell goods of value. The twist is that to a large extent it is the sovereignty cartel itself that creates the value being sold. It does so by colluding to require the particular forms of regulation that only it can provide. In this sense, regulatory universality fits Charles Tilly's description of state making as organized crime,[60] except that individual states are not requiring that economic actors pay them off, just that they pay off some member of the cartel. Meanwhile, the tension between the desire by some states to use the sovereign right to regulate in order to actually regulate, and the desire by others to use it as a source of income, creates interstitial spaces in the international political economy for illicit economic activity that the cartel allows (even as some states try individually to prevent) in order to defend the broader norm of the universality of sovereign regulation.

Another way to look at the phenomenon of sovereignty for sale is that it makes a successful claim to sovereignty potentially economically

---

[58] E.g., Kolstad and Søreide 2009.
[59] Kaczynski and Fluharty 2002. "Their waters" here generally refers to exclusive economic zones rather than territorial waters.
[60] Tilly 1985.

valuable to the individuals empowered to act in the name of the state. This view of the phenomenon takes us back to the discussion in the previous two chapters about who is sovereign. Since the value of what is being sold is created by the sovereignty cartel (even in the case of natural resources when it is the right of access, rather than the physical resources themselves, that is being sold) it is the cartel that decides who is legitimately sovereign. However, there are a variety of normative, as well as practical and political, bases on which individuals can claim sovereign right. In countries with well-established constitutional structures and processes, this decision is generally moot, as these processes identify who can act as sovereign in a way that the international community has no basis, either normative or practical, to challenge. But in countries where these structures and processes are weaker, claims made to the international community can matter. Furthermore, this process is recursive, inasmuch as international recognition of sovereign right can give actors the resources they need to establish effective domestic control, an observation to which we will return in the concluding chapter.

The Interstices of the Cartel

This set of arguments brings together several strands from the existing literature on offshoring and on illicit international economic activity. It explains why the offshore world that Palan talks about so often takes the form of regulatory havens in small sovereign states.[61] It helps to explain the patterns of regulatory control that DeSombre describes. Large-scale interstitial activity, both in the shipping industry that DeSombre discusses and elsewhere, requires access to those countries with big markets for that activity to be profitable. Those countries can, and do, regulate these activities to some extent. Why not regulate more? One answer is cost and economic efficiency, but that answer by itself is not sufficient to explain the resultant regulatory patterns.

---

[61] Offshoring does not always take this form. Sometimes it takes the form of regulatory havens carved out of, and kept separate from, the states that are the focus of the economic activity in question. Examples of such carving out include special export zones and second registries for international shipping, which have their own complicated relationships with norms of sovereign property.

Palan and DeSombre can explain the degree of regulation in the interstices of sovereignty by invoking arguments about economic efficiency and economic power,[62] but the resulting regulatory pattern, dominated by sovereign states as regulatory havens, cannot be fully explained without invoking ideas of sovereign legitimacy, sovereign property rights, and a sovereignty cartel.

Drezner's idea of "sovereignty for sale" is in essence the observation that the norm of sovereign right remains strong.[63] However, he does not address the question of why states participate in the reconstitution of this strength. The argument here addresses this question from three different perspectives. From the perspective of the sellers, sovereignty is a valuable commodity, often able to fetch a high price on the international market. It is, in other words, not only a property right, but a valuable good as well. From the perspective of the non-state actors who are the buyers of sovereignty, it explains why sovereignty, in particular the sovereignty of countries with few other real power resources, has economic value with respect to globalized economic activity in the first place. The sovereign right to regulate has the market value that it has because the cartel colludes to retain monopoly rights to a set of goods, both regulatory and material, that are necessary to international economic activity. From the perspective of other states, the ones that accept the legitimation of illicit economic activity by the regulatory havens, the argument here explains why they are willing to give up regulatory control; loss of practical control in specific cases is often worth the cost when it contributes to reproducing the broader principle of sovereign regulatory universality.

But not only does the sovereignty cartel help to explain illicit economic activity in the interstices of sovereignty, it helps to drive that activity. States at the same time claim the right to participation in collective governance and the right to autonomous governance, each claim drawing on different understandings of sovereign property rights. In the normative spaces between these claims are to be found economic opportunities, both for sovereigns and for other economic actors. Indeed, the illicitness of many of the activities discussed in this

---

[62] Palan 2003; Palan, Murphy, and Chavagneux 2013; and DeSombre 2006.
[63] Drezner 2001.

chapter is itself created by the tensions represented by the normative spaces between different understandings of property. Norms of sovereignty, and of sovereign property rights, are imprecise and varied, and are not necessarily internally coherent. States act to reconstitute these norms nonetheless, and the results can be messy.

8 | Normative Dissonance

What happens when states, colluding (self-consciously or not) as a sovereignty cartel, act to reconstitute norms of sovereignty that are themselves imprecise and varied, and not necessarily internally coherent? How can the cartel prosper in the face of internal contradiction not only in its practices but in the underlying norms? How do participants in international politics cope with the fact that the system is not normatively coherent and be able to effectively reconstitute its discourses nonetheless? How do states maintain ontological security when the ontological bases of sovereignty are internally contradictory?[1] Addressing these questions is key to understanding not only how the cartel does work, but also how it is possible for it to work.

One answer to these questions that is often cited in the international relations literature, as noted here in earlier chapters, is that the norms of sovereignty are an exercise in organized hypocrisy.[2] But this answer is unsatisfying in a number of ways. It fails to explain either patterns of the re-creation of norms through discourse and practice or the central role that questions of sovereignty often play in political discourse. Nor does it address the ontological purpose of sovereignty: if norms of sovereignty are exercises in hypocrisy, what is the purpose of sovereignty in the first place? A different lens through which to look at the question focuses on how political actors process normative incompatibility and contradiction. This chapter suggests such a lens, developing a psychological metaphor, which I call "normative dissonance," for how political actors deal with the normative contradictions of sovereignty that allows the cartel to function despite its fractured normative underpinnings. Normative dissonance reinforces rather than undermines ontological security by allowing a reaffirmation of the purposes

---

[1] On ontological security in international relations see, *inter alia*, Steele 2008 and Mitzen 2006.
[2] Krasner 1999.

of sovereignty and the state even when those purposes are internally contradictory.

We have seen to this point in this book that norms of sovereignty, and in particular norms of sovereign property rights, suffer from this sort of internal contradiction. This is the case both with norms of what kind of property sovereignty is, and norms of whose property it is. With respect to norms about what property is understood to mean, there is a contradiction in principle between contractual property practiced as multilateralism and Roman understandings practiced as exclusive domestic authority, particularly in the context of a sovereign states system with claims to regulatory universality. The latter requires that multilateral participation be an option that can be chosen by a state only when it is consistent with domestic autonomy and rejected at other times. The former, however, requires of states a willingness to participate in, and accept the results of, collective governance, because without collective participation the legitimacy of claims of universality of the sovereign states system cannot be upheld.

With respect to norms of whose property sovereignty is, there is a tension between on the one hand popular sovereignty, the idea that the state is in some way representative of the people, and on the other the fact that sovereign property is a potentially lucrative commodity to the people who personify the state. When there are potentially incompatible norms of legitimate sovereignty to choose from and the question of whose property a particular sovereignty is becomes an open one, there is a risk of competitive legitimate claims for that sovereignty. There are no clear normative rules for choosing among the competing norms (even when there are generally accepted procedural rules for identifying legitimate sovereigns).

How do political actors deal with these contradictions? One set of tools available to political scientists for dealing with the effects of internally contradictory, or in other words dissonant, information is provided by political psychology. Drawing on this set of tools, I offer in this chapter the concept of normative dissonance. This term is used here to refer to situations where actors in, and observers of, international politics hold in common two (or more) norms that are not fully mutually compatible. In such situations they will generally react in ways that minimize dissonance in norms discourse at the expense of fully analyzing the referent political situation of the discourse. The concept of normative dissonance draws heavily on (and is in fact a metaphorical use of) the theory of cognitive dissonance, as taken from psychology and political psychology. There are, however, two key differences. The first is that cognitive dissonance applies to processes of individual cognition. Normative dissonance begins with individual processes of cognition but describes those situations where intersubjectively held ideas are dissonant. The second difference is that cognitive dissonance can apply both to information (data) and to ideas that inform decision-making. Normative dissonance applies only to norms, not to cognitive inputs more generally.

The Metaphor of Normative Dissonance

What happens when two or more sets of norms, sets of commonly held intersubjective understandings about the legitimate basis of governance and rights of sovereignty, are incompatible? What are the political effects of such norm conflict? The norms literature in international relations, when looking at evolving conflicts among norms, has tended to assume that one will displace another.[3] It has focused more on how norms spread than on what happens when the old and the new coexist.[4] But in the case of the conflict discussed here, different and incompatible norms remain intersubjectively accepted concurrently; the incompatibility is not resolved because one norm atrophies. Where can we look to understand the effects of norm incompatibility when both norms retain intersubjective traction?

The literature on norms in international politics has tended to focus on the societal level of analysis, to look at norms as sociological artifacts rather than as aspects of individual cognition.[5] This approach is entirely reasonable; norms clearly are sociological artifacts that can only be intersubjective if they are broadly known, and as inputs into interests as well as actions they precede individual decision-making. However, they also operate through the mechanism of individual cognition; to become an intersubjective understanding, a norm must first be subjectively understood.[6] The societal level of analysis is where we must look to learn about the existence of norm conflict in the practice of international relations. Given, however, that intersubjective

---

[3] E.g., Finnemore 2004.   [4] E.g., Finnemore and Sikkink 1998.
[5] Srivastava 2019.
[6] For a more nuanced discussion of this claim, see Guzzini 2000.

beliefs and discourses differ from subjective beliefs primarily in that they are held in common by a group of people interacting within a system (in this case the international political system), looking at the literature on subjective beliefs and political behavior can also illuminate the political effects of norm conflict.

As such, one way of getting at the effects of norm incompatibility in international politics is through the cumulative effects of this incompatibility on subjective, which is to say individual, perception and cognition. The place to look for discussions of individual perception and cognition is in the literature on political psychology, and the central theories presented in this literature on incompatible perceptual inputs include theories of cognitive dissonance and cognitive consistency.[7] These cannot be applied directly as theories to questions of the social construction and political effects of norms, because societies are not people. But they can provide a useful metaphor, a lens through which to view the inconsistencies of sovereignty claims as other than simple hypocrisy.[8]

The theory of cognitive dissonance posits that people are made psychologically uncomfortable by dissonant, or mutually incompatible, information.[9] This is particularly the case once people have committed themselves to a specific course of action. The theory suggests that once people have committed themselves, they will attempt to justify their decision by reevaluating the information in a way that minimizes the dissonance. Two ways of doing this are by maximizing the difference between the dissonant pieces of information and by distinguishing dissonant information from underlying beliefs.[10] Maximizing the difference between the dissonant pieces of information involves reevaluating the information after the decision has been made, to increase *post facto* the perceived benefits of the choice made and decrease the perceived potential benefits of the choice not made.

Distinguishing dissonant information from underlying beliefs means that if you believe both A and B, and have to choose between behavior based on either A or B, you are likely to distance the behavior you did not choose from the underlying belief. This allows you to simultaneously hold both beliefs and minimize dissonance. Theories of cognitive consistency, meanwhile, suggest a "strong tendency for people to

---

[7] E.g., Jervis 1976.   [8] The hypocrisy reference is to Krasner 1999.
[9] Festinger 1957.   [10] Jervis 1976: 382–406.

see what they expect to see and to assimilate incoming information to preexisting images."[11] As an example in this context, if political actors have an image of sovereignty as absolute national autonomy, they are likely to see decisions about regulatory autonomy, such as signing a trade agreement with compulsory adjudication or voting on whether to leave the European Union, as a question of autonomy rather than as a question of regulatory participation (and are likely to perceptually maximize the benefits and minimize the costs of autonomy-maximizing decisions).[12]

The metaphor of normative dissonance draws on these theories, to suggest that people deal with incompatible norm sets, or more precisely with dissonant aspects of commonly held norm sets, by using similar cognitive strategies. Normative dissonance differs from the theory of cognitive dissonance in two key ways. The first is that it has a much narrower application. It refers to cognitive strategies for dealing with choices that draw on dissonant political norms (beliefs about how things should be done), not to dissonant informational input more broadly. Normative dissonance is thus about ways in which people tend to react, to deal with the incompatibility, when faced with incompatible norms. Once they have made a decision drawing on one norm rather than the other, they might then tend to redefine the norm not chosen, or reinterpret the perceived benefits of adopting the norm, to make it less appealing. They might also distance the behavior or opinion not chosen from the underlying norm, and to assimilate new information in ways that support both the redefinition and the distancing.[13]

The second key way in which normative dissonance differs as a process from cognitive dissonance is that it is a two-level process, involving both individual cognition and social communication. It is, in other words, a claim about political discourse as well as a theory of cognition. It builds on the theory of cognitive dissonance, but it then looks at the effects of the cognitive patterns predicted by that theory on political discourse.[14] Cognitive dissonance begins with a set of

---

[11] Jervis 1976: 117.   [12] See, e.g., Telegraph 2016.
[13] See Jervis (1976: 143–202) on assimilation of information to preexisting beliefs.
[14] There is an analogy here with theories of emotions in international relations and the way in which individual emotion affects intersubjective political practice. See, e.g., Sasley 2011.

potentially dissonant subjective beliefs. Normative dissonance begins with a set of potentially dissonant *inter*subjective, as well as subjective, beliefs. In other words, a prerequisite to the applicability of normative dissonance as a lens through which to look at norms of sovereignty is the existence of two (or more) political norms that a political community holds in common. This does not, of course, require that every member of the political community hold both norms equally. But it does require at minimum that both norms be recognized features of political discourse in the community.

The process of normative dissonance thus begins with the tendency of individuals to react to dissonant norms in a way described by the theory of cognitive dissonance. When the norms in question are commonly held within a political community, then individuals within that community will be reacting through similar cognitive processes to the same discourses of dissonant norms. It is through this similarity that a theory of cognition yields to a process of discourse. When particular political situations that require decisions highlight the dissonant aspects of commonly held norms, the theory of cognitive dissonance suggests that individuals will engage in predictable post-decision rationalizations.[15] In supporting a particular decision, individuals will engage in rationalizations that highlight the distance between the norms, and that dissociate the alternative decisions from underlying normative rationales.

But as long as not everyone supports the same decision, these predictable rationalizations will work from different directions. Supporters of a course of action based on one norm may engage in post hoc distancing of other norms, and supporters of an alternative course of action based on another norm are likely to engage in post hoc distancing from the first. Post hoc political discourse in reference to the decision is thus likely to adopt a particular pattern, in which participants in the discourse agree on the underlying norms that should inform political behavior. Despite this agreement, however, proponents will tend to talk past each other, because the cognitive defense mechanism underlying the discourse is not one oriented toward effective communication but rather is one oriented toward minimizing subjectively felt cognitive dissonance. It is this pattern of discourse, with commonly held normative bases but without effective communication

---

[15] Jervis 1976.

on the relationship between the normative bases and political decisions, that characterizes normative dissonance. The pattern means that participants in political discourse have available to them rationalizations for their preferred political choice that fail to address the underlying dissonance. This pattern is at the core of the example in the next section of this chapter, on multilateralism and globalization.

As with many ways to look at political discourse, the metaphor of normative dissonance refers to general patterns of discourse on a subject, not to the discourse of specific identifiable groups. It is predictive, not determinist.[16] It applies to political communities as wholes, and to all of those within those communities who hold and voice views on specific political decisions as individuals. Of course, some people will be more influential in creating patterns of political discourse in relation to specific decisions than others. Even those people most active in creating patterns of discourse, however, need a receptive audience, need to find a resonance for their ideas in order to be effective in creating discursive patterns.[17] Normative dissonance refers to these resultant patterns.

Critics of both political psychology and sociological approaches to the study of international relations might argue that the people most active in creating patterns of political discourse are not succumbing to psychological self-defense mechanisms; rather, they are engaged in strategic behavior. By this argument, they are self-consciously evoking certain norms in order to make their point. This is, in many cases, undoubtedly true.[18] But the fact that some discursive participants are being strategic in this sense does not mean that patterns of normative dissonance are not there. A strategy of evoking certain norms at the expense of others in support of political decisions is only effective insofar as the audience responds to the norms, and the audience is looking (consciously or subconsciously) for a way to place the relevant decisions in the context of the norms. In other words, the existence of a tendency to normative dissonance with respect to a particular decision

---

[16] It is, to use a common terminology, a cloud metaphor, not a clock metaphor. Almond and Genco 1977.
[17] See, *inter alia*, Goddard 2009 and Krebs and Jackson 2007.
[18] In fact, both Goddard 2009 and Krebs and Jackson 2007 argue in the context of sociological approaches that discourse is a form of power.

is a prerequisite for the effective strategic use of normative arguments that play off that dissonance.[19]

Multilateralism and Globalization

The rest of this chapter develops two examples of normative dissonance in the context of the sovereignty cartel. The first, in this section, looks at multilateralism and globalization as the expressions of contractual and Roman understandings of sovereign property rights in an era of popular sovereignty. Both popular and scholarly discourse on the political tension between multilateralism and globalization often elide the underlying normative tension by distancing the political expression from the underlying property right. The second, in the following section, addresses normative dissonance in questions of who is identified as sovereign.

Since the nineteenth century a normative basis both for claims of sovereign property rights and for the practice of sovereignty in international relations has been the idea of popular sovereignty, the idea that the state represents the people, who are ultimately sovereign. The idea of popular sovereignty, however, introduces a new question into discussion of sovereign property: who are the people on behalf of whom the state claims sovereign rights? How is the relationship between them and the sovereign to be conceived? Chapter 6 introduces this idea of popular sovereignty into the discussion of the sovereignty cartel and makes connections between conceptions of popular sovereignty and different understandings of the norms of sovereign property. In particular, it makes the argument that Roman and contractarian understandings of sovereign property underpin two distinct sets of answers to these questions: that the sovereign represents people as individuals via a social contract, and that it represents people as an aggregate, as a nation that is distinct from the sum of the individual citizens of the state.

The tension between the logic of social contracts and the logic of nationalism introduces contradictions into both the general discourse about and the practice of international politics. One place where such contradictions can be found is in the regulatory function of the state in the global governance of a wide range of issue areas, including the international political economy, the environment, and security issues.

---

[19] This is at the core of the empirical cases in both Goddard 2009 and Krebs and Jackson 2007.

In all of these issue areas, the claims of regulatory universality associated with the contemporary practice of sovereignty have for more than half a century been expressing themselves as multilateralism, as an increasing tendency for rules to be made cooperatively that are intended to apply to all those who participate in their making. Students of international organization often look upon multilateralism as a good thing – after all, it means countries cooperating rather than conflicting in areas of common concern. At the same time, the process of globalization is often criticized for undermining the ability of states to make their own decisions in areas of national concern.

These tensions speak directly to the discussion in the introduction of this book about sovereignty and globalization. That the norm of multilateralism (that states should in the first instance act collectively rather than individually) is so often viewed as benign, even by some of the people who view the result, globalization, as problematic, is an artifact of the tension between the two norms of social contract and nationalism as competing understandings of legitimate sovereignty. The social contractarian norm, when applied at the international level, suggests that rulemaking by common consent, which is to say multilateralist harmonization, is the most legitimate form of global governance. However, the nationalist norm generates a negative reaction to the resultant globalization.

What would the concept of normative dissonance suggest about the incompatibilities of nationalism and social contract theory at the level of global governance? It would essentially suggest that we should expect the discourses of anti-globalization and of multilateralism to speak past, rather than to, each other. More specifically, in the discourse of multilateralism, proponents of multilateralism are likely to distance themselves from nationalist norms, to argumentatively weaken the connection between globalization and the undermining of legitimate nationalism, and to interpret information about globalization in ways compatible with social contract theory. Similarly, in the discourse on globalization we should expect opponents of the process to distance themselves from social contract norms, to argumentatively weaken the connection between multilateralism and social contract, and to interpret information about globalization in ways compatible with nationalism, be that nationalism of a liberal or more virulent form.[20]

---

[20] See Haas 1997 for a discussion of liberal nationalism.

And in fact we see exactly this happening, both in the discourse of international politics, and in the academic study of international relations. In the discourse of international politics, for example, Stewart Patrick in *The Sovereignty Wars* describes more than a century of debate about sovereignty and multilateral commitments. Although he does not use the languages either of cartels or of cognitive dissonance, he argues that "although most Americans regard 'sovereignty' as sacred, they often use it to mean very different things – and talk past each other as a result. The way out of this predicament begins with realizing that sovereignty has distinct components, and that these don't always go together." *The Sovereignty Wars* can in this sense be read as the US political discourse case study for this chapter.[21]

In the academic study of international relations, proponents of multilateralism, for example, often deal discursively with the contradiction between nationalist and social contract norms by taking one of two approaches. The first is to distance themselves from nationalist norms, by focusing on the problems of nationalism, and by associating nationalism generally with its more virulent forms. In one of the seminal academic discussions of the norm of multilateralism, for example, John Ruggie repeatedly presents the economic system that Nazi Germany created with several Eastern European countries in the 1930s as the antithesis to multilateralism.[22] To the extent that the Nazi movement is commonly seen as the ultimate in virulent, unacceptable nationalism, this juxtaposition serves to cognitively reinforce multilateralist norms by radicalizing the dissonant nationalist norms.

The second approach weakens the link between multilateralism and the undermining of legitimate nationalism. One of the common ways in which this is done allows globalization to be interpreted by assumption in a manner that is not dissonant with national self-interest and autonomy. This is the way that the rational structuralist approach to multilateralism, often referred to as "neoliberal institutionalism" or simply "institutionalism," deals with norm incompatibility.[23] The neoliberal institutionalist approach assumes a national interest that is most efficiently furthered by multilateral cooperation. If liberal nationalism is assumed to favor multilateral cooperation, or at least the sorts of

---

[21] Patrick 2018: x.   [22] Ruggie 1992.
[23] The seminal work of this approach is Keohane 1984. The defining assumptions of this approach include rationality, state-centrism, and collective-action problems.

economic goals best furthered by multilateral cooperation, then any state that does not favor these goals is by definition illiberally nationalist, or as James Fearon phrases it, "pathological."[24] Globalization and liberal nationalism thereby become compatible by definition, by distancing an assumed national interest from the idea of a national interest as other than the sum of the economic interests of its citizens.

An example of this sort of neoliberal compatibility-by-assumption can be seen in the standard argument for free trade. Macroeconomic theory tells us that multilateral free trade should benefit the general welfare, defined as total economic output. Therefore, if a state does not support multilateral free trade, it must be acting against the common good and therefore against the good of the nation. The possibility that either the theory is wrong, or that welfare might be defined other than by economic output, is assumed away, and with it dissonance between nationalist and social contract norms.[25] We see the same effect in practice in the EU, with integrationists (and the European Commission) dedicated to neoliberal functionalism within Europe, leaving little room for any nationalism that does not conform with neoliberal norms (although at the same time being much more accepting of nationalist norms as they might apply at the European level).[26]

Those who oppose globalization (or aspects of it) often use similar techniques to deal with the tension between nationalist and social contract norms, but from different perspectives. Opponents of neoliberal globalization are, in effect, arguing for a renationalization (or relocalization) of international politics and international political economy,[27] an argument dissonant with some interpretations of a globalized social contract norm. Distancing the processes of neoliberal globalization from social contract norms can be done by focusing on the more communitarian continental variants of social contract theory at the expense of the autonomous individuality of the English model. In this view, it is the neoliberalism that has come into international relations under the guise of globalization, rather than globalization itself, that is being criticized: a more communitarian view of the social contract would not be dissonant with nationalist norms.[28]

[24] Fearon 1995.   [25] E.g., Bhagwati 1991.
[26] With predictable results on political identification; see Fligstein, Polyakova, and Sandholtz 2012.
[27] E.g., Mander and Goldsmith 1996.
[28] E.g., Broadhead 2002 and Paehlke 2002.

In the case of Brexit, contrarily, some opponents of the form of multilateralism that the European Union represents argue that it hinders rather than aids neoliberal globalization.[29] From this perspective, leaving the EU would allow the United Kingdom greater freedom to enter into a range of bilateral agreements to liberalize international trade and commerce. This argument seems at first glance to pit two versions of contractualist norms against each other, but upon closer examination it is in fact an example of decreasing normative dissonance by disconnecting a behavior (contracting international agreements) from the underlying dissonant norm (the collective sovereign ownership of universal international regulation).

Weakening the link between the process being criticized, globalization, and the dissonant norm, social contract, is also sometimes done by focusing on questions of democratic process. Democracy as currently practiced to a large degree comes to us through social contract theory; they are part of the same general norm set. Yet opponents of globalization often focus exclusively on democracy, minimizing other aspects of the social contract (such as due process and the rule of law) in ways that are generally not done in domestic political discourse. For example, many criticisms of international judicial and monetary institutions, such as the WTO's Dispute Settlement Mechanism and the International Monetary Fund (IMF), focus on their lack of democratic process.[30] Yet the equivalent domestic processes, courts and central banks, are intentionally undemocratic and are more likely to be accepted as justifiably so.

Similarly, international organizations are often criticized for not having directly elected executives and not having legislators elected by the population at large.[31] However, the former is true of parliamentary systems generally, and of a wide variety of administrative and executive organizations within most governments. The latter is true in any direct-election (as opposed to proportional representation) system. The legislative functions of international organizations are fulfilled, by and large, by representatives of governments, which in turn are supposed to represent their populations, much like the legislative functions in most democratic legislatures. There is a problem of representatives of countries where the government is not democratic, but this problem

---

[29] See, e.g., Paterson 2017.   [30] E.g., Korten 2001: 169; Weber 2001.
[31] See Moravcsik 2004 for an overview of this argument.

is rarely at the core of critiques of harmonization.[32] In other words, with respect both to the executive and judicial functions of international organizations, and with respect to their legislative functions, normative dissonance is addressed by holding international society to standards that are not applied to national society.

Thus the techniques for dealing with normative dissonance suggested by the literature on cognitive dissonance are to be found in both the multilateralism and the globalization discourses. In the former discourse, the techniques are used to reinforce social contract norms against dissonant nationalist norms; in the latter, the converse is true. But this pattern of normative dissonance is not just a matter of two sides to an argument talking past each other. People can participate in both discourses at the same time. Because the discursive results of normative dissonance are being driven by cognitive self-defense mechanisms, they serve to allow individuals to hold two dissonant norms at the same time without admitting to their mutual incompatibility. Normative dissonance means that discourses are available to individuals that allow them to participate in pro-multilateralism and anti-globalization discourses at the same time, each discourse engaging in a normative distancing from the opposite direction, without needing to accept the contradictions between the two discourses.

Interference and Responsibility

A story of normative dissonance can also be told about questions regarding who is recognized as the person of the sovereign, which provides the second promised example. Chapter 5 looks at the evolution over time of norms legitimating claims of sovereignty, claims to be recognized by the community of sovereigns as representing a state. These norms have moved from focusing on the family claims of the monarch to claims ranging from control of territory to respect for human rights. Such claims for recognition by the community of sovereigns are important in the practice of sovereignty in the contemporary international system; if successful, they give the claimant extensive rights to resources, to legitimate military activity, and to diplomatic representation. Much of the value of being a sovereign and member of

---

[32] But see Nye 2001.

the sovereignty cartel is therefore externally (internationally) guaranteed rather than being purely domestically generated.

This observation suggests a tension among three contemporary norms of sovereign property. The first is the norm that sovereignty guarantees to the actor (as distinct from the state) identified as sovereign by the community of sovereigns the property rights to resources and to the legitimate use of force, property rights that are not only respected by but also enforced by the sovereignty cartel. The second norm is the responsibility of states to respect the human rights of its citizens, ranging from the responsibility to abjure war crimes and crimes against humanity, to the responsibility to respect constitutional forms of political representation and expression. The third norm is against external intervention "in matters which are essentially within the domestic jurisdiction of any state."[33] All three norms can be found not only in the quotidian practice of contemporary international relations but also, and frequently, in international law as formally accepted by all full members of the sovereignty cartel.

One could make an argument for the compatibility of any two of these three norms. Domestic jurisdiction can be defined as not including state behavior that fails to respect human rights, allowing the possibility of a clear line at which external intervention is legitimate. One could similarly limit property rights to resources in situations where acting on those rights threatens specified human rights. There is little direct conflict between the norm against intervention and the norm of sovereign rights to resources.

However, the normative calculus becomes more fraught when all three norms are considered at the same time in the context of questions about who is sovereign, who gets to represent the state. The process of choosing a sovereign in an era of popular sovereignty should be an essentially internal affair, governed by the domestic constitutional structures of the state in question. When a claimant to sovereignty is clearly in breach of the norm of respecting domestic constitutional structures, such as when incumbents transparently rig elections or when members of the military stage a coup, the international community has been known to intervene. So far, this story is compatible with the clear line between autonomy and human rights at which external intervention is legitimate.

[33] United Nations 1945, Article 2 (7).

But the story is complicated by the norm of sovereign ownership of resources and of the exclusive sovereign right to the means of violence. This norm undermines the extent to which the determination of who is sovereign is in fact a domestic affair, in that it consists of the community of sovereigns privileging the existing internationally recognized sovereign with respect to alternative claimants. In other words, in any given situation in which there are multiple claimants to be the sovereign, the international community grants to one claimant control over the cash flow from natural resources and the right to maintain (and equip on the international arms market) military force and denies these things to the other claimants. When domestic constitutional structures are sufficiently robust, these sovereign rights make little difference, because the person of the sovereign cannot use these rights directly to subvert domestic political processes. Phrased differently, effective sovereignty is sufficiently diffused throughout the political structure that it is difficult to use it to subvert that structure.

When domestic constitutional structures are less robust, however, when the resources of sovereign right, both financial and military, can be used effectively to subvert or undermine constitutional structures (or when those structures do not exist in a meaningful way in the first place), sovereign right in effect means that the international community is interfering in domestic politics in a conservative way, by privileging the existing sovereign over alternative claimants. The sovereignty cartel can switch its recognition to an alternative claimant, but in doing so, it is interfering to the same extent by granting to the alternative claimant the property rights of sovereignty. The community of sovereigns can also disagree on whom to recognize as the legitimate claimant who should be granted sovereign property rights; this can often lead to violence, as can be seen in Libya in much of its post-2011 civil war.

Phrased differently, when there is no tension in practice between the norm of noninterference and the political rights of citizens in determining who is recognized as the sovereign in particular instances, the enforcement of sovereign property rights by the sovereignty cartel has no necessary effect on political outcomes. However, when there is a tension, then the enforcement of those rights in principle constitutes an interference in the domestic affairs of that state. One norm calls for keeping out of the domestic process of choosing a sovereign, and the other explicitly chooses sides. The norms are in direct conflict with each other.

The normative dissonance created by this conflict often generates the kind of cognitive and discursive coping mechanisms that theories of cognitive dissonance would suggest. One key mechanism is to ignore the dissonance by failing to acknowledge that external enforcement of the norm of sovereign property rights is in effect choosing sides in a domestic dispute. An obvious example of this move can be found in a statement by Jeremy Corbyn, then leader of the opposition Labour Party in the United Kingdom, opposing "outside interference" in Venezuela's 2019 constitutional crisis,[34] as if having the military, armed by the international community,[35] controlled by one sovereign claimant in that crisis did not already constitute interference. More broadly, though, a narrow focus on free and fair election processes in legitimating the identification of sovereigns in countries that are in democratic transition ignores the broader advantage that sovereign right can give incumbency in states where the institutional structure of politics and law is weak.[36]

Another mechanism for addressing normative dissonance in this situation is by only selectively deploying norms of sovereign responsibility in legitimating intervention in the domestic affairs of states. To a significant extent, this selectivity is both strategic and hypocritical, as suggested by the arc of debate on the concept of responsibility to protect.[37] But there is more to it than intentional hypocrisy. There is, among other things, a strong status quo bias. We are much more likely to see new threats to human rights than ongoing denials of those rights. A military coup can delegitimize a government, for example, but the same stigma does not apply to a sovereign regime that came to power through military means decades ago. A sovereign found to be cheating in an election can attract more opprobrium than a sovereign who does not hold elections in the first place.[38] Events, in other words, are much more likely to make our normative radar than nonevents. In the case of nonevents, normative dissonance is minimized by simply not seeing normatively problematic practice.

A third mechanism is distancing norms of who has legitimate claim to be sovereign from norms of what sovereigns can legitimately do. As

---

[34] Guardian 2019.
[35] In the sense that the military's weapons were mostly bought from international vendors that do not sell to non-state actors.
[36] See, e.g., Kelley 2008.   [37] For a sympathetic treatment, see Bellamy 2014.
[38] Kelley 2008.

an example, the international community can censure Bashar al-Assad for war crimes without retracting recognition of his claim as legitimate representative of Syrian sovereignty.[39] That recognition both enables the war crimes and helps to keep him in power. His behavior throughout the Syrian civil war suggests that his control of the sovereign property rights of Syria was considerably more important to him than any censure for abusing his sovereign position. And yet, the norm of human rights that plays a constitutional role in sovereignty was applied to him by the sovereignty cartel (albeit very unevenly) to question the conduct of his rule but not his right to rule in the first place. Normative dissonance worked in this case by distancing a particular behavior (war crimes) from the broader underlying norm (the constitution of sovereignty).

As a practical political matter, the pattern of dissonance discussed in this section tends only to come into play when there are credible alternative claimants to the role of representative of state sovereignty. At other times, the question of who is sovereign is governed by inertia: someone must represent the sovereignty of a recognized state within the sovereignty cartel, so in the absence of a challenger, the incumbent remains in place. The existence of credible alternative claimants in situations that create normative dissonance may be relatively rare, but it can also nonetheless be illuminating for questions of the normative structure of sovereignty (as well as being significant, sometimes critically important, moments for the countries involved).

Conclusions

The key theoretical conclusion of this chapter is that, quite simply, norms need not be mutually compatible. Conflicting generally accepted intersubjective ideas about legitimate governance can be held by the same groups of people at the same time. While there is no strong argument in the literature on norms in international relations that these norms need be compatible, few scholars have discussed the problem explicitly. The study of how norms work in international relations requires looking not only at the effects of individual norms and norm

---

[39] As of the time of writing, the United Nations still recognizes Assad's appointee, Bashar Ja'afari, as permanent representative of the Syrian Arab Republic, six years after concluding, in UN Security Council Resolution 2118, that the state had used chemical weapons.

sets, but also at the processes of interaction among norm sets, whether or not they are mutually compatible. The metaphor of normative dissonance is one way of doing so, but other ways are necessary as well to get at the effects of norm interaction that cannot be aggregated from the individual level.

More specifically to the study of sovereignty, the normative dissonance between the different understandings of property underlying contemporary norms of sovereignty points to a real problem with the discourses about globalization and multilateralism. It suggests that many of the disputes about the course and development of contemporary international organization are simply not resolvable, because the norms that they draw on really are to an extent mutually incompatible. Nor is this normative dissonance expressed as a debate between a pro-multilateralism camp and an anti-globalization camp, in which the two camps speak past rather than to each other. To the extent that the politically median participant in some contemporary polities participates in both discourses concurrently, discussion of global governance will remain not just contested but internally contradictory. As long as both nationalism and the neoliberal variant of the social contract remain core elements of the normative structure of global politics, the conflict between these norms will likely continue to play itself out as a profound dissatisfaction about the nature and course of a globalized international political economy.

The explicit recognition of patterns of normative dissonance in these discourses can be useful in addressing this subliminal dissatisfaction by bringing to the fore some of the points of tension that generate the dissatisfaction. Such recognition, for example, reminds those who are supportive of international organizations as engines of harmonization that nationalism is not an atavistic idea that is going away. Liberal nationalism is a key component of the normative structure of contemporary sovereignty and of the international system of which intergovernmental organizations are a part. In fact, liberal nationalism is undergoing a rehabilitation in places like Germany and Japan, where for a generation nationalism of any kind was considered problematic. Such a recognition points out to those who consider harmonization to be problematic that processes of international harmonization are not as far removed from accepted patterns of domestic governance in liberal democracies as they are often portrayed. More generally, it suggests to participants in both discourses that successfully merging the two requires overcoming the psychological tendencies associated with dissonance and tackling the question of norm incompatibility directly and communicatively. In other words, if we are to succeed at what Jürgen Habermas calls communicative reasoning,[40] we must be able to reason about, rather than subconsciously marginalize, norm conflict.

More broadly, both normative incompatibility and normative dissonance suggest that questions of both what the rights and responsibilities of sovereignty are and who is the legitimate sovereign are in principle not definitively resolvable. A resort to the cognitive mechanisms of normative dissonance in discourses of sovereignty suggests that participants in those discourses, while they may prioritize particular norms over others in specific instances, decisions, and practices, are not willing to formally eschew conflicting norms at the level of principle. It is not that there are no first principles in thinking about norms of sovereignty; it is that there are too many. Choosing among which norms of sovereignty to use in both informing and legitimating practices of sovereignty therefore both is and will remain contextual, political, and contingent. It is mechanisms like normative dissonance, which defuse tension among underlying norms of sovereignty, that allow the sovereignty cartel to succeed despite being built on an internally contradictory set of property rights claims.

[40] Habermas 1984. See also Risse 2000.

9 Conclusions

State sovereignty is complicated. It is not a specific thing, reduceable to a simple definition or concept. Nor is a sovereign states system reduceable to a set of component nation-states. Rather, sovereignty is a set of interrelated relationships and concepts that collectively underpin the contemporary international system. One lens through which to look at this set of things is provided by the analytic category of property rights, as intersubjective understandings, norms, and rules about what sovereigns have both rights and responsibilities to. What is clearer through this lens than through others is that sovereignty in the contemporary international system is not a stable background condition of international relations. It is valuable property, and in order to maintain that value, sovereigns act as a cartel to enforce their exclusive rights to sovereign property.

This lens has yielded several specific pieces of analysis across the chapters of this book. This piecemeal analysis leaves two tasks for a concluding chapter – first, to bring the pieces together into a coherent bigger picture, and second, to address the question that all works of analysis should answer: "So what?" What is learned from this analysis that we did not already know? This chapter works on these tasks in five sections. The first sets the stage by starting where so many discussions of state sovereignty start, the Peace of Westphalia, and discussing the relationship between the Peace as history and the Peace as metaphor. The second reviews the argument about different kinds of property and different kinds of property rights, and how these different kinds create both normative tension and a need for a sovereignty cartel. The final three address the "So what?" question in different ways, from the perspective of the sovereign states system in general, from the perspective of the global south specifically, and from the perspective of different species of international relations theorist.

Reifying Westphalia

In making the argument that we should focus less on the Peace of Westphalia in understanding contemporary state sovereignty, I manage to focus on it quite a bit in this book. On the one hand, simply ignoring it would make the case much more clearly that we can understand the contemporary international system without reifying a set of treaties signed almost a half millennium ago, which involved only a small corner of the world and very different forms of political authority than those that currently predominate. But Westphalia is the elephant in the room; it is so embedded in discussions of the contemporary sovereign states system that disentangling the myth from the Peace in a way that preempts misleading metaphors is necessary. The best response to reifying Westphalia, in other words, is to address the Peace rather than to ignore it.

There are three key dangers in reifying Westphalia. The first is that it leaves the impression that sovereignty is a straightforward thing, easily definable in a sentence or two. The danger in easy definition is that it reduces discussion of sovereignty to one dimension, taking from us a rich source of ideas and observations about how international politics work. It also leaves us with a single dimension that may not be particularly relevant to the aspect of international politics we wish to study, or for that matter to contemporary international relations at all. Nor does it give us a reasoned logic for focusing on that dimension beyond pseudo-historical metaphor. Even if the dimension is drawn from what is written in the Peace (and a single definition would need to be drawn from a narrow and simplistic reading of the text), it is not clear why that particular text should form the basis of our analysis of international relations half a millennium later.

This last point suggests the second danger of beginning with a Westphalian metaphor, that rather than being historically anchored in a set of events that happened almost 400 years ago, it might not be historically anchored at all. The claim that Westphalia guaranteed the treaty rights of sovereigns is, for example, historically tenuous; the claim that it guaranteed domestic autonomy to sovereigns is simply historically wrong. And yet this latter claim about what sovereignty means often uses a reified mythical Westphalia as justification. The resort to Westphalia as metaphor short-circuits both normative discussion, of what we *should* be talking about when we talk about sovereignty, and empirical discussion, of what we observe as the practices of sovereignty in contemporary international politics. Furthermore, this use of Westphalian myth as metaphor (rather than as history) in the definition of sovereignty leaves no basis for challenging that definition; to build a discourse of politics on myth empowers the mythmaker to define the terms of that discourse.

The third danger of reifying Westphalia is that it implies that the fundamental structures of international relations do not change over time. If "Westphalian sovereignty" is a thing, it is presumably the same thing that it was in 1648. This limits any discussion of change in sovereignty, or of the role of sovereignty in international relations, to questions of stronger or weaker; it short-circuits discussion of change in what the thing itself is. The use of the Westphalian metaphor thereby prevents us from seeing major changes in the practice of sovereignty. Furthermore, it conflates the politics of the northwest corner of Europe half a millennium ago with the global politics of today.

Two examples of such change over the course of the twentieth century illustrate this point: sovereign equality and sovereign universality. Sovereignty at the time of the Peace of Westphalia conferred a right to negotiate internationally to certain categories of ruler in the Holy Roman Empire but did not imply a formal or legal equality among sovereigns. This idea of legal equality did not fully develop until the rise of formal intergovernmental institutions, and with them the need for institutional voting rules. Sovereign universality, meanwhile, developed in the context of decolonization. The idea would have been anathema to the European imperial powers of the nineteenth century, and meaningless to seventeenth-century sovereigns to whom much of the world was simply unknown. And yet both formal sovereign equality and sovereign universality are constitutive of contemporary international relations.

What then can we take from the Peace of Westphalia as a set of historical documents rather than as myth? Reading the treaties that constitute the Peace as historical artifacts can inform us about the state of international law and the normative structure of international relations in parts of Europe in the middle of the seventeenth century. This can be useful both as an exercise in process tracing, helping us to understand a stage in the development of international relations, and as an exercise in comparative statics, helping us to understand what has changed between then and now. As historical context, it merits restating that the treaties were not self-conscious attempts to rewrite the legal and normative basis of international politics. They were attempts to end a war and mostly reflected, rather than changed, conditions on the ground at the time. They were, phrased differently, attempts to legally specify the property rights that various rulers (princes, kings, emperors, and states-general) laid claim to in the shadow of the war.

As it pertains to the arguments in this book specifically, the process-tracing exercise yields a few interesting observations. Westphalia is notable in that it does tend to cast the property rights of rulers in a less hierarchical, less feudal mold than earlier major European treaties and specifies some of those rights rather than assuming customary feudal rights. It thereby serves as an important marker (although by no means either the beginning or the end of the process) of creating an international relations of nonhierarchical and legally equivalent sovereigns, rather than one of customary and nested obligations. It also serves as evidence that sovereignty has long been discussed as a set of property rights; the starting point of the argument this book is in this sense not at all novel.

Furthermore, the two different understandings of property rights developed throughout the book, as the right to exclude and the right to participate, can both be found in the Peace. In explicitly limiting the rights of princes to enforce religion within their territories, the Peace implicitly recognized an understanding of property as exclusion, and of that right to exclude as circumscribed. However, the Peace also guarantees rights to participate internationally as explicit property rights of sovereignty. The specific property rights of sovereignty may well have changed substantially since the seventeenth century, but some of the underlying tensions in the ways in which sovereignty is understood as a right have remained. Reading Westphalia suggests that in studying the modern states system we can usefully ask how this tension between different understandings of property has changed over the years, and how it is being worked out in contemporary international relations. But it cannot tell us details about the specific content of sovereign right in contemporary international relations.

There have been several such changes over the course of the past century or so. The development of norms of human rights as counterclaims to sovereign right is a key example. Two other changes noted earlier, formal legal equality and the idea of sovereign universality, are similarly fundamental to understanding contemporary international politics. Neither of these are necessary developments of seventeenth-century European international politics or international law; they are all in ways products of the globalization of that system in the context of the popularization of sovereignty. They are both, though, fundamental to understanding how sovereign property rights work in contemporary international relations and how the sovereignty cartel functions to guarantee them.

Sovereignty as Property

Despite this digression through Westphalia, however, the core argument of this book is not about the historical development of the property rights aspects of sovereignty, but about property rights as a lens on contemporary state sovereignty. These property rights of sovereignty are examined here on two axes: what sovereign property is understood to mean and whose property sovereignty is. With respect to the former of these axes, what property means is understood here through two metaphors, variously referred to as the Roman and the English, property as exclusion and property as contract, the right to control and the right to participate, nationalism and multilateralism. These metaphors are by no means exclusive to norms of sovereignty, and the normative tensions they illustrate in international relations likely have analogues throughout capitalist economic systems. But that is a discussion for another book. The key point here is that while norms of property rights are constitutive of state sovereignty, what those rights are and what they mean is normatively contested.

With respect to the latter of these axes, these rights make sovereignty valuable property but do not always answer the question of whose property it is. There is in principle a clearer norm here than with the question of what we mean by property in a states system context – popular sovereignty, the idea that the state is the property of the people. But this norm in turn leaves unanswered the question of what we should understand "the people" to be and is furthermore layered on top of several centuries of different answers to the question of whose property sovereignty is, some of which still have normative resonance within the international system. Questions of "whose property" do not necessarily get asked that often, given that the identification of most sovereigns most of the time in contemporary international relations go largely uncontested. When they do get asked, however, the answers are often not normatively straightforward.

Since both axes on which the property rights of sovereignty are examined here represent sets of norms that operate concurrently rather than a range of possible outcomes, combining the two axes does not yield a neat, or even meaningful, 2×2 chart. The result of combining them is not a quadrant. Rather, it is a muddle, and from this muddle emerge two conclusions. The first is that maintaining this internally inconsistent set of rights requires active effort, which I call the sovereignty cartel. The second is that the internal inconsistencies are neither an aberration nor resolving themselves, but are an integral feature of the system, thereby creating normative dissonance.

Seeing sovereignty through the lens of property rights helps us to see both why sovereigns need a sovereignty cartel, and how it operates. Any small group of actors who arrogate to themselves a set of property rights to the exclusion of other actors will be tempted to collude to both maintain control of and increase the value of those rights. The rights in question are based on (at least) two different understandings of property, which translate into international relations as the right of individual sovereigns to control within their own borders and the right of sovereign states as a group to govern globally. The cartel acts to support both sets of rights, the former by arrogating to sovereigns exclusive rights to the use of force and the latter by claiming and enforcing a universal right to regulate.

These two sets of property rights are each valuable in their own right, and therefore each is worth colluding to reinforce. To an extent, however, and for reasons discussed in various places in this volume, they can also be mutually contradictory. This normative contradiction means that the system of sovereign property rights cannot rely on a compelling internal logic to support it. Nor can it rely on its structural position to replicate itself over the long term, because that position is built on a set of internal contradictions. This lack of a cohesive internal logic makes a strong cartel that much more important if the sovereign states system is to replicate itself.

This is where normative dissonance comes into the story. A sovereignty cartel could in principle replicate the system by simply overpowering a set of logical and discursive internal contradictions with brute force. This is in essence what Stephen Krasner argues in

Sovereignty: Organized Hypocrisy.[1] But such a system would be brittle, as political systems built on brute force tend to be. Better to simply pretend, on a day-to-day basis, that the contradictions are not there. Or, rather than say "pretend," with its connotations of conscious choice to build a mental reality distinct from one's physical surroundings, I should say instead act as if those contradictions are not there, by relying on a set of cognitive tools the study of which have been a staple of both political and cognitive psychology for decades.

Both a rights-owners' cartel and normative dissonance are, I would argue, general features of any system of politics built on a general recognition of a set of sovereign or exclusive rights accruing to some but not all actors. But then, any such system is likely to contain normative inconsistencies; large-scale social structures are always likely to be more complicated and multifaceted than can be captured by any single internally consistent set of norms. Norms will, therefore, come into conflict with each other. And in any system in which a set of rights accrues to some but not all actors, the privileged actors will need to collude in some way to protect those rights or risk losing them. In this sense, it would be surprising if a sovereignty cartel was not operating in the contemporary international system.

The cartel and the dissonant norms are in a way mutually supporting and mutually enabling. The dissonant norms make cartel behavior more necessary to support a system of rights that is normatively constitutionally weak. At the same time the cartel supports the continuation of the normative system despite its constitutional weakness by reinforcing the norms and the consequential rights claims with a set of practices that exclude other actors from those rights. It is through the cognitive processes suggested by the metaphor of normative dissonance that incompatible discourses of sovereignty can coexist without undermining the underlying norms. And it is through cartelizing behaviors that those norms can be reconstituted through practice.

The Sovereignty Cartel

The cartel has a set of straightforward effects, in which states collude to collectively monopolize the property rights of sovereignty. The

---

[1] Krasner 1999.

language of rights, of cartels, and of monopoly should not, however, be taken to indicate that states, as selfish actors distinct from the broader societies they govern and represent, are working primarily to arrogate to themselves as a group the governance equivalent of monopoly profits. There are good reasons, rooted in ideas like good governance and human rights, for limiting the right to the use of force in the enforcement of a political order (which is what sovereign property rights ultimately mostly come down to). And many participants in the day-to-day practices of the sovereignty cartel no doubt believe that what they are doing is participating in good governance rather than in the monopolization of property rights. The argument here is not that the sovereignty cartel is necessarily a bad thing. Rather, it is that the cartel metaphor allows us to understand international relations differently.

The members of the sovereignty cartel collude to reinforce their claim to the exclusive right both to the use of force and to regulation internationally. These claims are universal in scope, as they address all use of force and all regulation. They are not, however, universal in content, in that sovereigns in the contemporary states system accept formal limitations (not always honored in practice) on how, and against whom, they can use force, and the requirement (again, not always honored in practice) that they submit to the regulations they agree to. These property rights are claimed less through the mechanisms of what might be called high politics and more through the quotidian practices of diplomacy, multilateralism, and international law.

Furthermore, these are claims to right, not to necessary implementation. States may allow other actors access to the mechanisms of force or delegate the right to regulate domestically, subject to their international commitments. They may also simply not have the governance capacity to maintain a monopoly of force or to implement regulation domestically. And the right to regulate does not necessarily imply a desire to regulate, leaving space open for private authority in global governance. Whether this authority is in the form of creating standards or providing public goods such as refugee relief or food aid, however, it remains an authority that is either voluntary or delegated. Standards, for example, are voluntary unless sovereigns require them and lose their viability if sovereigns forbid them. Private authority in this sense is more about states not accepting responsibility for certain areas of governance rather than states ceding rights to them.

What is most notable about the sovereignty cartel is not that sovereign states claim these rights for themselves, but that they are willing to accord the same rights, as a category, to other recognized sovereign states, as a category, while not according them to anyone else. For example, while the United States (understood in this context as a corporate actor representing a state sovereignty) might not like what Iran does with its military, it recognizes that Iran (again, recognized as a corporate actor representing a state sovereignty) has a right to maintain that military, despite describing Iran as an enemy. Its primary complaint about Iranian military adventurism is that it supports uses of force by actors that do not formally represent sovereign states (and are therefore, by the logic of contemporary sovereignty, terrorists). The United States also recognizes the right of Ireland to be a legitimate headquarters for companies that do little real business there, even as it pressures those companies to be less enthusiastic about using Ireland as a tax haven.

Two upshots of the sovereignty cartel worth noting at this point shed light on aspects of contemporary international relations. The first has to do with claims to regulatory universality and the internal contradictions in the normative basis for these claims. Sovereign property rights both have states individually responsible for regulation within their borders and of their citizens, and states collectively responsible for regulation globally. However, there is a necessary gap between these claims to sovereign right. In part, this gap results from imperfect implementation of the claimed rights. States are neither able to perfectly implement regulation domestically nor agree on comprehensive regulation internationally. There are holes where states claim the right to regulate but are not able to do so effectively.

More fundamentally, however, the gap results from the tension between the two claims in a world in which other (economic) actors operate internationally. The claim to universal regulation relies on states, and only states, as the guarantors of regulation within their territories and for their citizens. It requires, in other words, that states cede to other states the right to regulate actors in some circumstances that they themselves regulate in others. This necessarily leaves interstices between national and universal regulation, where non-state actors can engage in regulatory arbitrage, and where even actors that want consistent regulatory standards can have trouble finding them. These interstices in the sovereign states system house a range of activities from the illegal to the self-regulated, and from activities that most states would prefer to prevent (like human trafficking) to activities that most states encourage (like banking). They have in common that they intersect with the gaps between national and universal regulation.

The key point here is that, seen through the lens of sovereign property rights, these interstices in the states system are not solely the result of poor implementation or political ill will. They are inherent to the normative structure of the property rights claims of contemporary sovereignty. They are in a sense the pressure valves that release some of the tension created between different kinds of claims of sovereign property right. This is the case whether the activities themselves are ones that states would like to eliminate but cannot do effectively (such as the narcotics trade), ones that states prefer to not have full regulatory control over (such as international shipping), or ones that states want individual control over in some instances and collective control over in others (such as international banking). These interstices, where both illicit activity and private authority happen, are not indicators that sovereignty is getting weaker. They are how the system lubricates the friction between what states claim collectively as sovereign right and what states undertake individually as foreign policy.

The second upshot of the sovereignty cartel worth noting at this point has to do with what might be called the empowerment effects of sovereignty. Among the property rights of contemporary sovereignty are exclusive rights to the use of military force and to regulation, but also what one might consider more traditional property rights, to property understood as material resources. Being recognized as sovereign by the other members of the cartel not only gives an actor a seat at the international table, it also offers assistance by the other members of the cartel in maintaining the exclusivity of the means of force and in profiting from those resources. It means that not only will the other members of the cartel recognize the sovereign's rights to the means of force and to royalties on its country's resources, they will often sell the weapons and enforce the sovereign's right to royalties against their own nationals.

The sovereignty cartel, in other words, in choosing to recognize specific actors as sovereign, empowers them at the expense of other actors that would use force, or regulate, or sell resources on an international market. When states have constitutional governments chosen by mechanisms seen as legitimate by the bulk of the population and have the governance capacity to maintain a legitimate monopoly of force in the enforcement of a domestic order, these empowerment effects in and of themselves likely do not make a major difference to political outcomes. In other cases, however, where the sovereign is not seen as legitimate by a significant portion of the population, where it survives on externally enforced rents, or when it does not have the governance capacity to enforce its writ throughout its territory, the empowerment effects of the sovereignty cartel may play a significant role in keeping the sovereign in power. These effects may also play a major role in the personal finances of the sovereign, such as when petroleum royalties or multilateral loans that are supposed to go to national coffers disappear into grand palaces or foreign bank accounts.

These empowerment effects mean that it is worth fighting over who gets to be considered to be the sovereign by the cartel. They also mean that the international community is necessarily integrally involved in disputes over who is identified as sovereign, because it has given the actor it identifies as sovereign a structural advantage. That actor has access to weapons and often to a funding stream from the sale of resources (that the actor may not be in any way involved in extracting) that are not available to alternate claimants to sovereignty. So when outside observers suggest, for example, that a political dispute is internal and therefore that outside actors should keep out of it, they are in fact taking the side of the incumbent sovereign, whom the international community is, in effect, supporting in the dispute through the recognition of that actor's sovereign right, and the political, financial, and military resources that come with that right.

Both of these upshots, that the interstices of sovereignty are integral to the contemporary states system and that the sovereignty cartel has the effect of empowering existing sovereigns at the expense of their competitors, suggest that it is both simplistic and inaccurate to think of the system as the interaction effect of a set of independent state actors. In important ways the cartel is constitutive of the sovereigns within it, and of the spaces both separating and connecting those sovereigns. The cartel makes it more difficult to weaken the role of states in international relations, but at the same time makes arguments for greater national autonomy from the multilateral system conceptually problematic.

The View from the South

To this point in the argument there has been little discussion of the role of the global south per se in the sovereignty cartel. There has, in places, been discussion of bigger and smaller states and of states more or less able to implement regulation domestically, but these axes do not map neatly onto north versus south. There has been some mention of decolonization but at the same time lengthy discussion of the European roots of the sovereign states system. Where does the global south fit into this picture, and how does the sovereignty cartel affect it specifically?

There are several ways to answer these questions, none of them straightforward. The sovereignty cartel as it is now practiced has its roots in European international relations and law but cannot be simply understood as a European imposition on the rest of the world. Once again the Peace of Westphalia provides a useful point of departure for this argument. The Peace is, in the context of norms of sovereignty, notable for supporting the idea that sovereigns could, in some circumstances, negotiate and treat with each other as legal equals. This marked a break with earlier European patterns of formal political hierarchy, and also marked a difference with politics as practiced in most of the rest of the world at the time, where international relations were characterized either by some form of suzerainty and vassalage, or by the absence of formal legal structures. The contemporary international system owes its legal roots to this idea, and this debt helps to explain why it is that these understandings of property are central to contemporary global norms of sovereign property rights.

However, most of the norms that underpin the contemporary practices of state sovereignty are nowhere to be found in the Peace and would not have resonated with the negotiators of that Peace. Many of these were noted earlier in this chapter, and include popular sovereignty, multilateralism, and regulatory universality. Incorporated in all of these norms in some way is the underlying principle that sovereigns represent people, that all people should participate in a sovereignty, and that all international relations should be brought within the sovereign states system. These norms evolved over the course of the twentieth century; some core principles of contemporary sovereignty are newer than the metaphor of Westphalian sovereignty would suggest. They evolved in the shadow of the rise both of nationalism and republicanism, both in

Europe and elsewhere, in the nineteenth century, and of the two world wars in the first half of the twentieth. Most importantly in this context, they evolved in the context of decolonization. The contemporary international system is, in this sense, the result of the negotiation of norms of sovereign equality on the one hand and of self-determination on the other.[2]

In other words, the contemporary sovereign states system, while it has some legal roots in early modern European politics, is a global phenomenon in its development.[3] In particular, it is an outcome negotiated among existing and aspiring sovereigns. Seen in this light, questions about whether this system adequately represents the interests of the global south beg the question of whose interests in the global south – the populations that are supposed to be sovereign, or the sovereigns recognized by the cartel? The discussion of empowerment effects in the previous section suggests that the answer may not be the same for both groups. This is particularly the case in places in which indigenous systems of government were undermined by colonial processes that left little governance capacity in their place.

The sovereignty cartel can (not to say that it necessarily will) have the effect of improving the quality of governance that states can deliver to their citizens, particularly states on the lower end of governance capacity domestically and power resources internationally. It does so through the straightforward mechanism of giving all sovereigns, and therefore in principle through them all citizens, a formal voice and vote in multilateral fora, something that would not necessarily be the case in an international system built on norms that did not include legal personhood and legal equality of states. It does so by creating restrictions on uses of military force by other states, which afford states unable to defend themselves militarily some protection against the outside world. It does so by creating some financial opportunities for states, through mechanisms ranging from regulatory offshoring to the creation of the category of sovereign debt.

The cartel can also have the effect of improving the quality of governance in states with relatively little governance capacity by giving sovereigns the formal right to regulate, rights that are often actionable

---

[2] E.g., Branch 2012 and Grovogui 1996.
[3] See Helleiner 2014 for an example of the negotiation of sovereign universality as a global process.

in other states. For example, it gives states rights under international law to natural resources within their borders and the right to enforce those rights. Similarly, it gives states rights to create pollution standards and some mechanisms for encouraging foreign actors to respect those rights.[4] The presumption that states have these rights by no means, it is true, guarantees that they will be respected. But like norms governing uses of force by states against each other, sovereign property rights, the right to govern "matters which are essentially within the domestic jurisdiction of any state,"[5] create a baseline for behavior that empowers states to govern.

Of course, some states fail to avail themselves of these possibilities. When the international community does not accord a ruler the full rights of sovereignty, as was, for example, the case in Iraq between the two Gulf wars, the possibilities are diminished. In other cases, the failure may be due to a lack of governance resources, or simply a lack of competence on the part of the sovereign and the supporting actors in state institutions. More common, though, may be that the failure originates in a disjuncture between the governance demands of popular sovereignty and the property rights of the sovereign. This observation points to the second major empowerment effect of the sovereignty cartel; it empowers the sovereign, as recognized by the other members of the cartel, with respect to other actors within the country.

This empowerment effect has already been noted. It gives the sovereign the right to equip an army and denies that right to other actors. It gives the sovereign the right to resource royalties even if those resources are physically controlled by other actors. It gives the sovereign the right to regulate and to a voice at the international table, and denies these rights to other actors. All of these rights are valuable, and the military rights can be used to reinforce the economic and financial rights. The sovereign is supposed to use these rights for the benefit of all, but many use them to benefit themselves (this is not a contentious observation). Some states have institutional structures better able to control these misuses of sovereign right than others.

What does this have to say about the sovereignty cartel and the global south? It suggests that we should be careful to disaggregate

---

[4] An example of such a mechanism is prior informed consent, as found for example in the *Rotterdam Convention on the Prior Informed Consent Procedure for Certain Hazardous Chemicals and Pesticides in International Trade*.
[5] United Nations 1945, Article 2 (7).

The Sovereignty Cartel and International Relations Theory 177

questions of sovereignty as the distance between the rights claims of the sovereign and the governance needs of popular sovereignty get larger. The sovereignty cartel has been very good to sovereigns, including those of the global south. It has given many sovereigns the means to stay in power, while at the same time making them rich (this is by no means true only in the global south). It merits stressing again that these are, in many instances, effects of sovereign right granted by the cartel, rather than domestically generated capabilities. The cartel has been much less effective in ensuring both popular sovereignty and effective governance in states where colonialism undermined governance structures. The sovereignty cartel empowers rulers to the extent that those rulers retain recognition by the cartel as sovereign. Whether it improves life for populations at large depends on both the goodwill and the competence of the sovereign, as well as on the ability of the institutional structures of the state to temper the sovereign.

The Sovereignty Cartel and International Relations Theory

The final task of this chapter is to revisit some of the specific issues discussed in the introduction to the book. There are four sets of conclusions about the sovereignty cartel in contemporary international relations to be drawn in this context. For students of foreign policy, the cartel as a framing explains the willingness of state actors to defer to states as a category, but not to other categories of actors, in a wide variety of quotidian multilateral practices. For students of globalization it suggests the danger of extrapolating from an increased role for non-state actors in the system to a decline in sovereignty. For students of the social structure of the international system, it points to the importance of looking not only at norms, but at the processes through which they are reconstituted by actors. And for students of sovereignty, it suggests that sovereignty is not only complicated, it is internally contradictory as well.

Foreign Policy

The sovereignty cartel provides a straightforward answer to a number of questions about what states understood as corporate actors, and the individuals who work within them, do in the conduct of their international relations on a quotidian basis. They act to reconstitute the sovereign states system, as well as their own place within it. They do this by recognizing only states as legal equals and by engaging in the myriad forms of international law that give only states legal standing, by participating multilaterally, and by according to other states a presumptive right to regulate that they deny to all other actors. With rare exceptions they accept the premise that sovereigns speak for their countries even when there is considerable evidence to the contrary, and they recognize the rights of sovereigns to material resources even when it is clear that those sovereigns are corrupt.

At one level these activities are easy to take for granted because they are so deeply ingrained in the day-to-day practices of foreign policy. At another level, however, they seem curious; they cut against both realist assumptions that it is the power of states with respect to other states that drives outcomes in international relations and liberal prescriptions that foreign policy be driven by ethical considerations. The sovereignty cartel is a realist lens inasmuch as it assumes that sovereigns look to maintain their power but parts with realism in that it looks at collusion across, rather than competition among, sovereigns to this end. This distinction can help bridge some of the gap in the study of international relations between the high politics on which realists tend to focus and the complex web of international relationships that account for the bulk of what foreign policy practitioners do with their time.

This observation can be illustrated by looking at the cartel from a different angle, that of states legitimating economic activity in the interstices of sovereignty. That smaller or poorer states are willing to cash in on the value of their sovereignty by legitimating some forms of illicit international economic activity is not surprising. What existing literatures, such as that on offshoring, have more trouble explaining is why the core countries in the system, those countries that could assert far higher degrees of control over many interstitial behaviors if they chose, put up with the loss of control that results from the sale of sovereignty by regulatory havens. The explanation offered here is that the core countries prioritize the idea of the sovereign right of states over practical control because the legitimation afforded to their own general governance patterns by the normative/legal ideal of sovereign exclusivity is of greater importance to them than control over specific instances of illicit behavior. This is not always the case – the desire for control in some specific issue areas trumps the negative effects of asserting control on the idea of the right of states to regulate. But it is often the case.

The operation of a sovereign states system of governance built on conflicting norms of property rights necessarily leaves interstices between governance and economic activity. Unpacking the concept of sovereignty can tell us quite a bit about why states react the way they do to these interstices, but these reactions in turn can tell us quite a bit about how to unpack the concept of sovereignty. It can, for example, shed light on the relative importance different states place on different aspects of sovereignty, and on the costs and benefits of different interstitial activities. More broadly, it suggests that states do in practice accord considerable importance to maintaining the norm of sovereign regulatory universality.

Globalization and Sovereignty

By the late 1990s many globalization theorists were arguing that globalization was displacing sovereignty as the central organizing feature of international relations, an argument that is made less often these days. One could attribute the decline of globalization and reassertion of sovereignty-as-control in contemporary international relations to several causes: to a reaction against transnational terror after 9/11; to a populist backlash against the migration associated with globalization; to the rise of a China not beholden to Western political norms, among others. All of these no doubt contributed (and continue to contribute) as proximate causes. The lens of the sovereignty cartel, however, suggests that arguments that globalization was undermining sovereignty were overstated even in the 1990s. The cartel was stronger than those arguments gave it credit for, and it meant that the apparent decline of sovereignty was ephemeral.

The cartel ensured that the sovereign state was at the center of, rather than being displaced by, processes of globalization even at the apparent peak of those processes. Much as the "sovereignty at bay" literature of the 1970s pointed to a temporary negotiating weakness by some states as they adapted to new economic forces rather than a secular decline of sovereignty,[6] the globalization literature of the 1990s marked a period of renegotiation of sovereign property rights rather than a decline in those rights. The norm of sovereign regulatory universality came out of the 1970s stronger than it was at the

---

[6] For a critical overview, see Vernon 1981.

beginning of the period, and the cartel ensured that this norm remained intact throughout the rise and fall of ideological neoliberalism and the Washington Consensus in the 1990s and 2000s.

During this latter period, many states reevaluated the costs and benefits of regulating with respect to specific issues but at no point conceded their right to regulate collectively if they so chose. When, in the 1990s, international finance was not seen as threatening the system, it was to a large degree left to self-regulate. When it came in the 2000s to be seen as a threat, the cartel was easily able to reclaim a stronger regulatory role.[7] Environmental issues such as forestry standards were left to private authority,[8] but others such as hazardous chemicals were subjected to formal sovereign scrutiny through mechanisms like prior informed consent.[9] This is not a patterns of state authority in principle getting weaker. It is a pattern of change in when states chose to claim their authority.

One could read a pattern of zero-sum struggle between the forces of sovereignty and globalization into the international relations of the past half-century, in which the cartel gives sovereignty an edge that the forces of globalization cannot replicate. A more nuanced view of international relations, however, is yielded by seeing them as different patterns. Globalization neither undermines nor supports sovereignty necessarily, and the sovereignty cartel is compatible with a variety of both levels and types of globalization. Seeing globalization through the lens of the sovereignty cartel highlights the ways in which states encourage or discourage processes of globalization while maintaining sovereign right as a central organizing feature of those processes.

The Social Structure of the International System

This last observation points to the conclusions to be drawn from this project for students of the social structure of the international system. It is a commonplace assumption among this group of scholars that international relations are a product of the simultaneous effects of social structure on political agents and of those agents on the structure. Neither is ontologically prior; neither can be seen by itself as the starting point for the study of international relations. In practice,

---

[7] E.g., Drezner 2007.   [8] E.g., Gulbrandsen 2010.   [9] E.g., Selin 2010.

however, it is difficult to study this process of what many of these scholars call co-constitution. So most of these scholars either study the effects of structures on agents by, say, looking at static sets of norms, practices, or discourses and their effects on political agents, or by looking at the role of agents, understood as political entrepreneurs, in changing those structures.

These efforts are each perfectly reasonable in their own terms. But collectively they give the impression that social structures change only when there is a conscious and concerted effort to change them. They suggest that existing social structures live on of their own accord unless changed. The sovereignty cartel suggests, however, that the social structures of international relations do not automatically perpetuate themselves. They remain intact because, and to the extent that, political agents reconstitute them through practice and discourse, and they are in turn changed, sometimes quickly but often slowly and gradually, by this process of reconstitution. Moreover, there may be useful lessons to be learned about patterns of international politics in studying processes of reconstitution of these social structures.

The particular social structure that is the focus of this study is the set of property rights associated with state sovereignty. Looking at sovereign right through the lens of the reconstitution of norms highlights and helps to explain both the quotidian practices that reinforce sovereign personhood as the cornerstone of international law and the spaces in international relations that do not quite fit into international law. It shows how these rights can coevolve with, rather than be threatened by, economic globalization. And it helps us to understand how the sovereign state system as a particular form of political organization responds to changing conditions, both material and normative, and thereby makes of itself a formidable structure capable of adapting to, rather than being threatened by, such changes.

Sovereign property rights are only one lens of many through which to look at the social structure of international relations. Many of these lenses allow us to look not only at the structures themselves, but at their processes of reconstitution. From this perspective the argument about sovereignty specifically can be taken as an example of what can be learned by studying the reconstitution, rather than the creation or effects, of social structure. These rights are a useful lens through which to study international relations but are not a uniquely privileged way of doing so. The study of international relations is in this sense like astronomy or spying. Improving one's lenses helps, but the more lenses used, the better the view.

Sovereignty

For students of sovereignty the conclusions that can be drawn from the argument here, beyond the observation that sovereignty as social structure needs to be continually reconstituted through practice, is that it is worth complicating sovereignty, rather than simplifying it into an easily definable single thing. Easy definitions increase formal analytic tractability, perhaps, but at the cost of telling us much about what is actually happening in contemporary international relations. Assuming that sovereignty means a single thing does not allow us to see the multiple, and often contradictory, behaviors undertaken and claims made under its guise.

Looking at sovereignty through the lens of property rights makes some of these complications clearer. It shows us that different claims of sovereign right are built on different normative foundations, different understandings of property. These different foundations do not ultimately yield a single or even an internally coherent normative structure to sovereignty and are not reconcilable. Nor is one or another more or less correct, or authentic, or historically grounded. Practices and discourses of contemporary sovereignty are therefore not normatively consistent, nor can they be. Understanding these practices and discourses requires that we see them as inherently normatively muddled, rather than trying to understand them as derogations of some imagined pure form of sovereignty.

The concept of a sovereignty cartel suggests that, above all, sovereignty is political. It is not a purely legal or moral category, although it draws on both legal and moral claims for legitimacy. It is not a standard against which behavior can be judged, because of its internal contradictions. It is (among other things) a claim on exclusive rights to a set of behaviors and resources, a claim that needs to be continually maintained through political action. Looking at this political action, at how these claims are made and reinforced, rather than arguing about what sovereignty might mean in the abstract, is how the concept of sovereignty can be of most use to us in understanding contemporary international relations.

References

Aalberts, Tanja 2004. "The Sovereignty Game States Play: (Quasi-)states in the International Order," *International Journal for the Semiotics of Law* 17: 245–257.

Abraham, Itty and Willem van Schendel 2005. *Illicit Flows and Criminal Things: States, Borders, and the Other Side of Globalization*. Indiana University Press.

Abrahamian, Atossa Araxia 2015. *The Cosmopolites: The Coming of the Global Citizen*. Columbia Global Reports.

Agamben, Giorgio 1998. *Homo Sacer: Sovereign Power and Bare Life*. Stanford University Press.

Ahrensdorf, Peter 2000. "The Fear of Death and the Longing for Immortality: Hobbes and Thucydides on Human Nature and the Problem of Anarchy," *American Political Science Review* 94: 579–593.

Al-Atawneh, Muhammad 2009. "Is Saudi Arabia a Theocracy? Religion and Governance in Contemporary Saudi Arabia," *Middle Eastern Studies* 45: 721–737.

Alchian, Armen 1991. "Property Rights," in John Eatwell, Murray Milgate, and Peter Newman, eds. *The New Palgrave: The World of Economics*. Macmillan.

Allan, Bentley 2018. *Scientific Cosmology and International Orders*. Cambridge University Press.

Allison, Graham and Morton H. Halperin 1972. "Bureaucratic Politics: A Paradigm and Some Policy Implications," *World Politics* 24: 40–79.

Almond, Gabriel and Stephen Genco 1977. "Clouds, Clocks, and the Study of Politics," *World Politics* 29: 489–522.

Ambrosius, Lloyd 1991. *Wilsonian Statecraft: Theory and Practice of Liberal Internationalism during World War I*. Scholarly Resources.

Anderson, Benedict 1983. *Imagined Communities: Reflections on the Origins and Spread of Nationalism*. Verso.

Andreas, Peter 2000. *Border Games: Policing the U.S.–Mexico Divide*. Cornell University Press.

  2004. "Illicit International Political Economy: The Clandestine Side of Globalization," *Review of International Political Economy* 11: 641–652.

Antarctic Treaty 1959. *The Antarctic Treaty.* Conference on Antarctica.
Associated Press 2019. "Many Latin American Governments Support Venezuela's Guaido," *New York Times*, January 23.
Baker, Ray Stannard 1922. *Woodrow Wilson and World Settlement*, Vol. 1. Doubleday, Page.
Barber, Benjamin 1995. *Jihad vs. McWorld: How Globalism and Tribalism Are Reshaping the World.* Ballantine Books.
Barbey, Christophe 2015. "Non-Militarisation: Countries without Armies," The Ålands Islands Peace Institute.
Barkin, J. Samuel 1998. "The Evolution of the Constitution of Sovereignty and the Emergence of Human Rights Norms," *Millennium* 27: 229–252.
  2003. *Social Construction and the Logic of Money: Financial Predominance and International Economic Leadership.* State University of New York Press.
  2010. *Realist Constructivism: Rethinking International Relations Theory.* Cambridge University Press.
  2013. *International Organization: Theories and Institutions*, 2nd ed. Palgrave Macmillan.
  2015a. "On the Heuristic Use of Formal Models in International Relations Theory," *International Studies Review* 17: 617–634.
  2015b. "Racing All Over the Place: A Dispersion Model of International Regulatory Competition," *European Journal of International Relations* 21: 171–193.
Barkin, J. Samuel and Bruce Cronin 1994. "The State and the Nation: Changing Norms and the Rules of Sovereignty in International Relations," *International Organization* 48: 107–130.
Barkin, J. Samuel and Elizabeth R. DeSombre 2013. *Saving Global Fisheries: Reducing Fishing Capacity to Promote Sustainability.* The MIT Press.
Barkin, J. Samuel and Patricia A. Weitsman 2019. "Realist Institutionalism and the Institutional Mechanisms of Power Politics," in Anders Wivel and T. V. Paul, eds. *International Institutions and Power Politics.* Georgetown University Press.
Barnett, Michael and Raymond Duvall 2005. "Power in International Politics," *International Organization* 59: 39–75.
Bartelson, Jens 1995. *A Genealogy of Sovereignty.* Cambridge University Press.
Barton, John, Judith Goldstein, Timothy Josling, and Richard Steinberg 2006. *The Evolution of the Trade Regime: Politics, Law, and Economics of the GATT and the WTO.* Princeton University Press.
Basel Committee on Banking Supervision 2010. *Basel III: A Global Regulatory Framework for More Resilient Banks and Banking Systems.* Bank for International Settlements.

Baumgold, Deborah 2005. "Hobbes's and Locke's Contract Theories: Political not Metaphysical," *Critical Review of International Social and Political Philosophy* 8: 289–308.
Bellamy, Alex 2014. *Responsibility to Protect: A Defense*. Oxford University Press.
Benhabib, Seyla 2005. "Borders, Boundaries, and Citizenship," *PS: Political Science & Politics* 38: 673–677.
Berman, Harold 1983. *Law and Revolution: The Formation of the Western Legal Tradition*. Harvard University Press.
Bhagwati, Jagdish 1991. *The World Trading System at Risk*. Princeton University Press.
Biersteker, Thomas and Cynthia Weber, eds. 1996. *State Sovereignty as Social Construct*. Cambridge University Press.
Bliss, F. Allen 1994. "Rethinking Restrictions on Cabotage: Moving to Free Trade in Passenger Aviation," *Suffolk Transnational Law Review* 17: 382.
Bloch, Marc 1961. *Feudal Society*. University of Chicago Press.
Bodansky, Daniel 1995. "Customary (and Not So Customary) International Environmental Law," *Indiana Journal of Global Legal Studies* 3: 105.
Bodin, Jean 1945 (1566). *Method for the Easy Comprehension of History*. Translated by Beatrice Reynolds. Columbia University Press.
Bogdanor, Vernon 1997. *The Monarchy and the Constitution*. Clarendon Press.
Boland, Vincent 2017. "Ireland's 'De-Globalized' Data Calculate a Smaller Economy," *Financial Times*, July 18.
Boxer, C. R. 1974. *The Anglo-Dutch Wars of the Seventeenth Century, 1652–1674*. Her Majesty's Stationary Office.
Branch, Jordan 2012. "'Colonial Reflection' and Territoriality: The Peripheral Origins of Sovereign Statehood," *European Journal of International Relations* 18: 277–297.
Bratspies, Rebecca and Russell Miller, eds. 2006. *Transboundary Harm in International Law: Lessons from the Trail Smelter Arbitration*. Cambridge University Press.
Broadhead, Lee-Anne 2002. *International Environmental Politics: The Limits of Green Diplomacy*. Lynne Reinner.
Brysk, Alison and Gershon Shafir, eds. 2004. *People Out of Place: Globalization, Human Rights, and the Citizenship Gap*. Routledge.
Buchheit, Lee 1978. *Secession: The Legitimacy of Self-Determination*. Yale University Press.
Bull, Hedley 1977. *The Anarchical Society: A Study of Order in World Politics*. Macmillan.
Burch, Kurt 1998. *"Property" and the Making of the International System*. Lynne Rienner.

2000. "Changing the Rules: Reconceiving Change in the Westphalian System," *International Studies Review* 2: 181–210.

Burchell, Graham, Colin Gordon, and Peter Miller, eds. 1991. *The Foucault Effect: Studies in Governmentality*. University of Chicago Press.

Burdick, Alan 2017. *Why Time Flies: A Mostly Scientific Investigation*. Simon & Schuster.

Burgerman, Susan 2001. *Moral Victories: How Activists Provoke Multilateral Action*. Cornell University Press.

Burgess, John 1890. *Political Science and Comparative Constitutional Law. Volume I: Sovereignty and Liberty*. Ginn & Co.

Burley, Anne-Marie 1993. "Regulating the World: Multilateralism, International Law, and the Projection of the New Deal Regulatory State," in John Gerard Ruggie, ed., *Multilateralism Matters: The Theory and Praxis of an Institutional Form*. Columbia University Press.

Capoccia, Giovanni and R. Daniel Kelemen 2007. "The Study of Critical Junctures: Theory, Narrative, and Counterfactuals in Historical Institutionalism," *World Politics* 59: 341–369.

Caulkins, Jonathan, Peter H. Reuter, Martin Y. Iguchi, and James Chiesa 2005. *How Goes the "War on Drugs"?* Rand Corporation.

Cerny, Philip 1998. "Neomedievalism, Civil War and the New Security Dilemma: Globalisation as Durable Disorder," *Civil Wars* 1: 36–64.

Chayes, Abram and Antonia Handler Chayes 1993. "On Compliance," *International Organization* 47: 175–205.

Chulov, Martin 2018. "'We Will Get Him: The Long Hunt for ISIS Leader Abu Bakr al-Baghdadi," *The Guardian*, January 15.

Clark, Ian 2005. *Legitimacy in International Society*. Oxford University Press.

Coase, Ronald 1959. "The Federal Communications Commission," *Journal of Law and Economics* 2: 1–40.

1960. "The Problem of Social Cost," *Journal of Law and Economics* 3: 1–44.

Coggins, Bridget 2014. *Power Politics and State Formation in the Twentieth Century: The Dynamics of Recognition*. Cambridge University Press.

Cooley, Alexander and Hendrik Spruyt 2009. *Contracting States: Sovereign Transfers in International Relations*. Princeton University Press.

Craig, Gordon 1971. *Europe since 1815*, 3rd ed. Holt, Rinehart and Winston.

Cronin, Bruce 1999. *Community under Anarchy: Transnational Identity and the Evolution of Cooperation*. Columbia University Press.

Croucher, Sheila 2018. *Globalization and Belonging: The Politics of Identity in a Changing World*. Rowman & Littlefield.

Croxton, Derek 2015. *Westphalia: The Last Christian Peace*. Palgrave Macmillan.

D'Amato, Anthony and Richard Anderson Falk 1971. *The Concept of Custom in International Law*. Cornell University Press.
DeSombre, Elizabeth R. 2005. "Fishing Under Flags of Convenience: Using Market Power to Increase Participation in International Regulation," *Global Environmental Politics* 5: 73–94.
  2006. *Flagging Standards: Globalization and Environmental, Safety, and Labor Regulations at Sea*. The MIT Press.
Dimitrov, Radoslav 2020. "Empty Institutions in Global Environmental Politics," *International Studies Review* 22: 626–650. https://doi.org/10.1093/isr/viz029.
Drezner, Daniel 2001. "Sovereignty for Sale," *Foreign Policy* 125: 76–77.
  2007. *All Politics Is Global: Explaining International Regulatory Regimes*. Princeton University Press.
Economist 2019. "Siege on the Mediterranean," *The Economist*, July 6-12: 39–40.
Ekelund, Robert and Robert Tollison 1981. *Mercantilism as a Rent-Seeking Society: Economic Regulation in Historical Perspective*. Texas A&M University Press.
Everitt, Anthony 2009. *Hadrian and the Triumph of Rome*. Random House.
Fairbank, John, ed. 1968. *The Chinese World Order: Traditional China's Foreign Relations*. Harvard University Press.
Farrell, Graham and John Thorne 2005. "Where Have All the Flowers Gone? Evaluation of the Taliban Crackdown against Opium Poppy Cultivation in Afghanistan," *International Journal of Drug Policy* 16: 81–91.
Fearon, James 1995. "Rationalist Explanations for War," *International Organization* 49: 379–414.
Ferrel, Robert 1985. *Woodrow Wilson and World War I: 1917–1921*. Harper & Row.
Ferrero, Guglielmo 1941. *The Reconstruction of Europe: Talleyrand and the Congress of Vienna, 1814–1815*. G.P. Putnam's Sons.
Festinger, Leon 1957. *A Theory of Cognitive Dissonance*. Stanford University Press.
Finnemore, Martha 1996. *National Interests in International Society*. Cornell University Press.
  2004. *The Purpose of Intervention: Changing Beliefs About the Use of Force*. Cornell University Press.
Finnemore, Martha and Kathryn Sikkink 1998. "International Norm Dynamics and Political Change," *International Organization* 52: 887–917.
Fligstein, Neil, Alina Polyakova, and Wayne Sandholtz 2012. "European Integration, Nationalism, and European Identity," *JCMS: Journal of Common Market Studies* 50: 106–122.

Franklin, Julian 1973. *Jean Bodin and the Rise of Absolutist Theory.* Cambridge University Press.
Friedheim, Robert, ed. 2001. *Toward A Sustainable Whaling Regime.* University of Washington Press.
Friedrichs, Jörg 2007. *Fighting Terrorism and Drugs: Europe and International Police Cooperation.* Routledge.
Gardam, Judith 1993. *Non-Combatant Immunity as a Norm of International Humanitarian Law.* M. Nijhoff Publishers.
Gee, Graham and Alison Young 2016. "Regaining Sovereignty? Brexit, the UK Parliament and the Common Law," *European Public Law* 22: 131–147.
Geitner, Paul 2004. "EU Signs $1.25B Deal with Philip Morris," *Associated Press*, July 9.
Gellner, Ernest 1983. *Nations and Nationalism.* Cornell University Press.
Gilley, Bruce 2006. "The Meaning and Measure of State Legitimacy: Results for 72 Countries," *European Journal of Political Research* 45: 499–525.
Gilpin, Robert 1981. *War and Change in World Politics.* Cambridge University Press.
Glaeser, Edward and Andrei Shleifer 2001. "The Rise of the Regulatory State," *National Bureau of Economic Research Working Paper 8650.* National Bureau of Economic Research.
Goddard, Stacie 2009. "When Right makes Might: How Prussia Overturned the European Balance of Power," *International Security* 33: 110–142.
Goldstein, Judith, Miles Kahler, Robert O. Keohane, and Anne-Marie Slaughter, eds. 2001. *Legalization and World Politics.* The MIT Press.
Gore, Charles 2000. "The Rise and Fall of the Washington Consensus as a Paradigm for Developing Countries," *World Development* 28: 789–804.
Grigorescu, Alexandru 2007. "Transparency of International Organizations: The Roles of Member States, International Bureaucracies, and Nongovernmental Organizations," *International Studies Quarterly* 51: 625–648.
Gros, Daniel 2013. "Banking Union with a Sovereign Virus: The Self-Serving Treatment of Sovereign Debt," *Intereconomics* 48: 93–97.
Gross, Leo 1948. "The Peace of Westphalia, 1648–1948," *American Journal of International Law* 42: 20–41.
Grovogui, Siba N'Zatioula 1996. *Sovereigns, Quasi Sovereigns, and Africans: Race and Self-Determination in International Law.* University of Minnesota Press.
Gruber, Lloyd 2000. *Ruling the World: Power Politics and the Rise of Supranational Institutions.* Princeton University Press.
Guardian 2019. "Chakrabarti Defends Jeremy Corbyn's Venezuela Remarks," *The Guardian*, February 3.

Guilfoyle, Douglas 2009. *Shipping Interdiction and the Law of the Sea*. Cambridge University Press.
Gulbrandsen, Lars 2010. *Transnational Environmental Governance: The Emergence and Effects of the Certification of Forests and Fisheries*. Edward Elgar.
Guzzini, Stefano 1998. *Realism in International Relations and International Political Economy: The Continuing Story of a Death Foretold*. Routledge.
  2000. "A Reconstruction of Constructivism in International Relations," *European Journal of International Relations* 6: 147–182.
  2005. "The Concept of Power: A Constructivist Analysis," *Millennium* 33: 495–521.
Haas, Ernst 1997. *Nationalism, Liberalism, and Progress, Vol. 1: The Rise and Decline of Nationalism*. Cornell University Press.
Habermas, Jürgen 1984. *The Theory of Communicative Action*. Translated by Thomas McCarthy. Beacon Press.
Hacking, Ian 1999. *The Social Construction of What?* Harvard University Press.
Hall, Rodney Bruce 1998. *National Collective Identity: Social Constructs and International Systems*. Columbia University Press.
Harper, Kyle 2011. *Slavery in the Late Roman World, AD 275–425*. Cambridge University Press.
Haufler, Virginia 2001. *A Public Role for the Private Sector: Industry Self-Regulation in a Global Economy*. Carnegie Endowment for International Peace.
Hegel, G. F. W. 1974. *Hegel: The Essential Writings*, Frederick Weiss, ed. Harper & Row.
Helleiner, Eric 2014. *Forgotten Foundations of Bretton Woods: International Development and the Making of the Postwar Order*. Cornell University Press.
Henkin, Louis 1979. *How Nations Behave: Law and Foreign Policy*. Columbia University Press.
Hobbes, Thomas 1991 (1651). *Leviathan*. Cambridge University Press.
Hobsbawm, Eric 1990. *Nations and Nationalism Since 1780*. Cambridge University Press.
Holland, Ben 2010. "Sovereignty as Dominium? Reconstructing the Constructivist Roman Law Thesis," *International Studies Quarterly* 54: 449–480.
Holland, Max 1994. "After Thirty Years: Making Sense of the Assassination," *Reviews in American History* 22: 191–209.
Holsti, Kalevi 1992. "Governance Without Government: Polyarchy in Nineteenth-Century European International Politics," in James N. Rosenau

and Ernst-Otto Czempiel, eds. *Governance Without Government: Order and Change in World Politics*. Cambridge University Press.

Hoppe, Carsten 2008. "Passing the Buck: State Responsibility for Private Military Companies," *European Journal of International Law* 19: 989–1014.

Hozic, Aida 2004. "Between the Cracks: Balkan Cigarette Smuggling," *Problems of Post-Communism* 51: 35–44.

Hurka, Thomas 2005. "Proportionality in the Morality of War," *Philosophy & Public Affairs* 33: 34–66.

Inayatullah, Naeem 1996. "Beyond the Sovereignty Dilemma: Quasi-States as Social Construct," in Thomas Biersteker and Cynthia Weber, eds. *State Sovereignty as Social Construct*. Cambridge University Press.

Jackson, Patrick Thaddeus 2011. *The Conduct of Inquiry in International Relations: Philosophy of Science and Its Implications for the Study of World Politics*. Routledge.

Jackson, Robert 1993. *Quasi-States: Sovereignty, International Relations and the Third World*. Cambridge University Press.

Jackson, 2007. *Sovereignty: The Evolution of an Idea*. Polity.

Jacobson, Harold, William Reisinger, and Todd Mathers 1986. "National Entanglements in International Governmental Organizations," *American Political Science Review* 80: 141–159.

Jervis, Robert 1976. *Perception and Misperception in International Politics*. Princeton University Press.

Kaczynski, Vlad and David Fluharty 2002. "European Policies in West Africa: Who Benefits from Fisheries Agreements?" *Marine Policy* 26: 75–93.

Kahler, Miles and David Lake, eds. 2003. *Governance in a Global Economy: Political Authority in Transition*. Princeton University Press.

Kalmo, Hent and Quentin Skinner, eds. 2010. *Sovereignty in Fragments: The Past, Present, and Future of a Contested Concept*. Cambridge University Press.

Kann, Robert 1950. *The Multinational Empire: Nationalism and National Reform in the Habsburg Monarchy, 1848–1918*. Columbia University Press.

Keck, Margaret and Kathryn Sikkink 1998. *Activists beyond Borders: Advocacy Networks in International Politics*. Cornell University Press.

Kelley, Judith 2008. "Assessing the Complex Evolution of Norms: The Rise of International Election Monitoring," *International Organization* 62: 221–255.

Keohane, Robert 1982. "The Demand for International Regimes," *International Organization* 36: 325–355.

1984. *After Hegemony: Cooperation and Discord in the World Political Economy*. Princeton University Press.

Khanna, Parag 2009. "Neomedievalism," *Foreign Policy* 172: 91.
Kissinger, Henry 1958. *A World Restored: Metternich, Castlereagh, and the Problems of Peace, 1812–1822*. Houghton Mifflin.
Klein, Daniel and John Robinson 2011. "Property: A Bundle of Rights? Prologue to the Property Symposium," *Econ Journal Watch* 8: 193–204.
Klotz, Audie 1995. *Norms in International Relations: The Struggle Against Apartheid*. Cornell University Press.
Klotz, Audie and Cecilia Lynch 2007. *Strategies for Research in Constructivist International Relations*. M.E. Sharpe.
Kobrin, Stephen 1998. "Back to the Future: Neomedievalism and the Postmodern Digital World Economy," *Journal of International Affairs* 51: 361–386.
Kocs, Stephen 1994. "Explaining the Strategic Behavior of States: International Law as System Structure," *International Studies Quarterly* 38: 535–556.
Kolstad, Ivar and Tina Søreide 2009. "Corruption in Natural Resource Management: Implications for Policy Makers," *Resources Policy* 34: 214–226.
Korten, David 2001. *When Corporations Rule the World*, 2nd ed. Kumarian Press.
Krasner, Stephen 1993. "Westphalia and All That," in Judith Goldstein and Robert O. Keohane, eds. *Ideas and Foreign Policy: Beliefs, Institutions, and Political Change*. Cornell University Press.
  1995. "Sovereignty and Intervention," in Gene Lyons and Michael Mastanduno, eds. *Beyond Westphalia: State Sovereignty and International Intervention*. The Johns Hopkins University Press.
  1999. *Sovereignty: Organized Hypocrisy*. Princeton University Press.
Kratochwil, Friedrich 1994. "The Limits of Contract," *European Journal of International Law* 4: 465–491.
  1995. "Sovereignty as *Dominium*: Is There a Right of Humanitarian Intervention?" in Gene Lyons and Michael Mastanduno, eds. *Beyond Westphalia: State Sovereignty and International Intervention*. The Johns Hopkins University Press.
Krebs, Ronald and Patrick Thaddeus Jackson 2007. "Twisting Tongues and Twisting Arms: The Power of Political Rhetoric," *European Journal of International Relations* 13: 35–66.
Lake, David 2003. "The New Sovereignty in International Relations," *International Studies Review* 5: 303–323.
Leander, Anna 2005. "The Power to Construct International Security: On the Significance of Private Military Companies," *Millennium: Journal of International Studies* 33: 803–825.

2011. "The Promises, Problems, and Potentials of a Bourdieu-Inspired Staging of International Relations," *International Political Sociology* 5: 294–313.

Lee, Daniel 2008. "Private Law Models for Public Law Concepts: The Roman Law Theory of Dominium in the Monarchomach Doctrine of Popular Sovereignty," *The Review of Politics* 70: 370–399.

Levi, Margaret, Audrey Sacks, and Tom Tyler 2009. "Conceptualizing Legitimacy, Measuring Legitimating Beliefs," *American Behavioral Scientist* 53: 354–375.

Locke, John 1960 (1688). *Two Treatises of Government*. Cambridge University Press.

Lumsdaine, David 1993. *Moral Vision in International Politics: The Foreign Aid Regime, 1949–1989*. Princeton University Press.

Luoma-Aho, Mika 2009. "Political Theology, Anthropomorphism, and Person-hood of the State: The Religion of IR," *International Political Sociology* 3: 293–309.

Lyons, Martyn 1994. *Napoleon Bonaparte and the Legacy of the French Revolution*. St. Martin's Press.

Macpherson, Crawford Brough 1962. *The Political Theory of Possessive Individualism: Hobbes to Locke*. Oxford University Press.

Mander, Jerry and Edward Goldsmith, eds. 1996. *The Case Against the Global Economy: And for a Turn Toward the Local*. Sierra Club Books.

March, James and Johan Olsen 1998. "The Institutional Dynamics of International Political Orders," *International Organization* 52: 943–969.

Mathias, Peter 1983. *The First Industrial Nation: An Economic History of Britain*, 2nd ed. Methuen.

McCourt, David 2016. "Practice Theory and Relationalism as the New Constructivism," *International Studies Quarterly* 60: 475–485.

McNamara, Kathleen 1997. "Globalization Is What We Make of It? The Social Construction of Market Imperatives," paper presented at the 1997 Annual Meeting of the American Political Science Association, Washington, DC.

1998. *The Currency of Ideas: Monetary Politics in the European Union*. Cornell University Press.

McNeill, William 1982. *The Pursuit of Power: Technology, Armed Force, and Society since A.D. 1000*. University of Chicago Press.

Mee, Charles Jr. 1980. *The End of Order: Versailles 1919*. Dutton.

Mitzen, Jennifer 2006. "Ontological Security in World Politics: State Identity and the Security Dilemma," *European Journal of International Relations* 12: 341–370.

Moore, Mick 2004. "Revenues, State Formation, and the Quality of Governance in Developing Countries," *International Political Science Review* 25: 297–319.

Moran, Michael 2002. "Understanding the Regulatory State," *British Journal of Political Science* 32: 391–413.
Moravcsik, Andrew 2004. "Is There a 'Democratic Deficit' in World Politics? A Framework for Analysis," *Government and Opposition* 39: 336–363.
Morgenthau, Hans 1940. "Positivism, Functionalism, and International Law," *American Journal of International Law* 34: 260–284.
  1948. *Politics Among Nations: The Struggle for Power and Peace*. Knopf.
Morris, Justin 2013. "Libya and Syria: R2P and the Spectre of the Swinging Pendulum," *International Affairs* 89: 1265–1283.
Mueller, Milton, John Mathiason, and Hans Klein 2007. "The Internet and Global Governance: Principles and Norms for a New Regime," *Global Governance: A Review of Multilateralism and International Organizations* 13: 237–254.
Mumford, Lewis 1961. *The City in History: Its Origins, Its Transformations, and its Prospects*. Harcourt, Brace.
Munn, Mark 2006. *The Mother of the Gods, Athens, and the Tyranny of Asia: A Study of Sovereignty in Ancient Religion*. University of California Press.
Murphy, Craig 2006. *The United Nations Development Programme: A Better Way?* Cambridge University Press.
Naim, Moises 2005. *Illicit: How Smugglers, Traffickers, and Copycats Are Hijacking the Global Economy*. Anchor Books.
Nayar, Baldev Raj 1995. "Regimes, Power, and International Aviation," *International Organization* 49:139–170.
Neumann, Iver 2007. "'A Speech That the Entire Ministry May Stand for,' or: Why Diplomats Never Produce Anything New," *International Political Sociology* 1: 183–200.
Newman, Peter 1978. *The Bronfman Dynasty: The Rothschilds of the New World*. McClelland and Stewart.
Nexon, Daniel and Thomas Wright 2007. "What's at Stake in the American Empire Debate," *American Political Science Review* 101: 253–271.
Nielsen, Richard 2013. "Rewarding Human Rights? Selective Aid Sanctions against Repressive States," *International Studies Quarterly* 57: 791–803.
North, Douglass 1981. *Structure and Change in Economic History*. W. W. Norton.
North, Douglass and Robert Paul Thomas 1973. *The Rise of the Western World: A New Economic History*. Cambridge University Press.
Nye, Joseph Jr. 2001. "Globalization's Democratic Deficit: How to Make International Institutions More Accountable," *Foreign Affairs* 80: 2.
Ohmae, Kenichi 1995. *The End of the Nation State, The Rise of Regional Economies: How New Engines of Prosperity Are Reshaping Global Markets*. The Free Press.

Olson, Mancur 1965. *The Logic of Collective Action: Public Goods and the Theory of Groups.* Harvard University Press.

Onnekink, David, ed. 2016. *War and Religion after Westphalia, 1648–1713.* Routledge.

Onuf, Nicholas Greenwood 1989. *World of Our Making: Rules and Rule in Social Theory and International Relations.* University of South Carolina Press.

Osiander, Andreas 1994. *The States System of Europe, 1640–1990: Peacemaking and the Conditions of International Stability.* Clarendon Press.

  2001. "Sovereignty, International Relations, and the Westphalian Myth," *International Organization* 55: 251–287.

Paehlke, Robert 2002. *Democracy's Dilemma: Environment, Social Equity, and the Global Economy.* The MIT Press.

Palan, Ronen 2003. *The Offshore World: Sovereign Markets, Virtual Places, and Nomad Millionaires.* Cornell University Press.

Palan, Ronen, Richard Murphy, and Christian Chavagneux 2013. *Tax Havens: How Globalization Really Works.* Cornell University Press.

Paterson, Owen 2017. "Don't Listen to the Terrified Europeans. The Singapore Model Is our Brexit Opportunity," *The Telegraph*, November 21.

Patrick, Stewart 2018. *The Sovereignty Wars: Reconciling America with the World.* Brookings Institution.

Peterson, M. J. 1988. *Managing the Frozen South: The Creation and Evolution of the Antarctic Treaty System.* University of California Press.

Pflanze, Otto 1963. *Bismarck and the Development of Germany: The Period of Unification, 1815–1871.* Princeton University Press.

Price, Richard 1997. *The Chemical Weapons Taboo.* Cornell University Press.

  1998. "Reversing the Gun Sights: Transnational Civil Society Targets Land Mines," *International Organization* 52: 613–644.

Prokhovnik, Raia 2007. *Sovereignties: Contemporary Theory and Practice.* Springer.

Raustiala, Kal 2000. "Compliance & Effectiveness in International Regulatory Cooperation," *Case Western Reserve Journal of International Law* 32: 387–440.

Ravishankar, M. N., Shan Pan, and Michael Myers 2013. "Information Technology Offshoring in India: A Postcolonial Perspective," *European Journal of Information Systems* 22: 387–402.

Rawlings, Gregory 2007. "Taxes and Transnational Treaties: Responsive Regulation and the Reassertion of Offshore Sovereignty," *Law & Policy* 29: 51–66.

Reno, William 2000. "Clandestine Economies, Violence and States in Africa," *Journal of International Affairs* 53: 433–459.
Reus-Smit, Christian 1999. *The Moral Purpose of the State: Culture, Social Identity, and Institutional Rationality in International Relations*. Princeton University Press.
Risse, Thomas 2000. "Let's Argue! Communicative Action in World Politics," *International Organization* 54: 1–40
Rousseau, Jean Jacques 1984. *The Basic Political Writings*. Translated by Donald Cress. Hackett.
  1986. *Political Writings*. Translated by Frederick Watkins. The University of Wisconsin Press.
Ruggie, John Gerard 1982. "International Regimes, Transactions, and Change: Embedded Liberalism in the Postwar Economic Order," *International Organization* 36: 379–415.
  1983. "Continuity and Transformation in the World Polity: Toward a Neorealist Synthesis," *World Politics* 35: 261–285.
  1992. "Multilateralism: The Anatomy of an Institution," *International Organization* 46: 561–598.
  1993. "Territoriality and Beyond: Problematizing Modernity in International Relations," *International Organization* 47: 139–174.
  1998. "What Makes the World Hang Together? Neo-Utilitarianism and the Social Constructivist Challenge," *International Organization* 52: 855–885.
Ruggie, John Gerard, ed. 1993. *Multilateralism Matters: The Theory and Praxis of an Institutional Form*. Columbia University Press.
Salter, Mark 2008. "When the Exception Becomes the Rule: Borders, Sovereignty, and Citizenship," *Citizenship Studies* 12: 365–380.
Sand, Peter 2004. "Sovereignty Bounded: Public Trusteeship for Common Pool Resources?" *Global Environmental Politics* 4: 47–71.
Sasley, Brent 2011. "Theorizing States' Emotions," *International Studies Review* 13: 452–476.
Schmitt, Carl 2005. *Political Theology: Four Chapters on the Concept of Sovereignty*. Translated by George Schwab. University of Chicago Press.
Schroeder, Paul 1994. *The Transformation of European Politics, 1763–1848*. Oxford University Press.
Scott, Gary and Craig Carr 1996. "Multilateral Treaties and the Formation of Customary International Law," *Denver Journal of International Law and Policy* 25: 71.
Seligson, Mitchell 2002. "The Impact of Corruption on Regime Legitimacy: A Comparative Study of Four Latin American Countries," *The Journal of Politics* 64: 408–433.
Selin, Henrik 2010. *Global Governance of Hazardous Chemicals: Challenges of Multilevel Management*. The MIT Press.

Sending, Ole Jacob, Vincent Pouliot, and Iver B. Neumann 2011. "The Future of Diplomacy: Changing Practices, Evolving Relationships," *International Journal* 66: 527–542.
Shaffer, Gregory 2012. "International Law and Global Public Goods in a Legal Pluralist World," *European Journal of International Law* 23: 669–693.
Sikkink, Kathryn 1993. "Human Rights, Principled Issue-Networks, and Sovereignty in Latin America," *International Organization* 47: 411–441.
Simmons, Beth 2009. *Mobilizing for Human Rights: International Law in Domestic Politics*. Cambridge University Press.
Simpson, Audra 2008. "Subjects of Sovereignty: Indigeneity, the Revenue Rule, and Juridics of Failed Consent," *Law & Contemporary Problems* 71: 191.
Slaughter, Anne-Marie 1997. "The Real New World Order," *Foreign Affairs* 76: 183–197.
Small, Melvin and J. David Singer 1982. *Resort to Arms: International and Civil Wars, 1816–1980*. Sage Publications.
Smith, Anthony 1983. *Theories of Nationalism*. Holmes & Meier.
Snidal, Duncan 1985. "The Limits of Hegemonic Stability Theory," *International Organization* 39: 579–614.
Spruyt, Hendrik 1996. *The Sovereign State and Its Competitors: An Analysis of Systems Change*. Princeton University Press.
Srivastava, Swati 2019. "Varieties of Social Construction," *International Studies Review* 22: 325–346. doi.org/10.1093/isr/viz003.
  forthcoming, *Hybrid Sovereignty in World Politics* (manuscript under review).
Steele, Brent 2008. *Ontological Security in International Relations: Self-Identity and the IR State*. Routledge.
Strang, David 1991. "Anomaly and Commonplace in European Political Expansion: Realist and Institutional Accounts," *International Organization* 45: 143–162.
  1996. "Contested Sovereignty: The Social Construction of Colonial Imperialism," in Thomas Biersteker and Cynthia Weber, eds. *State Sovereignty as a Social Construct*. Cambridge University Press.
Strange, Susan 1996. *The Retreat of the State: The Diffusion of Power in the World Economy*. Cambridge University Press.
Straumann, Benjamin 2008. "The Peace of Westphalia (1648) as a Secular Constitution," *Constellations* 15: 173–188.
Talmon, Stefan 1999. "Who Is a Legitimate Government in Exile? Towards Normative Criteria for Governmental Legitimacy in International Law," in Guy Goodwin-Gill and Stefan Talmon, eds. *The Reality of International Law: Essays in Honour of Ian Brownlie*. Clarendon Press.

Taylor, A. J. P. 1954. *The Struggle for Mastery in Europe, 1848–1918*. Oxford University Press.
  1961. *The Origins of the Second World War*. Hamilton Press.
Telegraph 2016. "EU debate: Boris Johnson says Brexit will be 'Britain's Independence Day' as Ruth Davidson Attacks 'Lies' of Leave Campaign in front of 6,000-strong Wembley Audience," *The Telegraph*, June 21.
Temperley, Harold 1966. *The Foreign Policy of Canning, 1822–1827: England, the Neo-Holy Alliance, and the New World*. Archon Books.
Teschke, Benno 1998. "Geopolitical Relations in the European Middle Ages: History and Theory," *International Organization* 52: 325–358.
Thomas, Daniel 2001. *The Helsinki Effect: International Norms, Human Rights, and the Demise of Communism*. Princeton University Press.
Thomson, Janice 1995. "State Sovereignty in International Relations: Bridging the Gap between Theory and Empirical Research," *International Studies Quarterly* 39: 213–233.
  1996. *Mercenaries, Pirates, and Sovereigns: State-Building and Extraterritorial Violence in Early Modern Europe*. Princeton University Press.
Tilly, Charles 1985. "War Making and State Making as Organized Crime," in Peter Evans, Dietrich Rueschemeyer, and Theda Skocpol, eds. *Bringing the State Back In*. Cambridge University Press.
  1992. *Coercion, Capital, and European States, AD 990–1992*. Blackwell.
Treaty of Münster 1648. *Peace Treaty Between the Holy Roman Emperor and the King of France and their Respective Allies*. British Foreign Office Translation. Viewed at The Avalon Project, Yale Law School, https://avalon.law.yale.edu/17th_century/westphal.asp.
United Nations 1945. *Charter of the United Nations*. Viewed at www.un.org/en/charter-united-nations/.
United Nations General Assembly 1948. *Universal Declaration of Human Rights*. United Nations 217 (III).
  1995. Agreement for the Implementation of the Provisions of the United Nations Convention on the Law of the Sea of 10 December 1982 Relating to the Conservation and Management of Straddling Fish Stocks and Highly Migratory Fish Stocks. United Nations A/CONF.164/37.
  1998. *Rome Statute of the International Criminal Court*. United Nations A/CONF.183/9.
  2005. *2005 World Summit Outcome*. United Nations A/RES/60/1.
  2012. *Status of Palestine in the United Nations*, United Nations A/67/L.28.
United Nations Security Council 1991. *Resolution 687*, United Nations S/RES/687.
Vattel, Emer de 2001 (1834). *The Law of Nations or, the Principles of the Law of Nature, Applied to the Conduct and to the Affairs of Nations and of Sovereigns*, Jospeh Chitty, ed. Cambridge University Press.

Vernon, Raymond 1971. *Sovereignty at Bay: The Multinational Spread of U.S. Enterprises*. Basic Books.
  1981. "Sovereignty at Bay Ten Years After," *International Organization* 35: 517–529.
Vincent, R. J. 1986. *Human Rights and International Relations*. Cambridge University Press.
Vorhölter, Julia 2012. "Negotiating Social Change: Ugandan Discourses on Westernisation and Neo-Colonialism as Forms of Social Critique," *The Journal of Modern African Studies* 50: 283–307.
Walker, R. B. J. 1993. *Inside/Outside: International Relations as Political Theory*. Cambridge University Press.
Waltz, Kenneth 1979. *Theory of International Politics*. Columbia University Press.
Weber, Martin 2001. "Competing Political Visions: WTO Governance and Green Politics," *Global Environmental Politics* 1: 92–113.
Weber, Max 1968. *Economy and Society*. University of California Press.
Webster, Sir Charles 1931. *The Foreign Policy of Castlereagh, 1812–1815: Britain and the Reconstruction of Europe*. G. Bell and Sons.
  1934. *The Congress of Vienna, 1814–1815*. Thames and Hudson.
Wendt, Alexander 1999. *Social Theory of International Politics*. Cambridge University Press.
  2004. "The State as Person in International Theory," *Review of International Studies* 30: 289–316.
Wiessner, Siegfried 2008. "Indigenous Sovereignty: A Reassessment in Light of the UN Declaration on the Rights of Indigenous People," *Vanderbilt Journal of Transnational Law* 41: 1141.
Wight, Martin 1972. "International Legitimacy," *International Relations* 4: 1–28.
  1977. *Systems of States*. Leicester University Press.
Wilson, Charles 1967. "Trade, Society, and the State," in Edwin Rich and Charles Wilson, eds. *The Cambridge Economic History of Europe, Vol. IV: The Economy of Expanding Europe in the Sixteenth and Seventeenth Centuries*. Cambridge University Press.
  1968. *The Dutch Republic and the Civilization of the Seventeenth Century*. McGraw-Hill.

Index

Absolutist legitimation, 88
Agamben, Giorgio, 19
Albania, 129, 138
anarchy, 18, 23
Anschluss, 93
Antarctic Treaty, 45, 68
Antarctic Treaty System, 46
Antarctica, 45–46, 71
Assad, Bashir, 61
Augsburg, Treaty of, 23, 33, 86–88, 103
Austria, 88, 91, 93

Bank for International Settlements (BIS), 67
Basel Accords, 67–68
Basel Committee on Banking Supervision, 67
Belgium, 90
Bodin, Jean, 37, 58, 115, 130
Bretton Woods, 33, 118–119
Brexit, 74, 155
Britain, 134
Bronfman family, 126

cabotage, 133
Cameroon, 73
Canada, 73, 126, 136
Caribbean, 66, 128
Central Europe, 116
China, 46, 52, 73, 101, 123, 179
    Imperial, 58, 65
Coase, Ronald, 39–40
Coase Theorem, 39–40
cognitive dissonance, 12, 145–150, 153, 156, 159
Cold War, 4–5, 81, 84, 95–99, 103
collective sovereign responsibility, 138
community of states, 47, 59, 81–82, 85, 115

comorros, 138
competitive liberalism, 118
Congress of Vienna, 84, 89
Contract law, English, 14
Corbyn, Jeremy, 159
corporate actors, 42, 46–48, 60–61, 64, 73, 76, 79, 119
    States as corporate actors, 53, 55, 57, 73, 75, 171, 177
Council for Mutual Economic Assistance (Comecon), 94
critical theory, 19
Czechoslovakia, 93

decolonization, 10, 165, 174–175
democracy, 92, 155
    liberal/market, 97, 114
    representative, 64, 114
democratic liberalism, 3
DeSombre, Elizabeth R., 125, 141
diplomats, 8, 54, 61, 76
Drezner, Daniel, 125, 142
Durkheim, Emile, 72
dynamic density, social, 72

Eastern Europe, 153
El Salvador, 99
English contract law. *See* Contract law, English
Eswatini, 47
European Commission, 154
European states system, 22, 80, 110
European Union, 63, 99, 129, 148, 155
Exclusive Economic Zones (EEZs), 68, 77, 139

Fearon, James, 154
flags of convenience, 66–67, 80, 125, 128, 133, 138

199

France, 23, 83, 88, 91
French Revolution, 88

Gaza, 96
General Agreement on Tariffs and Trade (GATT), 119
Germany, 88, 90, 161
global commons, 55, 69–71, 78
  Governance of, 56, 68
global governance, 2, 9, 124, 151, 161
global public goods, 1
global south, 163, 174–175, 177
globalization, 154–156, 161, 177, 179–180
  neoliberal globalization, 118–119, 154
Grand Coalition, 88
Great Depression, 119
Great Powers, 88, 90
Great Recession of 2008, 118, 123
Greek revolt of 1821–1829, 90
Gross Domestic Product (GDP), 66, 105
Grotius, Hugo, 23
Guatemala, 99
Gulf Cooperation Council (GCC), 101

Haas, Ernst, 114
Habermas, Jürgen, 162
Haiti, 99
Hapsburg Empire, 93
Hegel, Georg Wilhelm Friedrich, 83, 92, 111
Helsinki Accords, 99
Hobbes, Thomas, 107–108
Holy Roman Empire, 23–24, 88, 103, 165
Hong Kong, 45
Hozic, Aida, 125
human rights, 14, 18, 57, 70–71, 82, 98–100, 114, 157, 159, 170
  human rights discourses, 99–100
  human rights norms, 156, 160, 166

indigenous sovereignty, 136
institutional liberalism, 3
institutionalism, 153
integrationists, 154
International Civil Aviation Organization (ICAO), 134
International Committee of the Red Cross (ICRC), 63
International Convention for the Regulation of Whaling, 68
International Criminal Court (ICC), 100
international law, 100, 106, 110, 116, 120, 130, 132–133, 137–138, 157, 165, 167, 170, 176, 178, 181
  customary international law, 71, 138
  international legal personhood, 1, 6, 26
  international legal sovereignty, 20, 36
international maritime law, 133
International Monetary Fund (IMF), 155
international organizations, 62, 74, 99, 155, 161
international political economy, 1–2, 5, 7, 66, 69, 73, 101, 124, 136–137, 140, 151, 154, 161
International Seabed Authority, 68
international society, 82, 95, 156
International Telecommunications Union (ITU), 73
International Union for the Conservation of Nature (IUCN), 63
Iran, 171
Iraq, 45, 100, 176
Ireland, 66, 171
Islamic State, 61
Italy, 90

Kashmir, 96
Knights Templar, 45
Krasner, Stephen, 11–12, 20–21, 23, 36, 47–49, 51, 102, 168

Labour Party (UK), 159
Lake, David, 20, 45
Legislators, 75, 155
Legitimacy, 4, 23, 26, 36–37, 43, 52, 80, 82–83, 92–93, 182
  external legitimacy, 131
  internal legitimacy, 131
  international legitimacy, 65, 84
  legitimated sovereignty, 82
  state legitimacy, 94, 96, 99

Leviathan, 107
liberal nationalism, 114, 117, 153, 161
Liberia, 67, 128
Libya, 99, 158
Lichtenstein, 47
Locke, John, 108, 114, 117, 120
Louis XIV, 86

Macpherson, C.B., 108, 117
Macroeconomic theory, 154
Maduro, Nicolás, 71
Mediterranean Sea, 128
microstates, 134
modern state system, 58, 115–116
Montevideo Convention on the Rights and Duties of States, 43
multilateral cooperation, 7
Münster, Treaty of, 23–24

Naples, 90
Napoleonic Wars, 88
Nationalism, 90–94, 112–113, 117, 151–154, 161, 167, 174
Navigation Acts, 134
Nazi Germany, 153
neocolonial international norms, 74
neoliberal institutionalism, 153
neoliberalism, 40, 154, 180
neomedievalism, 4–5, 9, 15
Netherlands, 116
Neumann, Iver, 29
New York, 104–105
nonintervention, 8, 100
non-state public actors, 9
normative dissonance, 12, 15, 120, 144–146, 148–151, 155–156, 159–162
norms, 4, 11, 30–35, 56–60, 71–78, 81–101, 103, 105, 110, 112–114, 117–123, 131–142
    norms of sovereignty, 12–15, 18–29, 45–54
North America, 71
North Atlantic Treaty Organization (NATO), 94
North Korea, 113
Norway, 91

Onuf, Nick, 53
Organization of the Petroleum Exporting Countries (OPEC), 8

Osiander, Andreas, 23
Osnabrück, Treaty of, 22–23
Ottoman Empire, 93

Palan, Ronen, 125
Palestine, 63
Palestinian Authority, 70
Paris Agreement, 2015, 56
Patrick, Stewart, 153
Peace of Westphalia. *See* Westphalia, Peace of
Persian Gulf, 112
Piedmont, 90
Poland, 90
politicians, 75
pollution havens, 127
popular sovereignty. *See* Sovereignty, popular
possessive individualism, 108, 112, 117, 122–123
private international regulation, 69
Prohibition Era, 126
property rights, 21–28, 35, 70, 72, 77–78, 84–87, 102–107, 113, 123, 130, 136, 151, 157–160, 162
Prussia, 88, 91

real property, 106–107
realism, 2, 18, 36, 58, 83, 178
recognition cartel, 9, 13, 42–44, 47, 65, 77
Republicanism, 88, 174
Responsibility to Protect (R2P), 99, 101, 159
Reston, Virginia, 67
Revolutions of 1848, 91
Rhineland, 93
Roman law, 14, 106–108
Rome Statute of the ICC, 60
Rome, Imperial, 58, 65
Rousseau, Jean Jacques, 83, 111, 117
Ruggie, John Gerard, 29, 153
Russia, 88

San Francisco, 122
Saudi Arabia, 113
Saxe-Coburg family, 90
Schmitt, Carl, 19
self-determination, 95, 114, 175
social contract theory, 114, 117–118, 120, 152, 154–155

social institutions, 7, 94
South America, 71
South China Sea, 52
sovereign regulatory authorization, 137
Sovereign rights, 45–50, 52, 56, 70, 77–78, 151, 157–158
  Principle of sovereign right, 3
  Sovereign right to regulate, 57–66, 69, 72, 135, 140–142
Sovereignty
  absolute sovereignty, 23
  De facto, 20
  De jure, 20
  external, 20, 25, 37, 115–116
  interdependence, 20
  internal/domestic, 20, 25, 37, 115–116
  popular, 3, 14, 110–113, 121, 139, 145, 151, 157, 167, 174, 176
sovereignty for sale, 132, 137, 140, 142
Soviet Union, 98–99
Spain, 90
stateness, 43
Sudetenland, 93
Supranational organizations, 85
Suzerainty, 174
Sweden, 23, 88, 91
Syria, 61, 160

Taiwan, 45, 63
tax havens, 66, 127
Thirty Years War, 22–23, 84, 86, 88
Thomson, Janice, 20, 36
Tokyo Round Agreement of the GATT, 119
transnational corporations, 43, 66
transnational terrorism, 179
Turkmenistan, 113

United Arab Emirates, 138
United Kingdom, 74, 159
United Nations, 81, 96
United Nations Convention on the Law of the Sea (UNCLOS), 52, 72
United Nations Development Programme (UNDP), 99
United Nations Security Council, 63

United Nations Security Council Resolution 687, 46
United Nations Straddling Stocks Agreement, 72
United Provinces, 116
United States, 46, 60, 67, 126, 128, 136, 171
Universal Declaration of Human Rights (UDHR), 70

Vanuatu, 47
Vassalage, 62, 174
Venezuela
  2019 constitutional crisis, 159
  President of, 71
Versailles settlement, 33, 92
Vienna, 33, 88
Vienna System, 89–90

Waltz, Kenneth, 26
War on Drugs (United States), 131
Warsaw Pact, 94
Washington Consensus, 180
Weber, Max, 43, 58–59, 64, 130
West African states, 140
West Bank, 96
Western Europe, 103, 128–129
Westphalia, Peace of, 13, 17, 20–23, 33, 86, 103, 115, 163–165, 174
Westphalian metaphor, 164–165, 174
Westphalian sovereignty, 13, 25, 28, 165, 174
Westphalian system, 11, 87–89
Wight, Martin, 82
Wilson, Woodrow, 92
Wilson's Fourteen Points, 91
World Trade Organization (WTO), 119
World War I, 93
World War II, 93
WTO Dispute Settlement Mechanism (DSM), 155
Wyoming, 104–105

Yugoslavia, 99

Zero-sum game, 96, 105, 134, 180

Lightning Source UK Ltd.
Milton Keynes UK
UKHW022028130821
388723UK00015B/206